Red River Women

Sherrie S. McLeRoy

Republic of Texas Press

Library of Congress Cataloging-in-Publication Data

McLeRoy, Sherrie S.
    Red River Women / by Sherrie S. McLeRoy.
        p.   cm. — (Women of the West series)
    Includes bibliographical references.
    ISBN 1-55622-501-6
    1. Women pioneers—Red River Valley (Tex.-La.)—Biography.
    2. Women pioneers—Texas—Biography.   3. Red River Valley
    (Tex.-La.)—Biography.   4. Texas—Biography.   I. Title.
    II. Series: Women of the West series (Plano, Tex.)
    F392.R3M38   1996
    976.6'603'0922 — dc20
    [B]   96-7326
                                      CIP

Republic of Texas Press is an imprint of Wordware Publishing, Inc.
No part of this book may be reproduced in any form or by any means
without permission in writing from Wordware Publishing, Inc.

Printed in the United States of America

ISBN 1-55622-501-6
10 9 8 7 6 5 4 3 2 1
9605

All inquiries for volume purchases of this book should be addressed to
Wordware Publishing, Inc., at 1506 Capital Avenue, Plano, Texas 75074.
Telephone inquiries may be made by calling:

(214) 423-0090

For my daughter,
Ann Elizabeth

Contents

Introduction

They have been called "gentle tamers," though some of the more outrageous women of Texas would probably have disdained being called "gentle" anythings. The conventions of the Victorian world decreed that they live sedately amongst children, teacups, and servants, an ornament to one man and his home, pleasant to look at but no longer really necessary for the survival of the family in the brash Industrial Age.

But the Texas frontier dared its women to adhere to society's rules and then threw in their way every conceivable obstacle: Indians, heat, blue northers, bugs, wind, isolation, and violence. Some women met that challenge, countless others withered and died in the trying.

And some took the challenge and flung it back in Texas' teeth.

Red River Women tells the stories of eight of those defiant women, who endured and thrived because they had the strength, the intelligence, and the guts to make their mark in a society ruled by and for men. In proper Victorian tradition, they tended to use wiles and charm to get what they wanted, but if that didn't work, they did what they wanted anyway.

These eight women share several links. All were born during the Victorian era (1837-1901), and the cultural mores of that period ruled their formative years, if not their entire lives. They were not the stereotype we "moderns" tend to have of Victorian women: frail, languid, in constant need of smelling salts and fainting couches. Instead they typify the energy and savvy of the era's frontier, and they dared to venture from the genteel, urban confines of the East and South to carve new lives on the edge of civilization.

They share a simple link of geography, too, for all lived on the bawdy, brawling Red River for at least some critical part of their years.

The accomplishments of these eight women in business, literature, education, and social work are remarkable even by today's more liberated standards, but, shamefully, their achievements are little known. Only two of the eight have been the subject of biographies: Sophia Porter in an earlier work by this author, and Enid Justin, in an autobiography she dictated to a writer. Their labors have been overlooked and they themselves branded as "minor historical figures, not worth writing about."

But the women who have followed in the footsteps of these eight, and hundreds of others like them, owe them much.

It is time they understand that debt, hence this book.

ABOUT THE BOOK

Red River Women began as an outgrowth of my research for *Black Land, Red River: The Pictorial History of Grayson County, Texas* (Donning Publications, 1993). I was amazed at the many fascinating women who really stood out in this county's history; for some reason, Sherman and Grayson County have attracted a disproportionate number of achievers and rebels. So I dug deeper, widened my search outside the county, and had more fun than should be legal in piecing together the stories of these eight Red River women.

I had first encountered Sophia Porter years earlier when I came to Sherman as director of the county historical museum. I had previously worked at Galveston's "Ashton Villa" and never thought to find another woman who flaunted as many rules as the redoubtable Bettie Brown. But here was Sophie, and she made Miss Bettie look positively tame.

Shy, quiet Lydia McPherson tried to live as obscurely as she could, and I had to ferret her out from deeds and newspaper columns and a rare copy of her book of poetry. She just wanted to write in an age that discouraged women from composing anything more difficult than a social letter.

And I was astonished to find that no one had ever written a biography of Lucy Pickens, the flamboyant Queen of the Confederacy. If there's not the makings of a rip-roaring novel in her life, I'll be very surprised.

Telling the terrible story of Olive Ann Oatman, just a child, was difficult for the mother of a daughter herself. Documentation of Olive's life in Sherman is sparse. Normally, that challenge would simply have set me to digging deeper, but I felt strangely reluctant to do that to Olive. Surely she deserved peace and anonymity if anyone did.

Lucy Kidd-Key. Now there was a Southern woman down to her fingertips, one who didn't hesitate for a second to use her "womanly qualities," as she called them. She got what she wanted, and people thanked her for letting them give it to her. That takes brains.

As with Lucy Pickens, I was amazed that no one had written Ela Hockaday's story. Sadly, in Bonham, where she grew up, few people even know of her anymore. "Didn't she go off to Dallas and start a school?" several people asked me. "But it's closed now, I think."

Dearest to my heart is Edna Gladney, for our daughter is adopted through the Gladney Center. Not a day goes by that I don't say a silent "thank you" to Aunt Edna. I sat in the Sherman Library reading her masterful demolition of the county commissioners court and laughed out loud, to the dismay of the other patrons.

Enid Justin I knew the least when I started and enjoyed the most. She had enough guts for a dozen women and didn't hesitate to call a spade a shovel.

These are the eight I selected, but they are by no means the only outstanding women of the Red River Valley; it would take several volumes to tell all their stories. Their "sisters" raised cattle, built schools and hospitals and monuments, and sang opera on world stages. They studied law, exhorted the masses, sculpted and painted treasured works of art, and marched for every woman's right to vote. Red River women were tough, they were survivors.

They had to be.

Acknowledgements

This book would not have been possible without the help of many people.

First, Republic of Texas Press editor Mary Elizabeth Goldman, who developed the concept for this new "Women of the West" series.

A big thank-you to my husband and daughter, Bill and Ann, who actually manage to live with an author; Bill even does double duty as my personal editor—and we're still married. And thank you to the Monday night gang, a bunch of women who know how to tear apart a manuscript, but in a nice way.

To the staffs of the Sherman Public Library/Genealogy Room, Austin College Library and Archives, the Red River Historical Museum of Sherman, and the Dallas Public Library/Genealogy Section, where I do so much of my research. Also the staffs of the Bryan County Historical Society (Calera, Oklahoma), Edgefield County (South Carolina) Historical Society, Texas Woman's University Library/Women's Collection, Center for American History (Austin, Texas), Mount Vernon Ladies' Association library, Oklahoma Historical Society library, the DeGolyer Library at Southern Methodist University (Dallas), the South Caroliniana Library of the University of South Carolina at Columbia, and the Public Information Office of USC-Aiken.

Thanks to Ellen Wilson (Development Office) and Kayte Steinert-Threlkeld (vice president, Public Information) of The Gladney Center; Christy Bednar (Director of Development) at The Hockaday School; Doris Floyd (Personnel Manager) and the employees of Nocona Boot Company; Marsha Taylor, Enid Justin's niece, for sharing photos with me; Jane Dumas Chester, Edna Gladney's niece for sharing family photos and memorabilia; and Ruth Briggs and Mr. Bender of the Harrison County Historical Museum in Marshall.

Sherrie S. McLeRoy

CHAPTER ONE

Sophia Suttonfield Aughinbaugh Coffee Butt Porter

"Set your peg and work toward it."

. . . Sophia Porter

Was she the Jezebel of legend and story? Or was she just a beautiful woman with too much natural charm for her own good? Probably no one will ever know. What is certain is that Sophia Porter was an astute businesswoman with an eye to the primary need of a developing nation: land.

And while she didn't change Texas history, she sure did liven it up.

FRONTIER CHILDHOOD

From the beginning Sophia's life was spent on the edge of civilization. Fort Wayne, where she was born on December 3, 1815, was in the middle of a military reserve and surrounded by Indian lands that comprised most of the modern state of Indiana.[1] When Sophia's parents arrived at Fort Wayne in 1814, nineteen-year-old Laura Taylor Suttonfield was one of only five women among nearly sixty men.

Laura, who was born in Boston in 1795 and grew up in Detroit,[2] later recalled that her life at Fort Wayne was spent amidst "soldiers, savages and pioneers, encumbered with the care of a large family, pressed with poverty and the privations of a frontier country, sickness and death of loved ones and more than half a century of constant unremitting toil. . . ."[3]

The large family[4] had begun in 1814 when Laura presented her Virginia-born husband William with a son. But the boy died only a few weeks after Sophia was born. William Suttonfield, a veteran of the War of 1812, was discharged from the Army shortly afterwards, and he moved his family just outside the fort to an 18' by 30' log home. It was adjacent to the stone structure where he operated a trading post with the Indians and from which he supplied the fort itself. William also carried the mail from Fort Wayne to Chicago and eventually opened a tavern and hotel. He was one of the first to buy lots when the new town was platted in 1824, served on its board of trustees, and subscribed to the First Presbyterian Church.

In this setting of an isolated military post, Sophia grew to young womanhood. Her earliest existing photograph depicts her in her thirties, long after she'd left Fort Wayne: a beautiful woman with dark hair and with a high forehead and square jaw she inherited from her mother. As a teenager, she must have been stunning. Surrounded by soldiers, with few other women present, she must have also been a constant temptation. Some authors[5] believe she began her "career" with men here; but no documentary evidence to prove—or disprove—that has been found.

Holland Coffee's first trading post has been reconstructed in Lawton, Oklahoma. The Texas post in which Sophia lived was probably identical.

(Author photo)

JESSE AUGHINBAUGH

Sophia and her other siblings attended the County Seminary on Calhoun Street. In 1832, when Sophia was a vulnerable sixteen-going-on-seventeen, a new headmaster arrived, Jesse Augustine Aughinbaugh; a little over a year later, in July of 1833, Sophia married her teacher.

Little is known about Jesse, partly because Sophia herself later tried to hide his tracks: in at least one instance, she even skipped him entirely and listed her second husband as her first. Jesse was probably from a Pennsylvania Dutch family, though Sophia once described him as a high ranking Prussian army officer. That he was Catholic is indisputable, for Fort Wayne records show that he was soon forced to resign from the Seminary because of the fuss that resulted from the town's only teacher being Catholic.

There is no further mention of Jesse for nearly a year after their marriage, when the local newspaper carried an advertisement for J. A. Aughinbaugh & Co., druggists (June 1834).

And almost another year passed before the couple turned up in the newspaper again, as the honorees at a "Social Party" given by William and Laura Suttonfield on April 1, 1835. This was probably a "bon voyage," for in late June the Aughinbaughs arrived in Nacogdoches, Texas, then still a part of Mexico. Jesse's entry certificate from the Mexican government,[6] issued on July 8, listed him as married and "of very good morality" and granted him a league of land (4,428.4 acres) near the Trinity River in modern Houston County.[7]

And then Jesse disappeared.

He was never listed on a Texas census, nor does he appear in any of the standard reference books on the state's history and genealogy. One of the few hints to his subsequent life is an 1854 deed in which *Jose* Augustine Aughinbaugh, of San Patricio County, sold Jesse's original land grant. There is also a recurring story that his son visited "Glen Eden," Sophia's Red River home, after her death.

Did Jesse desert his wife in Texas? Or did she leave him? One 1936 newspaper story about her life reported that Jesse was "a German officer who deserted her . . . at Old Washington" (Washington-on-the-Brazos). In his book *The Day of San Jacinto*, Frank Tolbert noted that Juan Almonte's journal referred to a lone Prussian who turned up at Santa Anna's camp just before the Battle of San Jacinto; Tolbert speculated that this could have been Jesse since Sophia herself also was in the area.[8]

But Sophia's companion and housekeeper in later years, Belle Skelly Williams Evans, said her mistress never talked about Jesse or their marriage, so it is likely no one, then or now, knew the truth of it.

SAM HOUSTON

A large body of folklore says she took to prostitution in order to survive on her own. While there is no "hard" evidence for this, it is a logical assumption in view of the limited choices for work available to women at the time. Hazel Greene, in a 1941 article, wrote that Sophia eventually turned up in a band of refugees, a story that agrees with the legend that she was caught in the infamous Runaway Scrape. For Sophia, who had come with her husband to the land of promise, was now in the middle of the Texas Revolution.

She would later boast of being the first woman on the battlefield at San Jacinto on April 21, 1836 and of ministering to a wounded Sam Houston. Belle Evans recalled that Sophia would regale friends and servants, formed up "in a circle around the old fireplace," with "stories of Mexican warfare, Indian massacres, and the refugee camp where she met and nursed General Sam Houston back to health."[9] Tolbert's account of the meeting notes that Sophia and Sam had met earlier in Nacogdoches and that "she did some practical nursing for Houston, sponge-bathing his face and combing his hair for him."[10]

Interestingly, there is no mention of her in any of the general's published letters or biographies, leading some to speculate that they were more than friends and that Houston was too embarrassed in his later Baptist years to write about her. Just exactly what kind of relationship these two shared is not clear and, again, Sophia never talked about it except as a friendship. But rumors about her and Houston persisted for years and may have led to the death of her second husband.

HOLLAND COFFEE

It was probably Houston who placed her in the care of Sam and America Lusk after San Jacinto. Lusk (1800-1861) was from Alabama but had moved to Tennessee where he met and married America Coffee (1801-1872) of McMinnville. They emigrated to Texas in 1834 and settled a farm at Washington (-on-the-Brazos). According to *The Handbook of Texas*, Lusk joined the Texas army in 1835 and "was detailed to guard the women and children during the Battle of San Jacinto."

America Coffee Lusk descended from an old Virginia family that had once been friends with Thomas Jefferson; it is no surprise that one of her brothers was named for him and another for George Washington. But it was her younger brother Holland who would play the next part in Sophia's life; and he is easily the most complicated and magnetic of her husbands.

Born in Tennessee in 1807, Holland Coffee left McMinnville at the age of twenty-two, with his friends and partners James Randolph and Silas Colville, to head west. They stopped at Fort Smith, Arkansas to open what would be their first trading post. Over the next few years, Holland and Silas took on several other partners as they crisscrossed modern Oklahoma and north Texas in search of sites for new posts. In 1834 they accompanied the Dodge Expedition under General Leavenworth to present-day Fort Sill and the Wichita Mountains. Later that year, they established a post on the Red River in Tillman County, Oklahoma and, soon after, one on Cache Creek near modern Lawton and then another on Walnut Bayou in Love County.[11] In 1837 Holland purchased a league of land for $350 from George Ivey on the south side of Red River (in modern Grayson County, Texas) near the junction of the Faw (False) Washita River, where he would build his last and most famous trading house.

By 1835 Holland Coffee had become well known among the Plains tribes of that region, by whom he was feared and respected. But in 1835 came the first of the complaints about him, this one from James Bowie, that Coffee and Colville helped the Indians that raided across the Red River into Texas.[12] There were even rumors that he planned to attack San Antonio and La Bahia with his Indian allies. Yet after a false rumor of his death in 1836, a government official characterized him as "bold[,] enterprizing [sic], intelligent and industrious, and no mean character."[13]

Coffee and Colville's posts soon became popular with the warriors who wished to sell cattle and horses and to ransom captives, all taken on raids. In 1837, for example, Holland "traded" 400 yards of calico and a large quantity of blankets, beads, and other trade goods for a Mrs. Crawford, captured near Bastrop with her children. But he was unsuccessful at ransoming Mrs. John Horn, who later wrote that Holland wept when the Comanche refused to trade, and that he gave her and her children clothing and flour.[14]

The Texas House Standing Committee on Indian Affairs gave more credence to Bowie and Coffee's enemies, for they recommended that fall (1835) that Coffee's Texas post be closed or placed under surveillance. Holland traveled to Houston to answer the charges against him, which he did so successfully that they were dropped. In addition, he was reimbursed $691 for "monies expended in purchasing Texian prisoners from the Indians."[15] President Sam Houston also appointed him as a commissioner to negotiate a treaty with several North Texas tribes.

Family genealogies state that in 1837 Holland also assisted his brother Thomas Jefferson Coffee in his appointment by President Andrew Jackson "to remove the Indians, the Cherokees and the Choctaws, from north Miss[issippi] to the Indian Territory."[16]

How and where Holland met Sophia Aughinbaugh is a matter of debate, but it was likely at the Lusk home in Washington, sometime in 1836 or 1837. Even what happened next is open to speculation.

Did they marry twice?

DIVORCE: PART ONE

By Sophia's own account, she and Holland married in 1837 and traveled 600 miles by horseback from Washington, through Nacogdoches, back to Coffee's Trading House on the Red River.[17] But no marriage license has ever been found. Yet there still survives a bill of sale from February 1838 in which "Sophiah Coffee" purchased a slave from John Rogers of Fort Smith. And Mrs. Dilue Harris wrote in her "Reminiscences" that Holland and his wife were present in Houston at the Washington's Birthday Ball on February 22, 1838.

Five months later, Sophia returned to Houston to seek a divorce—from Jesse Aughinbaugh. Had she thought him dead, only to discover Jesse was still alive? Or had she and Holland taken advantage of the confusion regarding the validity of the old Mexican marriage laws under the new Republic, laws which would have made her marriage to Jesse illegal since it was not performed in the Catholic Church?

Whatever the reason, Sophia petitioned Judge James Robinson of Harris County District Court for a divorce on July 25. She showed, to Robinson's "satisfaction," that Jesse resided "out of the jurisdiction of this court."

Unfortunately, all the original court records for this case, other than the summation in the Minute Book, have been lost. Still extant is the notice Sophia placed in *The Telegraph & Texas Register* at the court's direction which notified Jesse of her petition and asked him to appear at October Court to answer it. Only by "reading between the lines" of the later Minute

Book entry can one determine that Jesse did, indeed, appear: "It is therefore . . . ordered . . . by the Court that the Plaintiff [Sophia] take nothing by her Bill but that *the Defendant [Jesse] recover of the Plaintiff all costs by him about his suit in this Behalf Expended.*" (author's italics)[18]

While she waited through the summer of 1838 for the district court's decision, Sophia operated a boardinghouse for Army recruits. Folklore again says she was catering to the men's more base needs; but it is possible that she's been confused with the colorful Permelia (or Pamela) Mann, who owned the Mansion House Hotel and was indeed charged with prostitution. Quartermaster records in the Texas State Archives show three payments, totaling $800, made to Sophia *Aughinbaugh* "for rent of quarters for the recruits at Houston" between August 16 and December 16, 1838. However, they do not describe the house or its location, and early Houston city records are equally unhelpful. Since Sophia's name does not appear on the roll of Houston taxpayers for that period, she probably leased or rented the property.

Holland, meanwhile, was at Fort Gibson, conferring on Indian matters; at Bonham to deal with a contested land claim; and at Shawneetown (near modern Denison), negotiating a treaty with the Keechi, Tawakoni, Waco, and Tawehash tribes in his capacity as President Houston's commissioner. That summer, he was also elected from Fannin County to the Texas Legislature. His continued absence from Houston over most of the period in which Sophia ran the boardinghouse indicates that she did so alone. There are no records of complaints from the Army about the facilities, so she presumably operated it in an efficient manner.

DIVORCE: PART TWO

By the time Holland arrived to take his seat in the Legislature in November, Sophia had grown tired of dealing with the court to no avail and took her petition to the Legislature. If a divorce suit was scandalous enough in court, this action placed her beyond the pale and caused more discussion among the legislators than the homestead bill.[19]

Ezekiel Cullen of San Augustine presented her petition in the House on November 27, and it was referred to a special committee comprised of Cullen, Louis Cooke of Brazoria, and G. W. Hill of Robertson County. Two days later, it came back up on the floor and narrowly missed being rejected; among those voting in favor of the bill was Holland Coffee. But on November 30, it was indefinitely postponed. The petition then went to the Texas Senate, introduced there by President Pro Tem Stephen Everitt of Jasper and Jefferson Counties, on December 3. The Senate, however, shilly-shallied more than the House had. Sophia's bill was referred to one special committee, which reported favorably, and then to a second, chaired by Edward Burleson of Bastrop County. It was subsequently "laid on the table until called up" three times.

On December 27, Isaac Burton moved to take up "the bill for the relief of Sophia Aughinbaugh" but was voted down. Stephen Everitt then forced a second reading, but the vote tied at five to five. On the twenty-ninth, it passed to a third reading but, two days later, was again "laid on the table."

By this time, Sophia must have been sorely exasperated, and, it is said, her old friend Sam Houston stepped in to move the process along now that his term as president was over. On January 4, 1839, the Texas Senate passed the bill by a vote of six to five. After four days of further deliberations, the House followed suit—with Holland Coffee voting aye.[20]

When Harris County District Court finally dismissed her case in May, Sophia and Holland were long since married, legally this time, by Sam Lusk, and back on the Red River. Holland's wedding gift to her was, prophetically, one-third of a league of land.[21]

LIFE ON THE RED

In recounting her history forty years later to the Old Settlers Association of Grayson County, Sophia described her life on the Red River from 1839 until 1845. The nearest neighbor, she told them, was twenty-five miles away at Warren's Trading House, and their own post was "guarded by a few settlers and the Texas Rangers." Horses had to be watched while the slaves plowed to prevent Indians from stealing them, and firearms were stacked under a tree during preaching for easy access in case of attack.

The Coffees lived in the fort "in a lap board house with puncheon floor and our table consisted of a dry goods box with legs in [sic] it." Sophia grew and picked the cotton herself for her first quilt, and Holland "placed" it out in squares for her to quilt. A rag rug she made herself and another dry goods box for a wardrobe were the extent of the furnishings, and, she recalled, "I was the happiest woman in Texas."[22]

This was despite the fact that the Indians were about to drive them from their home. No sooner had the couple returned from their wedding trip than Holland set out to negotiate a new treaty. But Fannin County's population continued to decline to a hundred settlers, and even Holland was on the verge of pulling out when Texas Secretary of War Albert Sidney Johnston recommended that a new line of forts be built on the western frontier. To connect them, the Republic would build the Military Road.

In 1840, under the command of Colonel William Cooke, the troops building that road from Austin to the Red River erected a supply post, Fort Johnson, near Coffee's Trading House. They represented a badly needed boost to Holland's business, buying from him such necessities as shirts, tobacco, gunpowder, padlocks, wooden buckets, and tools. The post also bought foodstuffs from Coffee's.[23]

Unfortunately, the Army either didn't pay him for supplies charged there or, in some cases, paid only in land scrip.[24] That, coupled with his own purchases of land and slaves, and loans he had taken out from his brother Thomas Jefferson Coffee, left Holland badly in debt. By this time, he had also dissolved his partnership with Silas Colville, and they divided the land they jointly owned in the Washita Bend area near the trading post.

By the spring of 1841, the soldiers had left and Indian raids had intensified; Holland joined James Bourland's militia company under General Edward Tarrant for the spring campaign. Perhaps uneasy about the outcome, he wrote a will on May 7 in which he left his entire estate to his "beloved wife Sophia." That summer, after the militia built Bird's Fort (between modern Fort Worth and Arlington), Sophia must have joined him, for the troops named the lake close by the fort, Lake Sophia, because "it, too, was a heavenly body."[25]

Back on the Red River, their life resumed its old course. Holland continued to buy and sell land, to purchase more slaves to work the new properties, and to be involved in lawsuits from Bonham to Nacogdoches. Sophia had her own business interests, buying a slave girl for $500 and land on Iron Ore Creek for $230, among other purchases. After the Civil War, she would sell that land for more than $6,500, a tidy return on her investment.

Coffee's Trading House grew in importance as settlers began to fill North Texas. The Snively Expedition outfitted there in 1843; two years later, Holland platted the land around the post and began to sell it in lots as the town of Preston. Drovers moved the first few herds of cattle up the Preston Road, as Cooke's 1840 route came to be called for its terminus at Coffee's. Holland had opened a ferry in 1839 at the Rock Bluff crossing on the Red River and acquired the estate of his old partner, Silas Colville, after he was killed in a gunfight.[26]

In the winter of 1845-1846, Holland hired on with Pierce Butler's expedition to negotiate an Indian treaty at Comanche Peak in Somervell County. Butler and his co-commissioner, M. G. Lewis, rendezvoused at Coffee's in January 1846, while Holland sent runners to tell the Indians of the upcoming council. He then accompanied the expedition to Comanche Peak and recruited the hunters who provided the party with meat. Holland also supplied much of the food and trade goods given to the attending Indians.[27] Because of his fluency with their languages, he may also have handled some interpretation between the whites and Indians.

That same winter, he hired a party of Mormons traveling from Illinois to Central Texas to build the Coffees a house located a mile from the post and the Rock Bluff crossing. By April 1846 they had completed Glen Eden, a two-story house of oak logs with a pitched roof, fieldstone chimneys at either end, and a stone foundation forty-eight feet long that supported four rooms—two up and two down—and a dogtrot hallway.

Living with Holland and Sophia in the new house were Tennessee and Mary Jewell, young daughters of his sister Elizabeth. She and her husband, George Jewell, had emigrated to Fannin County from McMinnville, but both died soon after their arrival in Texas.

Construction of Glen Eden only added to Holland's growing debts. Traveler William Quesenbury visited in the fall of 1845 and wrote that he found him "much changed but as noble as ever." Was this a reference to the burden of worry he carried over his debts? Or was it, as folklore says, jealousy over Sophia and her attentions to the soldiers and other men who now visited Glen Eden regularly? And how much of a role did Holland's regular absences on business and Indian affairs play in their marital discord?

DEATH OF HOLLAND COFFEE

While Holland was at Comanche Peak with Butler, Sophia was at home entertaining fourteen-year-old Eugenia Coffee from Mississippi, the daughter of Holland's brother George Washington Coffee. The girl soon met Charles Ashton Galloway, a merchant from Fort Washita (near modern Durant, Oklahoma), and they married on May 13, 1846. Four days later, while he was on a visit to Fort Washita, Holland made a codicil to his 1841 will and wrote that he was "apprehensive that surrounding circumstances may soon terminate my life."

The true origin of the quarrel between Holland and Charles Galloway has been lost over time. In one version, Sophia grew angry over remarks Galloway made about her past liaisons—including Sam Houston—and goaded Holland into the fight, declaring she would rather be married to a dead hero than a live coward. In another she wished to "get rid" of Holland so she could marry Justice of the Peace Thomas Murphy, who actually married her sister Frances the following year. In yet another version, she was carrying on with every soldier that came through Preston and drove her husband wild with jealousy.[28]

One of the few real clues is in the court records of Grayson County. In the fall of 1847, Thomas Murphy was indicted for "malconduct of office" because he had "knowledge of the intention and determination of one Holland Coffee to perpetrate and commit an unlawful assault upon one Charles A. Galway [sic]" and "unlawfully and contemptuously" did nothing about it.[29]

A descendant of Eugenia's believes that Holland felt Galloway had taken advantage of her extreme youth. What Holland didn't know, she contends, was that Eugenia had rushed into the wedding because she didn't want to go back to Mississippi. Her mother was remarrying, to a man old enough to be the girl's grandfather; Eugenia feared he would be strict and decided that her own marriage, as soon as possible, was the best answer.

On October 1, 1846, Holland and Charles met in the streets of Preston in an "Indian duel:" a fight to the death. One observer reported that Holland was armed with a bois d'arc stick, bowie knife, single barrel pistol, six-shooter, and a double barrel shotgun loaded with buckshot. Holland called Charles out into the street from his brother's store; Charles replied, "yes, sir" and those were the only words spoken. "Galloway came to the door," the witness wrote, "and Coffee knocked him down and then got under him by the head and commenced operations to kill; Galloway got out his knife . . . and struck upwards; he made three licks . . . and each lick was a mortal one. Coffee fell off Galloway dead, and so tight was his grip that he carried Galloway with him, Galloway not much hurt." The witness concluded by reporting that Holland "had said he would kill Galloway whenever he could find him off the reserve," *ie.*, the Indian Territory.[30]

Charles was later acquitted in Grayson County court: a clear case of self-defense, the jury found. The *Northern Standard* of Clarksville wrote of Holland after the trial that he was "warmly esteemed by a large circle of friends . . . noted for great frankness and natural nobleness of character . . . remarkable for the considerate kindness of feeling more ordinarily attendant upon refined society . . . a warm friend and true hearted gentleman."

GEORGE BUTT

Sophia buried Holland in a brick mausoleum on the hill behind Glen Eden. His will left her more than five thousand acres of land, nineteen slaves, herds of horses and cattle, his businesses at the post and in Preston, as well as Glen Eden. What she soon discovered was that he'd also left thousands of dollars of debt. She tried to recover but by December of 1847 was forced to mortgage the house and more than a thousand acres to Thomas Coffee.[31]

And she married a third time.

No record of her marriage to George N. Butt of Virginia has been found, but Mrs. Helen Morrison Cummins of Sherman later recalled attending the wedding reception at Glen Eden. Additional evidence lies in a deed signed "Sophia Butt" that dates to early December of 1847.

But was her relationship with George a business one?

On Valentine's Day 1848, soon after their marriage, she and George filed a contract in Grayson County Court. He gave her $1,708 to cover her due notes, assumed another $2,228 in notes, gave her an outright $2,000 in cash, and agreed to educate Tennessee and Mary Jewell. In return, Sophia gave him 1,438 acres of land and three slaves: a good deal on her part and a highly unusual marital contract.

George Butt had been born in Princess Anne County, Virginia in 1813 and may have met Sophia in New Orleans; but that, too, is uncertain.[32] George seems to have gotten into trouble with debt at an early age. An 1841 deed of trust shows that he owed money on several notes; to secure them, he pledged livestock, a horse cart and its harness, all his household and kitchen furniture, all his poultry, and all his "present crop of oats and corn now growing."[33] Some of the money he invested in Glen Eden may have been inherited from his father on the latter's death in 1849.

Contemporary accounts indicate that George was arrogant and persnickety. Army explorer Randolph Marcy, returning from his 1849 expedition, stopped at Glen Eden for provisions. George looked at the tattered and dirty man "in a very curt and indifferent manner" and wanted nothing to do with the stranger until Marcy introduced himself. George

The earliest known photograph of Sophia,
circa 1850, with third husband George Butt.

(Courtesy Red River Historical Museum, Sherman, Texas)

then became gracious and placed "his corn, hay, house, and everything it contained" at Marcy's disposal.[34]

George insisted that Sophia, rather than the servants, set the dining room table to his specifications. Known as Major Butt (apparently a courtesy title), he was passionate about railroads, invested in mostly worthless rail company stock, and was a delegate to the 1853 railroad convention which formulated transportation policy for Texas. He bought more slaves for Glen Eden, received grants of land from the Peters Colony, and purchased other land such as the old Shawnee-town site.

He also had a temper and was charged with assault with intent to murder in 1849. The case was moved from Grayson to Collin County Court and eventually dismissed more than a year later when a key prosecution witness failed to appear. Surviving records do not give more particulars. George was also the defendant in several suits for debt, and he himself charged others with damages and trespass. Between 1849 and 1859 he was involved in at least ten cases in Grayson County, two of which went to the Texas Supreme Court.

One of these he filed jointly with Sophia in 1858, charging Benjamin Franklin Colbert and Alexander Browne of the Indian Territory with interfering in their operation of Holland Coffee's Rock Bluff ferry. Colbert, a Choctaw Indian, operated a competing ferry downstream. Overruled, the Butts went to the Supreme Court; Sophia eventually dropped the suit in 1866.

The census records of 1850 listed the Butts' worth at more than $18,000. Over the next decade, they expanded Glen Eden, covered it in siding brought from Jefferson, Texas, and added long galleries to the front and back, as well as a kitchen and wine cellar. Sophia indulged her love for plants—she is credited with having the first rose garden in the county—by building a rock garden on one side of the house and a pit-style greenhouse on the other. An orchard of more than a hundred fruit trees stretched from the rear of Glen Eden to the cemetery hill, while grape and berry vines covered the south lawn, destined for jams and pies and potent liquors to fill the wine cellar. In the front yard stood a magnolia tree grown from a seedling given Sophia by Sam Houston. And just before the Civil War broke out, she planted a line of catalpa trees down the driveway with seeds sent her from California by Albert Sidney Johnston.

She and George filled Glen Eden with furnishings and china from New Orleans and even developed a large flock of peacocks that strutted across the lawn and ended their days as feather fans and baked peahen. Visitors recalled parties that went on for days and the fine food and wines served there: you never knew, said one, what was under the domed covers on the plates.

The Butts' entertained the famous and the soon-to-be-famous. Randolph Marcy often stopped there on his trips west and was responsible for bringing a military supply depot to Preston. Fitzhugh Lee, nephew of Robert E. Lee and later governor of Virginia, is said to have recuperated from an Indian wound there. In 1855 the U.S. Second Cavalry passed through Preston on its way from St. Louis to a new post in San Antonio. On Albert Sidney Johnston's staff were Captain Kirby Smith, Lieutenant John B. Hood, Lieutenant J. E. B. Stuart, and Lieutenant Colonel Robert E. Lee (who was not with the company at that point).

One of the most enduring stories about Sophia is that she entertained both Lee and Ulysses S. Grant.[35] One newspaper article from 1929 even pointed out that Lee had used the rocking chair and Grant the mohair sofa.[36] There is, however, no evidence to indicate that either man visited Glen Eden. Possibly the original confusion rose from the fact that Lee was on the staff of the Second Cavalry, which did stop there. This story seems to have gained credence after Sophia's death when it was repeated by Aaron Coffee, Holland's nephew, to the *Denison Herald*. He even reported that Grant had invited Sophia to his presidential inauguration, but that she had "lost" the letter.

The Butts paid for this luxury with the cotton they began to grow in earnest in the 1850s and with the sale of land. By 1861 Glen Eden and the other properties were valued at nearly $26,000, but the good times were soon to be over.

CIVIL WAR

The war quickly touched Grayson County and the Red River with conflicts between Unionists and Secessionists. The Indians grew bolder, and inadequate numbers of Confederate and militia troops had to protect hundreds of miles of frontier against tribes, Jayhawkers, and deserters.

In the winter of 1863-1864, William Quantrill led his troop of Confederate guerrillas from Kansas and Missouri to winter in Grayson County. At first welcomed with open arms, the men soon became violent and split into several bands. One, commanded by Quantrill himself, camped near Glen Eden on Big Mineral Creek while another located fifteen miles away in Sherman.

On Christmas Eve, several of the younger men got drunk and came into Sherman, riding their horses into Ben Christian's Hotel where Sophia was attending a dance. One guerrilla bet another that he could shoot the tassels off her hat without hurting her; he did so, and Sophia, reported observers, never stopped dancing.[37]

Early in February 1864, George went into Sherman on business and never returned. Searchers found his body a week later lying to the side of the Sherman-to-Preston road. Days later, Sophia spotted Fletch Taylor, one of Quantrill's men, wearing George's watch, and she raised the cry with the Confederate authorities in Bonham. Taylor admitted killing George but claimed it had been done on Quantrill's orders. According to another of the guerrillas, George "had been very active in trying to have every able bodied man in the county forced in the ranks of the Confederate army;"[38] but it's likely his murder was committed for robbery and not for political reasons.

Sophia buried George in Sherman's West Hill Cemetery and later placed a flat stone over his grave, in the fashion of Tidewater Virginia where he had been born. On the stone was inscribed: "Thou art gone, no more we meet/ No more our longing looks repeat/ Then let me breathe this parting prayer/ The dictate of my bosom's care/ This is of love the final close/ Oh God the fondest last adieu."[39]

If their marriage started as a business relationship, the poem indicates it ended as something warmer. But this proved not to be love's "final close" after all in Sophia's life.

CONFEDERATE PAUL REVERE

By now, with wartime inflation running rampant, Sophia's estate was valued at $45,400, with $18,000 of that in slaves alone. She fought off at least one Indian attack during this period behind a barricade of cotton bales and continued to plant cotton in hope of retrieving some money after the now inevitable Confederate downfall.

The adventure which earned her the title of "Confederate Paul Revere" does not appear in any report in the *Papers of the War of the Rebellion*. But the story did surface during the Texas Centennial in an interview with an elderly ex-Confederate who claimed to have been there.

James Bourland, commander of Texas' Frontier Regiment, passed through Glen Eden with his troops on their way back to Fort Washita. He warned Sophia that Federal troops were behind him. They did, indeed, arrive and she invited them in for dinner and then a tour of her wine cellar, an invitation the Yankees accepted with alacrity. When they were all drunk, she locked them in the cellar, saddled up a reluctant mule, and tore off to the north after Bourland, fording the icy Red River. Legend says she rode all the way to Fort Washita, but that's not likely in view of the distance. Still another says she stripped to her underwear and swam the river, summoning the Confederates with a whistle when she reached the northern shore. In reality, she probably used the mule and stopped at a sympathetic home in the Territory where she either found or sent word to Bourland to pick up the prisoners.[40]

LOVE'S FINAL CLOSE

The Red River country had finally become too dangerous even for Sophia, now fifty years old, and she packed her remaining gold in tar buckets and set out with her slaves for Waco, the nearest refuge town.

There she met James Porter, a Confederate cavalry officer and a widower from Missouri who was on his way to Mexico to join Emperor Maximillan's army.

Born in Kentucky in 1809, Porter had served as a judge in Independence, Missouri; hence, he became known in Grayson County as "Judge Porter." In Independence he'd operated a Santa Fe mail contract business known as Hall & Porter, but he lost it at the outbreak of the war because of his Southern sympathies. His wife, Mahala, was dead and his daughter, Vestia, married to a Kansas City physician when he met Sophia and decided to stay in Texas. They were married by Rufus Burleson, president of Baylor College, on August 2, 1865 and returned to Glen Eden from Waco that fall.

Sophia's capital investment in slaves was now gone and her estate plummeted in value to about $12,000. But she still had land, and it was that which sustained her.

She and James began to buy and sell land, often picking up new tracts cheaply at sheriffs' auctions. The sale of the Iron Ore Creek property and her still-valuable lots in Preston gave them seed money and helped increase their holdings by a third within a year. Land resold quickly to the many new families moving into Texas after the war.

In 1869 Sophia returned to Fort Wayne to see her mother on what was probably her first visit home since she left thirty-four years earlier. And under James Porter's influence, she decided to "get religion." At a camp meeting one night, either in Sherman or Shawneetown, she ran down the aisle in an orange satin dress and threw herself at the feet of the Reverend John Witherspoon Pettigrew McKenzie, a Methodist minister who had founded McKenzie College in 1841.

McKenzie knew Sophia and her history, and he was not impressed by this public act of repentance. He informed her, recalled witnesses, that she would have to do good deeds for twelve years before he'd let her into his church. And he wasn't hopeful even then, for "the sun, the moon, and the stars" were all against her becoming a Christian. Unabashed, Sophia went to the Reverend J. M. Binkley of Sherman's First Methodist Church. He accepted her into the congregation, and they remained good friends for the rest of her life.[41]

Now Glen Eden, once the site of lavish parties, continued to be a social mecca, but Sophia, greyhaired and answering to "Aunt Sophia," no longer permitted dancing. She and James gave money and/or land to several churches in the Preston area "in consideration of the love we bear for the cause of Christ and from an earnest desire to promote his heritage on earth." In 1879 she became one of the founding members of the Grayson County Old Settlers Reunion, an association of surviving early settlers who gathered each August to visit and recall old times. According to the minutes, she brazenly lied about her age on at least one occasion, claiming she was sixty when she was actually seventy-six years old.

It is these placid years in the 1880s and 1890s that Belle Evans recalled so vividly after she came to Glen Eden in 1885. Sophia, said Belle, "was very proud and was immaculate in her appearance, and she carried herself as straight as an Indian . . . [She] was as changeable as the Texas winds. She was gracious or curt as the mood struck her. She was a tempest of temperament but altogether lovely and lovable."[42]

Despite the painful rheumatism that plagued her, Sophia continued to entertain, even after James Porter died in 1886 following a long illness. She surrounded herself, recalled Belle, "with the notable persons of the day from whom she could learn of the state of politics and social life of Texas."

The servants both feared and adored her, and "five or six Negroes hovered over the table at meal time to fulfill her every wish." She ran a strict household, requiring Belle to check the servants' mouths to make sure they weren't stealing fruit from her prize berry vines.

DEATH OF SOPHIA PORTER

Sophia Suttonfield Aughinbaugh Coffee Butt Porter died peacefully in her sleep on August 27, 1897 after a short illness. She was eighty-one. Reverend Binkley conducted her funeral service at Glen Eden, and hundreds of mourners and spectators camped in the woods around the house like "an old-time camp meeting."

The hearse was pulled by four black horses draped in black net, and Sophia herself was laid to rest in a pink satin dress trimmed with black lace. After the funeral, which cost $170, she was buried beside James in Preston Cemetery. His

A collage, circa 1890, of Sophia and her
Red River home, "Glen Eden."

(Courtesy Red River Historical Museum, Sherman, Texas)

tall columnar monument reads simply, "He made home happy;" hers asserts with pride that she was a "Pioneer of Texas since 1835."

The Sherman and Denison newspapers vied with each other to eulogize the woman some had once considered a whore. "An aged saint . . . an ornament to society in every respect . . . a magnificent example of the Spartan mothers of the old South . . . one of the most noted women in the pioneer history of Texas. . . ."

Sophia's will left half her household goods and livestock, as well as land already conveyed her, to Holland's surviving niece, Mary Jewell Moseley of Midland, Texas. The other half and several tracts of land went to her longtime overseer, Confederate veteran Captain J. H. Williams, who would marry Belle two years later. Williams was appointed trustee of several notes due Sophia, with instructions on how they were to be spent; $1,628 was to renovate the Methodist Church in Preston Bend, and $500 was "to assist Russell Noble to an education." When Noble repaid that loan, the money was to go to the Rescue Home for Fallen Women in Dallas. She also gave 337 acres of land to Southwestern University, a Methodist school in Georgetown, Texas. The *Sherman Register* reported dutifully that Sophia "distributed her possessions well and carefully, where it [sic] would do the most good."

Her personal estate was valued at $1,953 and included 11 cows, 46 hogs, several horses and mules, the "contense" of a china cabinet, furniture, 5 stands of bees, 25 gallons of wine, and 120 pounds of ham. The total estate, including lands and notes payable, came to more than $18,000.

AFTERWORD

After Sophia's death, Glen Eden was bought and sold several times before being purchased by Judge Randolph

Bryant of Sherman. He and his wife opened it to the public as a historic site during the Texas Centennial of 1936. That same year, the state erected a historical marker at the site of Holland Coffee's trading post.

But even then discussions were underway that would mean the end of Glen Eden.

For decades, residents of Grayson County had suffered floods and damage when the Red River went on a rampage and overflowed its banks. In 1939 the United States Congress appropriated $5.6 million to build Denison Dam and Lake Texoma as a flood control and hydroelectric power project. The damsite was to be located at the site of Baer's Ferry, only a few miles downriver from Preston and Glen Eden.

In the early months of 1942, with completion of the dam imminent, Judge Bryant began to dismantle the house, numbering the logs and moving them to higher ground. For Glen Eden, built close to the Red River, would be flooded when impoundment of the lake began. Bryant's plan was to rebuild the structure and open it as a museum of Grayson County history.

Unfortunately, Bryant's dream was never realized. Through several unfortunate circumstances, many of the main beams of aged oak and walnut were burned, and other components used to build several houses in the area. Portions of the structure were acquired by a Denison antiques dealer and, upon her death several years ago, were moved to Grayson County Frontier Village, an outdoor museum of the county's historic buildings.

Even Holland Coffee's brick mausoleum is now gone. His body was moved in 1960 to a plot in Preston Bend Cemetery and the original tomb destroyed. The new burial site is a few feet outside the fence which marks the graves of Sophia and James Porter.

Sophia was also honored with a historical marker in 1965 which describes her as the "Confederate Paul Revere," a reference to her escapade with the Yankees and the wine cellar. The text of the marker credits her actions with helping to "prevent Federal invasion of north Texas."

Of Sophia's empire, there are few other physical remnants left today, and most of her land along the river is under water. The Sherman Public Library houses a collection of documents which includes the deed to Holland Coffee's first property in this area, George Butt's railroad stock, and bills of sale for several Glen Eden slaves. The Red River Historical Museum in Sherman has some clothing, furniture, china, and photographs, most acquired from Belle Evans' family.

But almost a century after her death, Sophia's legacy and her legend live on in North Texas. The land that was once hers is now farms and subdivisions and resort communities along Lake Texoma. Her many fans affectionately call her "Sophie" and still argue heatedly over the details of her life and adventures, trying to fill in the gaps that lack of records and Sophia herself left. And more than one has stood by her grave and asked questions that will never be answered.

Notes—Chapter One

1   Inexplicably, her tombstone lists the date as 1813.

2   When a young girl, Laura and her father were captured near Mackinac by British troops and held some time as prisoners. At sixteen, she eloped with William Suttonfield; the young couple lived for two years in Upper Piqua, Ohio, where William supervised the pack trains that hauled Indian and military stores to Fort Wayne. After the War of 1812, Suttonfield was sent to Kentucky to serve under Major John Whistler, who would later build the fort where Sophia was born. The 1816 Suttonfield home was probably the first to be built in the town of Fort Wayne itself. William died in 1836; Laura lived until 1886.

3   Willa G. Cramton, *Women beyond the Frontier: A Distaff View of Life at Fort Wayne* (Historic Fort Wayne, Inc., 1977), 18.

4   Jane, born 1816, married a teacher, Myron Barbour; Sarah, born 1819, married James Galbraith. Frances married Thomas Murphy in 1849 at "Waltooga Hall" in Grayson County, Texas. Another brother, George, went to California as a '49er with his brother-in-law Myron. Other siblings were Anna and Acey.

5   For example, see Jack Maguire's article on Sophia in *Legendary Ladies of Texas*.

6   Another certificate granted that same day was to Robert Potter; the life of his famous wife, Harriet, strangely parallels Sophia's. And on July 6, entry was claimed by Jacob Snively, who would later provision his ill-fated expedition to harass Mexican traders on the Santa Fe Trail from the trading post of Sophia's second husband, Holland Coffee.

7   Nacogdoches Archives: 1835 Entrance Certificates. Original in General Land Office, Austin, Texas.

8   Frank Tolbert, *The Day of San Jacinto* (New York, 1959), 188-189.

9   Mrs. M. E. Jackson, "Shots Clipping Tassels from Her Hat Failed to Mar Dance Here for Aunt Sophia, Mistress at Glen Eden." *Dallas Morning News*, May 2, 1939.

10 Tolbert, *ibid.*, 188-189.

11 The second post has been reconstructed on the grounds of the Museum of the Great Plains in Lawton.

12 John H. Jenkins (editor), *The Papers of the Texas Revolution, 1835-1836: Volume I* (Austin, 1973), 301.

13 Grant Foreman, compiler, "Copies of Manuscripts in the Office of the Commissioner of Indian Affairs, Washington, DC," Volume 1, 67.

14 Josiah Wilbarger, *Indian Depredations in Texas* (Austin, 1889).
Audy J. and Glenna Middlebrooks, "Holland Coffee of Red River," *Southwestern Historical Quarterly* Volume 69 (Austin, Texas), 149, 159-160.

15 *The Laws of Texas: Volume I* (Austin, 1898), 16.

16 From a Coffee family genealogy prepared by Mrs. Ernest McLemore, daughter of Eugenia Coffee. Private copy given author by a family member.

17 There are many stories about this marriage. One says it took place in Waco, but that town had not yet been founded. Aaron Coffee, Holland's nephew, said after Sophia's death that they married in Bonham in 1840; but very little of his account in the Denison newspaper is correct. And a Lusk family genealogy says Sophia was the widow of an army officer when Holland met her.
"Incidents as Related by Mrs. Sopha Poter [sic]," Minute Book 1 of Grayson County Old Settlers Association (Sherman, Texas), September 5, 1879, 49.

18 *The Telegraph & Texas Register* (July 28, 1838).

19 In June 1839, a Robert Hanks sued Sophia in Harris County. The complaint? "Marriage of the Defendant [Sophia] suggested." The Minute Book states that the

Court decided "that the Husband be made party to this suit and ordered to appear and answer at the next term. . . ." Which husband? Jesse or Holland? Existing records do not say. The case was finally dismissed in December 1840 with Hanks paying all court costs. His identity and his relationship to Sophia have not been determined. (Minutes of the District Court, 11th Judicial District: Book B, 1838-1841 (Harris County, Texas), 212, 516.)

20   "Journal of the Senate of the Republic of Texas; First Session of the Third Congress, 1838." (Houston, 1839).
"Journal of the House of Representatives of the Republic of Texas (1) Regular Session of the Third Congress November 5, 1838 (2) Called Session of September 25, 1837." (Houston, 1839).

21   Holland's other accomplishments in this, his only legislative session, included: named a trustee of the newly established DeKalb College in Red River County; introduced a bill to appropriate $20,000 for Indian expenses; introduced another bill to locate a seat of justice in Fannin County; introduced a resolution questioning the disposition of money appropriated by the previous Congress for Indian affairs; presented a report to the Committee on Indian Affairs that charged that many of its agents were "utterly destitute of a knowledge of the Indian;" and voted against a motion to thank Sam Houston for his "able service" as first president of the Republic of Texas.

22   "Incidents as Related by Mrs. Sopha Poter [sic]," *op. cit.*, 49.

23   Records of the Army Quartermaster: First Regiment/Fourth Brigade in the Texas State Archives, Austin, Texas: dated October 23, 1840; December 10, 1840; December 16, 1840; January 23, 1841; March 12, 1841; March 15, 1841.

24   Years after Holland's death, Sophia finally received a partial cash payment.

25   A. C. Greene, "Bird's Fort: The Beginning," *Dallas Morning News* (September 7, 1984).

26   In 1848 Sophia was forced to file suit against Colville's heirs to clear her title to these lands and those divided after the partnership split—more than 5,000 acres that formed the bulk of her holdings.

27   Carolyn Thomas Foreman, "Pierce Mason Butler," *Chronicles of Oklahoma* (Volume 30, 1952), 20.
      Grant Foreman, "The Texas Comanche Treaty of 1846," *Southwestern Historical Quarterly* (Volume 51), 319-322.
      Records of the Office of Indian Affairs: "Ratified Indian Treaties: (Microfilm) Roll 4: 1838-1853," National Archives, Fort Worth, Texas.

28   Jack Maguire, "Sophia Porter: Texas' Own Scarlett O'Hara," *Legendary Ladies of Texas* (Texas Folklore Society, 1981), 75-76.
      Winnie Allen and Corrie Walker Allen, *Pioneering in Texas: True Stories of the Early Days* (Dallas, Texas, 1935), 84-85.
      Bright Ray, *Legends of the Red River Valley* (San Antonio, 1941), 45-67.

29   Minutes of Grayson County District Court, Fall Term 1847.

30   Letter from A. M. M. Upshaw of the Chickasaw Agency to Major William Armstrong, October 6, 1846. Copy in Holland Coffee Collection of Sherman Public Library, Sherman, Texas.

31   By deed of December 7, 1847, she sold Thomas 1,087 acres "whereon the said Sophia Coffee now resides" for $2,166, payable in two notes. One of those notes was eventually assumed by her brother-in-law Sam Lusk, whom she repaid in 1853.

32   Republic of Texas poll lists for 1846 show a G. N. Butt in Cass County.

33   Princess Anne County, Virginia Deed Book 40, pages 195-196.

34 Randolph B. Marcy, *Thirty Years of Army Life on the Border* (Philadelphia, reprint 1963), 346-348.

35 Both Lee and Grant served in Texas during the Mexican War; Lee returned in 1855.

36 *Dallas Morning News* (July 14, 1929), 3.

37 Richard S. Brownlee, *Gray Ghosts of the Confederacy: Guerrilla Warfare in the West, 1861-1865* (Baton Rouge, 1958), 139.

Jackson, *op. cit.*

38 *Ibid.*

39 George Butt's tombstone lists his death date as 1863, though the best available evidence, gleaned from books on Quantrill and from the president of the Quantrill Society, indicates it was 1864.

40 Allen, *op. cit.*, 88-89.

Ray, *op. cit.*, 45-67.

Dallas Morning News (July 14, 1929), 3.

Sherman Democrat (May 3, 1937).

41 Maguire, *op. cit.*, 78.

42 Homer de Golyer, "Sophia Porter's Texas Adventures Read Like Arabian Nights Chapters," *Dallas Morning News* (April 11, 1942).

CHAPTER TWO

Lydia Starr Hunter McPherson

"Our motto—Light First in Order—is
a good clue to our design."

. . . Lydia McPherson

In an age that had not yet given birth to Nellie Bly or Katharine Graham, Lydia McPherson was an anomaly: a woman in the man's world of newspaper publishing.

There was only a scant handful of female publishers in this country when Lydia established the first of the four newspapers that would bear her name on the mastheads. Her efforts in both journalistic and literary circles earned her praise from many, ridicule from some. But no man could wrest from her the title she won in more than three decades of work: "First Woman Newspaper Publisher in Texas and Oklahoma."

FAMILY BACKGROUND

Lydia Starr was born in Belmont County, Ohio[1] on August 11, 1826, one of six children of William F. and Sarah Lucas Starr. Her father was born in Virginia in 1796 and appears on various census records as a shoemaker (1850) and a farmer (1860). Sometime prior to 1820, he married Sarah Lucas of Maryland. Of their heritage, little is known other than that their "ancestors came from England and Scotland" to America in the late seventeenth century and were "farmers, lawyers, ministers and statesmen." Some, like Lydia's parents, settled in the Midwest, others "on the Pacific Coast."[2]

When Lydia was three years old, the Starrs moved ninety miles west to Jersey (Licking County), near Columbus. About 1838, William Starr moved his family once more, to Keosauqua in Van Buren County, Iowa, a town on the Des Moines River just north of the Missouri state line. After she graduated there at the age of seventeen, Lydia returned to Ohio to teach at "a select school" in Ashland for the princely sum of one dollar a week.

DAVID HUNTER

When and where she met David Hunter is uncertain. A stonemason, Hunter was born September 2, 1825 in Hunters Valley (Perry Country), Pennsylvania, the son of John and Sarah Yocum Hunter. He married Lydia at her father's new home in Birmingham, Iowa on May 3, 1849, and they returned to Keosauqua to set up housekeeping. Over the next decade, she gave birth to four children: Emorelda (Emma) in 1850, John Lucas (Luke) in 1853, Granville Owen (G. O.) in 1857, and Edwin Chester (E. C. or Chet) in 1859. Lydia and David's last child, Mary Wright Hunter, was born in December of 1862 but died weeks later on January 14, 1863.

The only known photograph of Lydia, circa 1890.

(Courtesy *Sherman Democrat*, Sherman, Texas)

The family's means were modest: the 1860 census valued David Hunter's real estate holdings at $600 and his personal estate at $150.

Their private life was tempestuous. David beat Lydia regularly, a fact Luke testified to in a Keokuk, Iowa court when his mother sought a divorce in 1869. The dissolution of her twenty-year marriage became final on August 24, and soon the relationship between Lydia and Luke also began to deteriorate; it would remain uneasy for many years.

Lydia moved the family to Oskaloosa, a town north up the Des Moines River from Keosauqua. There, to help support them, G. O. apprenticed at *Welch's Reform Leader*. In Oskaloosa, Lydia became known as "a Christian woman of culture and fine literary taste"[3]; it may have been here that she began to write professionally, but that is uncertain.

David Hunter disappeared from official records after the divorce, leading descendants to speculate that he either changed names or went by his middle name for legal purposes. Family legend says that he visited Lydia and the boys years later in Sherman, Texas. California relatives (descended from one of David's brothers) believe he returned to Texas and died there in 1904 in an unknown location.

TO THE INDIAN TERRITORY

In 1874 Lydia packed up her family[4] and moved to Caddo in the Choctaw Nation of the Indian Territory (now Oklahoma). What prompted her to choose that location is unknown. But it's likely that life in the Territory was not what she was accustomed to.

Named for the Indian tribe that once hunted in the nearby hills, Caddo (population 400) was a rough, tough town on the Missouri, Kansas & Texas Railroad and the closest rail point to Fort Sill. Game was still plentiful in the area, and thousands of skunk pelts were shipped from Caddo each year for the Eastern fur market. The town swarmed with soldiers going to and from Fort Sill. Because the Territory was dry, there were no saloons but rather "several places that had the semblance of a saloon, minus door blinds, foot rails and real liquor" on Buffalo Street. There, Jamaican ginger beer and concoctions of lemon extract were the drinks of choice. When combined with chewing tobacco and a military diet, E. C. Hunter later recalled, they "produced a breath a squirrel could climb."[5]

Caddo's streets were filled with freight wagons carrying supplies to Territory forts and reservations, with "tanked up" Indian boys and "bad white men." Cattle from the rich grazing lands of the Choctaw and Chickasaw nations were herded through town to be loaded onto rail cars. Lawlessness was rife; in a two-year period, at least fifteen murders were committed in and around Caddo.

GRANVILLE McPHERSON

One claim to civility that Caddo did have was a newspaper.

The *Oklahoma Star*[6] was established in January 1874 by W. J. Hemby. In April, Hemby sold the paper to his editor, Granville McPherson, who chose the newspaper's new motto—Progress and a Higher Civilization—and was the man who would play the next role in Lydia's life.

Born in Tennessee circa 1827, Granville moved to Saline County, Arkansas, married a woman known in the records only as Sophronia, and settled down as a farmer.[7] A decade later the family was living in Little Rock, where Granville worked as a surveyor. He had apprenticed to a printer in his youth, and it was in Little Rock that Granville returned to journalism, working on the *Herald* and the *Advocate*. There he met poet and soldier Albert Pike, who gave him his first instructions in Masonry. Granville rose quickly through Masonic ranks and served as Worshipful Master of Little Rock's Magnolia Lodge from 1858-1860, as Junior Warden of the Lodge of Perfection in 1858, and in several other important capacities.

Sophronia died just before the outbreak of the Civil War, possibly in giving birth to the McPhersons' last child.

Granville next appeared on April 18, 1861 as one of the signers of a declaration "To the People of Arkansas," which stated that Lincoln's recent actions had forced them to embark on a rebellion against his "weak and perfidious Administration."[8] When hostilities began, Granville joined the Confederate Engineers Corps. In the summer of 1862 he made his first trip to the Indian Territory on a surveying expedition to the Wichita Mountains.

On their return eastward in September, the engineers camped at Sulphur Spring in the Choctaw Nation, and there Granville met his second wife. Her name is unrecorded, but she would figure in a later newspaper battle as "the white widow of a dead Indian." She and Granville probably married late in 1863. But she and two of their children died; a son, Ben J., and a daughter survived.

And what of Granville's first family, back in Arkansas?

According to a descendant, he simply deserted them.

After the war, Granville spent some years wandering around the Territory and New Mexico before he turned up at Fort Washita in the early 1870s and opened a mercantile store. From there he made his way the short distance to Caddo and the *Oklahoma Star*.

MARRIAGE AND JOURNALISM

When he bought the *Star* in 1874, Granville McPherson had developed a passion that would guide his newspaper career in Caddo: seeing the Indian Territory become a United States Territory, governed by federal, rather than tribal, laws.[9]

Within a few months of his purchase there appeared a new writer in the pages of the *Star* who agreed wholeheartedly with his philosophy. As "Urania," her nom de plume, Lydia took wholeheartedly to the task of convincing Territory folks that Granville McPherson had seen the future.

By the time Urania's first essay was published in January 1875, she and Granville had already married, on December 18 at his old home in Fort Washita. Where and when they met is unknown. The first public intimation of their new relationship came in the March 12, 1875 issue of the *Star* in which Urania relates the conversation of the previous Saturday while she and Granville were in bed together and discussing the snowstorm outside.

It was a remarkably risque story, given the times and the fact that their marriage notice did not appear in the *Star* until May 20, more than two months later. Of course, Caddo was a small town, and everyone may well have known by then that Urania and "the Devil," as Granville was known, had married.

It is probably not a coincidence that, with Urania's appearance, the style of the *Star* changed also; it became longer, with more columns and more dramatic headlines. Whether Lydia had come to Caddo with journalistic experience, or Granville simply saw a natural talent in her, is unclear; but he soon began turning more and more of the daily work over to her.[10]

Soon Granville had the leisure to devote to his Masonic duties[11] or succumb to what he called his indifferent health and to spend days, even whole weeks, "entirely prostrated" upon his bed while Lydia put the paper together. Still appearing in its pages as Urania, Lydia published her first issue on May 20, 1875, styled herself "a humble contributor," and respectfully solicited "the prayers of the press." Perhaps it is no wonder that her wedding notice also appears in this issue. The following week Granville returned. "We feel it a simple duty," he wrote, "to express our gratitude to Urania for the able manner in which she conducted the *Star* last week, in the capacity of editor. We deem ourselves truly fortunate in having one competent to occupy the editorial chair when circumstances require it."

How he reconciled living with a "competent" woman and holding decidedly unsympathetic views toward suffragists is unrecorded. Granville took every opportunity to lambaste modern females in such comments as these: "Now what has Leavenworth City been guilty of that it should be subjected to such a dire calamity as a lecture by Victoria Woodhull?. . . Did anybody ever see a woman who knew how to fold a letter or sharpen a pencil? . . . We have always looked upon Caddo as being under the care of a special Providence and now are satisfied of it, since Elizabeth Cady Stanton passed by on her way south without stopping to give us a lecture."[12]

Granville disliked "niggars" as much as he did "modern women" and prophesied that the upcoming Civil Rights bill would result in many dead. "It won't win," he wrote. "All the legislating you can do will never put a niggar on an equality with a white man." Urania's views on the subject were not published.

LIFE AT THE *STAR*

In its early days, the McPhersons' relationship, both at work and home, seems to have been remarkably smooth, given Granville's penchant for bombast and oratory. Lydia described her husband as "a man of prepossessing appearance, winning manners, fine address and Anglo-Roman type of features." She cheerfully stepped in whenever health or travel took him from the office, though her name did not appear on the masthead until February 8, 1876[13] and not until July 6 was her byline as Mrs. L. S. McPherson on an article.

In "Star Lights," the local people and events column, Lydia occasionally twitted her husband on his health problems. "People generally hunt a thing where they think they lost it," she wrote early in 1876, "but the editor-in-chief of the *Oklahoma Star* has gone north, to hunt the health lost in his office. If he should be fortunate enough to overtake it, we hope he will take better care of it than he has in the past." A few weeks later, she inserted a mock advertisement offering "$1,000 payable in thanks" for anyone locating the "lost, strayed, or stolen" editor-in-chief. Even her Hunter sons got into the fray; G. O. and E. C. were the *Star's* printers and apparently liked Granville: "Hope when you come back you'll be fat as a pig and sleek as a mole."

Lydia and Granville also joked about life in Caddo, as one could do in a small town frontier newspaper. "A French chemist has found that bed bugs can be made into the richest and most delicious perfumery. If he will come, or send an agent to the *Star* office, we will agree to furnish him, at the very lowest figures, enough to keep every lady in Paris smelling loud for a whole year." Even the perennial "empty pockets of a newspaper editor"[14] were subject for columns, and the *Star* carried periodic notices that firewood, flour, meal, eggs, potatoes, "or in fact anything else in the eating line" were acceptable substitutes for the price of a subscription. Granville frequently wrote of growing old, and Lydia was moved to comment on the event when she was finally forced to wear spectacles: "time tells and we have had to come to it at last."[15]

Their life had its more serious disturbances, too. In March of 1876 little Flora McPherson became gravely ill and nearly died. Granville was also sick and Lydia nursed both him and the child, while also putting out the paper. Who was Flora? Was she Lydia's child? Probably not. Lydia's obituary lists all her children, both deceased and living; but it does not include Flora. She most likely was Granville's child by his second wife. He made several references in "Star Lights" to missing social occasions to stay "with the little ones at home," which suggests that he and Lydia were raising Flora and her brother Ben. What is also unclear is whether these are Granville's children by the second wife, or hers by her first husband, the "full-blooded Indian."

URANIA'S JOURNALISTIC STYLE

Lydia produced original poetry for the *Star*, selected verses from other poets, and also wrote genteel, "literate" essays on such topics as "Jealousy, the Green Eyed Monster" and "The Soul's Perfection is the Crown of Virtue."[16]

But in her editorials, Urania pulled few punches. Writing of Caddo's 1875 Fourth of July celebration, she tackled President Ulysses Grant's proposal to remove the "wild" Indian tribes from the western states to the Territory, a move opposed by many who feared the deleterious effect it would have on the Five Civilized Tribes and, consequently, on white settlers. "Standing as we do outside of the U. S., and threatened by the President with something worse than the seven plagues of Egypt, - the settlement of the wild tribes among us (-) it should not be a matter of much surprise, if we celebrated Independence Day more for the sake of our own social gratification than for the glorification of our oppressors. . . ."

Granville, and later Lydia, waged a constant war with Richard Shanks, an official with the Bureau of Indian Affairs whom Granville openly accused of corruption and of hate-mongering between whites and Indians.[17] Shanks, in return, often threatened to shut down the paper. In an editorial on the proposed intercourse law, which would prohibit whites from buying livestock in the Territory, Urania concluded by attacking the bill's proponent. "Excuse the *Star* Mr. Shanks for not paying you all the attention due you. We feel particularly suppressed. In fact we can hardly get our breath. We had no idea that the United States had such 'Great Shanks' that it could reach away down here and kick the *Star* into pi, if it chirped about Mr. Special's (*ie.,* Shanks) public maneuvers. . . ."[18]

To "Simon Scribbler," who complained about her essay on the good accomplished by whites in the Territory, she replied tartly: "Though a WOMAN, my pen is pitted . . . The standard of morality in the states, from which the white settlers must come, is far more elevated than the standard of morality is now in this territory; and if the few white people here has [sic] done so much for the Indians, what may we not hope for, when the full tide of civilizing influences are brought to bear in their favor?"[19]

Pungent and no-holds-barred commentaries such as these were often followed by examples of Urania's humor. On reading in the *Southern Kansas Advance* that "a literary lady is apt to run a hair pin into her pies to see when they are cooked," Urania responded with a laugh. "Ah! I thought literary ladies never made pies! Caught in your own net[,] gentlemen! Who ever heard of the husband of a literary lady having indigestion from eating too much mince pie!" In a facetious editorial entitled "Destruction of Birds at the Shrine of Fashion," Urania proposed adorning ladies' hats with centipedes, horned toads, scorpions, and other such creatures, all of which were readily available in the Territory.[20]

Granville applauded his wife's outspoken editorial stands and took public pride in her abilities. While on one trip, he wrote her: ". . . anything you may choose to say will be heartily endorsed by me. The *Star* in my absence is entirely under your control, and I feel perfectly satisfied of your ability to defend it. . . ." He then invited the editor of the rival McAlester paper, the *Vindicator*, to take his best shots and to "be no ways backward on account of my absence." Two months later, in a reply to another charge by the *Vindicator*, Lydia, for the first time, signed herself "L. S. McPherson, Ass[istan]t Editor" and challenged the other to discuss any subject "that will improve the morals, enlighten the minds, refine, or in any way aid in the elevation and advancement of our country." Her only stipulation was that he not "sink the subject with slang and vulgarity. . . ."[21] Granville responded gleefully on his return that her editorials had "struck home to the hearts of our opponents. . . ."

Other newspapers also respected Lydia's talents. The editor of the *Moberly* (Missouri) *Enterprise-Monitor* referred to her as "a lady of intelligence," and the *Fort Smith* (Arkansas) *Herald* commented that, in Granville's absence, "the accomplished associate [editor] makes a first-class, readable paper."

BREAK-UP OF A MARRIAGE

Through the summer of 1876, business at the *Star* continued running smoothly. Lydia wrote her first major article under her own name on July 6, four full columns that explored the history of the Indian Territory. In the September 14 issue, she railed against profanity and the abuse of individuals in the newspapers of the day; better to learn, she wrote, "the beauty and force of chaste language."[22] By this time, Granville had taken on a partner, Colonel E. C. Boudinot, an Indian himself and a vigorous campaigner for Indian rights and a federal territory. Boudinot's title was editor, Granville's editor and proprietor, and Lydia remained associate editor. Granville began traveling more and more, and Boudinot was frequently in Washington, so the burden of running the *Star* fell on Lydia.

Perhaps her husband's increased travels also were symptomatic of problems either beginning in their marriage or now coming to the surface. In August, Lydia wrote a very revealing comment about several good friends who dropped by to visit on a night when she was alone, "sick and heavy hearted," dreaming of "home, happiness and friends forever gone." For his part, Granville complained that he was a slave to the paper and never got a vacation, but the columns of the *Star* show he was away more than in Caddo over that summer. On September 14 he wrote that he was headed north "in search of health and rest, something he finds but little of at home." Was that a reference to his hectic public and Masonic life, or to a lack of domestic tranquility? A week later, he was moved to write about his first two wives and to comment that the second was loved "as a woman had never been loved before," surely a slap in the face to his third and current wife.

As the fall progressed, Granville's complaints about his health and his enemies continued, while Lydia's signed and attributable contributions to the *Star* declined markedly. In November came the first published hint that matters had gone seriously awry, when the masthead was changed to list only "G. McPherson, Ed. Prop.;" The partnership with Boudinot had apparently dissolved. Lydia's last identifiable article appeared a week later, on the sixteenth. By early December the marriage and the business had broken apart. Granville moved the paper to McAlester, changed its name to the *Star-Vindicator* (he bought out his old rival), and went into business with B. R. Bibb. In January he complained about strained relations with his family, reporting that he had gone to Caddo "to see our babies and take them their Christmas presents;" but weather prevented him from traveling beyond the town, where he stayed with friends. A week later he remarked pathetically that "no Christmas gifts came to us either."

Granville's admission makes it clear that he and Lydia separated before Christmas of 1876; she retained custody of the children, and she moved somewhere outside of Caddo. The split was not an amicable one, as is further attested by his statement that readers of the new *Star-Vindicator* "may reasonably expect to find a marked improvement in the quality of matter contained in its columns," a direct insult to Lydia, who had published many of the *Star's* fall issues.

FIRST FEMALE PUBLISHER IN OKLAHOMA

Lydia, meanwhile, did not waste time mourning either Granville or her ruined marriage. About the end of December, she and her three sons, who had been the *Star's* printers, established their own newspaper, the *Caddo International News*. The masthead of the one surviving issue lists Mrs. L. S. McPherson as Editor and the Hunter Brothers as Publishers.[23]

In the *News*, Lydia utilized many of the stylistic characteristics of the *Star*. "City and Country" carried local tidbits, as had "Star Lights;" and she continued to campaign for civic improvements such as sidewalks. But bearing in mind the controversy that had surrounded the McPhersons' earlier political leanings, Lydia now softened her stance somewhat. "While we firmly believe that this people would be safer and happier under a Territorial Government, and as citizens of the United States . . . we do not intend to make our paper a dictator, or a fanatical party leader. . . ."

Her theosophical beliefs probably determined the paper's motto, Light First in Order. "As in the days of creation," she wrote, "after light came the good the true and the beautiful, so may it be with the International News." Prosaically, the *News* also offered job printing, and a year's subscription cost $1.50.

And what happened to Granville? He continued to publish the *Star-Vindicator* in McAlester through 1878. Then he packed up his Washington hand press and moved to Blanco County, Texas. Territory records do not indicate when or even if he and Lydia divorced[24], but Granville appears on the 1880 Texas Census with a new wife and four stepchildren. Mary Kate helped him publish the *Blanco Star-Vindicator*, where he continued to attract enemies. The editor of the *San Marcos Free Press* accused him of hypocrisy and alleged that Granville posed "as an enemy to prohibition [but was] an inveterate whisky soaker." If true, his drinking may have been one of the causes of his separation from Lydia. Granville McPherson died in Blanco in 1887.[25]

GONE TO TEXAS

Lydia and her sons published the *International News* for only a few months before deciding to leave the Territory and move south across the Red River to Texas. There are several different accounts of why they chose to do so: that Lydia had "wearied of life among the tribes," that "they had heard of [the] enterprising village" of Whitesboro and "decided to establish a newspaper here," and lastly, that Whitesboro businessmen, impressed by their success in Caddo, invited them to come. Probably some combination of all these factors is close to the truth.[26]

The family loaded their army surplus, hand-operated printing press on a covered wagon and followed "Indian trails" to the Red River, which they "crossed on a barge,"[27] and arrived in Whitesboro in April 1877. A history of those early days that later appeared in the *Sherman Democrat* reported that Lydia and the boys "were given a warm welcome by the inhabitants although most of them had never seen a printing press before."[28]

Whitesboro, in western Grayson County and on the eastern edge of the Cross Timbers, had first been settled in the 1840s. The town grew rapidly in the next decade when both the California Road and the Butterfield Overland Stage line passed through it. By the time Lydia arrived, it was a bustling town of about four hundred, with a small police force and about twenty professionals and businesses. There were several saloons but no formal church until the Presbyterians organized one in 1878. And if Lydia had hoped to get away from the Indians, she must have been disappointed, for Whitesboro merchants did a brisk business with the Indians who routinely traveled back and forth across the Red River.

Lydia and the boys (now 22, 20, and 18 years old) rented a small frame building and set up shop to print the *Whitesboro Democrat*, a weekly newspaper like the *Caddo International*

News; the first issue appeared May 17, 1877. But with Lydia's name on the masthead as editor, the *Democrat* became "so far as [is] known the first newspaper in Texas published by a woman."[29] Lydia most likely stayed with the same format that had proved successful in Caddo. The *Dallas Weekly Herald* described the first issue as "a spicy sheet full of interesting reading matter, a first-class local paper," and wished the *Democrat* "the abundant success it justly merits."[30]

Soon after establishing the paper, the family purchased a used Washington hand press from the *Sherman Courier* to replace their antiquated machine. And in November 1878, Lydia bought a lot for $25 to be paid in advertising and printing, $25 in cash, and a note for $25 due in six months.[31]

HOME TO SHERMAN

A little over two years after they arrived in Texas, Lydia sold the *Whitesboro Democrat*[32] and moved her family for the last time, traveling eighteen miles east to the Grayson County seat, Sherman, where they would remain the rest of their lives.

Sherman, established in 1848, was fast becoming the "Queen City of the Prairies," a banking, mercantile, educational, and railroad shipping center with ties that stretched west to the Panhandle and north into the Indian Territory. George A. Dickerman, a former journalist himself and now county clerk, had persuaded Lydia that the time was right to move to Sherman: aside from the growth taking place in the town, its newspapers were going through turmoil, with one moving to Gainesville, a second unwilling to take a political stand, and the third Republican in a predominantly Democratic county. There was room, said Dickerman, for a "politically correct" paper.

And so the *Sherman Weekly Democrat* premiered on August 14, 1879, four pages handset on the Washington press brought from Whitesboro and printed on paper stock remaining from the last issue in that town. Lydia again was editor, Dickerman came to work for her as Associate Editor, and G.O. and E.C. were the "publishers"—E.C. gathered news and his brother ran the office.[33] They operated out of a room on the second floor of a building on Houston Street (no longer standing) and proudly proclaimed a somewhat obscure logo on the masthead: The Animating Spirit of a Collective Body. The first issue carried Lydia's philosophy of journalism: "We do not propose to convert the paper into a battle ax or kill off our enemies . . . but we do propose to convert it to every good work and to make it emphatically a peoples' paper. . . ."

THE *DEMOCRAT*

Unfortunately, few issues of Lydia's papers have survived; most of the early Sherman ones were lost in a 1911 fire. But a facsimile of the September 4, 1879 issue exists. As was customary, the *Democrat* carried reprints of news items from other journals (including *Poultry World*) and a column of oddities entitled "Texas Gleanings" with such reports as the discovery of a petrified human bone in Hamilton County and a Bell County hen that laid an egg within an egg.

Unattributed essays that smack strongly of Urania's style characterized the wit of the competing *Chronicle* as cheap and shoddy, praised the Democratic party as still "the only reasonable hope of the country" despite the corrupt men running it, and memorialized Colonel James Bourland of the Confederate Frontier Regiment as controversial and notorious but an honest man who "doubtless did what he believed to be right. . . ."

The *Democrat's* statement of purpose proclaimed it to be "The Friend of the People and the Gazetteer of Current

Events, the Exponent of the People's Wishes, Sentiments and Interests, and a General Advertising Medium . . . Democratic in politics, liberal in religious sentiment, moral in tone and high in purpose."

Lydia and the boys were quick to reprint praise for their efforts that had already appeared in the *Graham City Leader*. "This excellent paper edited by Mrs. L. S. McPherson, is one of the very best on our exchange list . . . [she] is a very fine writer, and we are glad to see her talents and energies employed in a business in which she can be of great service to the people of Texas." Interestingly, the *Leader* went on to editorialize about the role of women, stating that Texas women "should use their influence in extending the circulation of the *Sherman Democrat*." It chastised the state government for not hiring women even though the federal system had "always found them faithful and prompt in the discharge of their duties. *Woman's sphere is where she can exercise her good sense and fine judgement in promoting the welfare of the country. . . .*" (author's italics)

Also surviving is the April 21, 1881 issue. Although the masthead lists only the Hunter Brothers, an article on the illegal lease of land in the Indian Territory bears a strong resemblance to Lydia's style and would be consistent with opinions she formed while living in Caddo, concluding as it does by bemoaning "the sacred rights of the poor Indian!"

After two years the *Democrat* moved to the corner of Houston and Crockett in what is today the oldest surviving commercial structure in Grayson County (built in 1858). In the basement was a saloon, the post office occupied the first floor, the newspaper the second, and the Masonic Lodge and a dance hall were on the third floor (now missing). And while retaining the weekly edition for some time, Lydia and her sons expanded to a daily paper.[34] About 1890 the *Democrat* moved again to the opposite side of the courthouse square after acquiring a new cylinder press whose vibrations disturbed the other clients. It remained there until 1921; the Hunters had sold the paper the previous year.

The *Sherman Democrat*'s second location on the courthouse square.

(Courtesy Red River Historical Museum, Sherman, Texas)

LYDIA AND THE WORLD

The expansion of the newspaper in 1881 was just the start of a busy civic and professional period for Lydia, then fifty-five years old.

She joined the Texas Press Association, founded in Sherman in 1873. Lydia was one of three women who joined at the '81 Houston convention—the first Texas women to do so—and she was elected a corresponding secretary. Mrs. Bella French Swisher, editor and publisher of Austin's *American Sketch Book: An Historical and Home Magazine*, described this historic occasion. The men, she wrote, were not expecting women, but someone finally pointed out that Mrs. Swisher was "one of the two lady newspaper proprietors in Texas," the other being Lydia. No rooms had been engaged for either woman, and Lydia hadn't even been able to get an identifying badge when Swisher found her.

The final insult was when the twelve women attending as visitors or delegates were barred from the evening banquet because one of the editors "had some thing to say about 'women,' which he did not want them to hear. . . ." Mrs. Swisher was not impressed. Despite this inauspicious beginning, Lydia, with her son E.C., did attend the 1883 and 1884 conventions which were held in Dallas.

Other honors followed. In 1884 Governor John Ireland appointed her an Honorary Commissioner to the World's Industrial and Cotton Exposition at New Orleans. Of the eighty or so commissioners from Texas, only five were women. Two years later, Lydia was elected a Texas delegate to the World Press Association meeting in Cincinnati, Ohio.

The family's long loyalty to the Democratic party was rewarded in 1886 when President Grover Cleveland appointed Lydia Sherman's postmistress, the city's first Democrat since the Civil War; E. C. served his mother as assistant postmaster.[35] During her four years in that office, she presided over the inauguration of Sherman's free mail delivery (1887).

After retiring from that position, Lydia embarked on a four-month-long trip through the western United States and wrote a column about her travels for an Oregon journal. Her experiences found their way into her poetry; "Sierra Nevada" and "Dreams by the Pacific" are just two poems clearly based on this trip that she wrote for *Reullura*[36], a book of verse published in 1892 by Charles Well Moulton of Buffalo, New York.

She dedicated the book to her sons. Almost a hundred pages long, *Reullura* reflects a classical education and Lydia's own strong faith but is more workmanlike than brilliant. Its subject matter ranged broadly from typically Victorian nature themes to the death of Queen Victoria's son Leopold. In "An Answer," she sharply criticized Great Britain for deserting Gordon at Khartoum: "You dozed above your beef and bread/ While Arabs held that hero's head/ Impaled upon a barb of steel. . . ." In another she describes Abraham Lincoln's death: "For while our flag in glory waves/ O'er Richmond's ruined wall/ The world's best friend lies cold in death/ Beneath a funeral pall."

At some point she began work on a novel, *Phlegethon*[37], but it was never published and its subject matter is unknown. Lydia also contributed regularly to such publications as *Cosmopolitan* (not the current one by that name), *Youth's Companion*, the *Toledo Blade*, and the *Chicago Advance*. She also continued to write for the *Democrat*.

HOME LIFE

In 1887 Lydia had purchased a lot from George Dickerman for $500 on Travis and Mulberry Streets in Sherman and built a "prim cottage" there. It is no longer standing, but, in a 1954 article in the *Sherman Democrat*, her granddaughters recalled visiting her there. The house was fragrant with potpourri she made from summer's rose petals, and Lydia's collection of rocks, picked up on her travels, was exhibited on the corner what-not shelf. The girls regarded their grandmother, with some awe, "as a woman far ahead of her time."[38]

With Lydia lived her granddaughter Mary, born in Iowa in 1872.[39] Mary later went to work at the *Democrat* as a printer before marrying Calvin Williamson about 1896 or 1897 and leaving for her own home. In 1900, after Cal lost his job as a machinist, he and Mary and their two young children moved back in with Lydia as did her son Luke for a brief time.

The other two sons had also married by now: G.O. to Frances Jane Webster, daughter of a Whitesboro pioneer, and E.C. to Harriet Dickerman of Illinois.[40]

DEATH OF LYDIA

Towards the end of her life, probably beginning in the spring of 1902, when she wrote her final will, Lydia was afflicted with a "long illness," its nature undetermined.[41] During that time, she turned over all her right and title to the *Democrat* to E.C. and G.O. in appreciation of their care for her. She finally died on December 2, 1903 at her home on Mulberry Street; the funeral service was preached from there the following day. Lydia McPherson was seventy-seven years old.

Her will specified that her sons sell the house to carry out her cash bequests: $50 to daughter Emma Mendenhall, $100 to granddaughter Mary Williamson (then living in Tishomingo, Indian Territory), and $200 to Luke's widow Mattie and her children. G.O. and E.C. were to divide whatever money was left.

To Mary she left most of her household furnishings, and her clothes and table linens were to go to Mary and her mother. And the grandchildren were each to receive a memento: a counterpane, a framed picture, etc. The most specific directions involved her library: "Take my library and my big trunk to the Democrat office and keep them one year. Then divide the books or keep them after giving each grandchild one or two books. Give Luke Junior [her grandson] my big dictionary. Keep the old Bible in the Office." It is believed that the trunk and any remaining books were destroyed in a later fire.

The total estate was valued at a very modest $1,450: $1,000 for the house, $300 in cash, and household goods of $150. E.C., as his mother's executor, sold the land and house in May 1904 to the trustees of the Presbyterian Church for $1,250.[42]

And so ended the life and career of one of Texas and the Southwest's pioneering—but little known—journalists. Two of her newspapers are still being published today, a tribute to the diminutive woman who believed that they existed to help better their communities.

Notes—Chapter Two

1   Lydia's obituary in the *Sherman Register* lists her birth-place as Camden, Ohio, between Cincinnati and Dayton; but census records corroborate the Belmont County location. Lydia herself later wrote that she was "born amid the Beech and Sugar woods of Ohio, near the Virginia border," which would be Belmont County, near Wheeling.

2   *Sherman Democrat*, obituary of G. O. Hunter, October 28, 1948.

3   *Oklahoma Star*, May 20, 1875.

4   Emma had married Josh Mendenhall by this time and lived in Coon Rapids, Iowa.

5   *Dallas Morning News* Magazine Section, February 20, 1921; February 27, 1921.

6   The *Star* was the first official newspaper of the Choctaw Nation and the first in the Territory to use the Choctaw phrase "Oklahoma" in its title; actually two words, it translates as "Red People."

7   Granville and Sophronia's other children were Kinnia (1852), Granville (1855), Wilford (1858), and Payton (1860).

8   *The War of the Rebellion*, Series 1, Volume LIII, 672-3.

9   The Indians of the various nations that made up the Territory were subject only to their own tribal laws. Settlers who were not Indians or married to Indians were not considered citizens, and had virtually no law enforcement at all. This accounts for the severe crime problems in some Territory towns, as well as the lack of records from this period, since most Indian nations did not require legal records such as marriages to be kept. Land belonged to the nations and their citizens; non-citizens could only rent or lease property, and, consequently, there are no deed records either.

10   Elizabeth Brooks, in her 1896 book *Prominent Women of Texas*, writes that this was the beginning of Lydia's journalistic career and that her experience at the *Star* "was enriched by many incidents of thrilling interest."

11   Granville helped found the Caddo Lodge in 1873 and served as its first Worshipful Master. One of the Lodge's main goals was to combat the town's lawlessness, and Granville used the *Star* to editorialize against the Territory's criminal element. He believed that a stronger government and the settling of "a good class of white people" among the Indians would deter crime, a stance which made him unpopular in certain circles. A year after organizing the Caddo Lodge, he and eight other prominent Masons met in Caddo to organize the Indian Territory's first Grand Lodge, consisting of Eufaula, Caddo, and Atoka; Granville was its first Grand Master (1874-1876).

12   *Oklahoma Star*: February 19, 1875; November 9, 1875; December 14, 1875.

13   "G. McPherson, Editor & Proprietor. Mrs. L. S. McPherson, Assistant Editor." Volume III, No. 3, *Oklahoma Star*.

14   Territory newspapers were often strapped for cash since they could not depend on obtaining governmental or legal notices, principal sources of income in other areas. And because the Nations' citizens were chronically poor, commercial advertising was also limited. The *Star's* subscription rate was $1.25 per year, "Invariably in Advance." Late in 1875 the paper began advertising that it was now doing "job work," *i.e.*, miscellaneous printing such as notices, stationery, etc.

15   *Oklahoma Star*: July 23, 1875; March 28, 1876; January 4, 1876.

16   One attempt at improving the *Star's* cash flow came in the February 22, 1876 issue. "To every marriage notice sent to this office for publication, we will add, for every green-back accompanying [the] notice, a fine stanza of

original poetry. So you can have a whole song, or a piece an inch long, which ever you choose. Send on the green backs." Unfortunately, Urania's service was not much in demand in Caddo's economy.

17 Granville's dislike of Shanks reached a head in May 1875 when Shanks stated publicly that McPherson had no right to be in the Nation since "his first wife [*author's note: actually his second*] was only a white woman who had been married to an Indian; and his last wife [*i.e., Lydia*] a white woman he married by telegraph . . ." Few records illustrate Granville's character better than his various responses. In first repeating the slander, he wrote about his wedding to Lydia: "What more clearly indicates your mean, unprincipled nature than the manner in which you mention our marriage? None but a cur of the lowest degree would have said anything about it. . . ." (May 27, 1875) When the editor of the *Sherman Register*, another foe, picked up the story, Granville replied: "Even if it were to come to our ears that the editor of the *Register* had been married to the 'black widow of a dead negro' . . . we could never so far forget the duties of a gentleman as to throw it in his face," a backhanded slap that he proceeded to repeat several more times. (July 23, 1875) He went on to assert that "the secret of our wondrous love for the Indian" derived from his children by the second wife.

18 *Oklahoma Star*, June 4, 1875.

19 *Ibid.*, August 27, 1875.

20 *Ibid.*, November 9, 1875; January 11, 1876.

21 *Ibid.*, January 25, 1876; March 7, 1876.

22 Grace Ernestine Ray, in her comprehensive history of *Early Oklahoma Newspapers* (1928), attributes the first article to Granville; but it is clearly signed "L. S. McPherson." In the second, she presumed that L. S. had to be a man, since women in this period did not write for newspapers.

23   Elva Shartel Ferguson, on whom Edna Ferber based her character of Sabra Cravat in *Cimarron*, is generally credited as being Oklahoma's first woman newspaper publisher. But she and her husband did not arrive in the Territory or establish the *Watonga Republican* until 1892.

24   Several biographical sketches describe Lydia as twice widowed. Does this indicate that they never divorced and that she was trying to hide the fact to retain respectability? Or that Lydia hated her second husband so much that she wished him dead?

25   Mary Kate Rountree McPherson continued to run the Blanco paper another year, then moved it to Kyle in Hays County. Her son, Lee J. Rountree, later a renowned journalist himself and a state legislator, started his career by helping his mother. Mary Kate and Granville had at least one child together, a son also named Granville, who was born in 1882. The senior Granville's grave was lost until 1961 when the Grand Lodge of Oklahoma located it and erected a marker.

26   Frances E. Willard and Mary A. Livermore, editors, *A Woman of the Century*.
       Sherman Democrat, August 29, 1954.

27   This was likely at Colbert's Ferry, north of modern Denison.

28   *Sherman Democrat*, August 29, 1954.

29   *Galveston Daily News*, June 25, 1893; Willard and Livermore, *op. cit.*

30   *Dallas Weekly Herald*, May 26, 1877.

31   A handwritten note at the side of the deed entry records the note paid on January 1, 1881. Lydia advertised the lot for sale in the September 4, 1879 issue of the *Sherman Weekly Democrat* and finally sold it in 1885 for $60.

32   The name was changed to the *Weekly News*; today it is published as the *Whitesboro News Record*.

33   Luke stayed at the *Democrat* for a while then struck out on his own and worked for several other papers includ-

ing the *Savoy Star*, which acquired the old Washington press when the Hunters replaced it. Luke died in 1901, leaving his wife Mattie with seven children. She and her sons, at least two of whom had worked at the *Democrat*, started their own printing business, Mrs. L. Hunter & Sons. Luke's son Pierce, who started at the *Democrat* as a printer, returned there about 1909 as advertising manager to work for his uncles.

34 The *Sherman Democrat* is still published today.

35 She is still the only woman to have served a full term in that capacity.

36 "Reullura" may be derived from the Middle English "reule:" (1) a general principle governing morals and conduct (2) a moral precept or (3) a set of rules governing the whole of morality. (*The Middle English Dictionary*) Lydia may have written another volume of poetry, but it apparently was never published.

37 "Phlegethon" is from the Greek and means burning, blazing. It was also the name of one of the five rivers of Hades. (*Oxford-English Dictionary*) Several obituary notices for Lydia in 1903 reported she "was on the eve" of bringing the novel out.

38 *Sherman Democrat*, August 29, 1954, Section 4, page 2.

39 It is not clear who Mary's parents were.

40 E.C. died in 1934; after he and G.O. sold the *Sherman Democrat*, E.C. became president of Reynolds-Parker Company in Sherman. He was a Mason and a director of the Commercial National Bank and wrote a series of articles for the *Dallas Morning News* in 1921 about growing up in the Indian Territory and the changes happening there. He and Hattie (1864-1941) had a daughter, Gail.

G.O. died in 1948. A member of Woodmen of the World, he and Janie (1865-?) had four daughters, Grace, May, Alma, and Annie.

41 She wrote another will in November but later revoked it in favor of the earlier document.

42 Lydia's house appears to have been on the north side of Mulberry, on the present site of the Sherman Public Library parking lot. First Presbyterian's original building was a frame structure on Travis and Pecan, built in 1874; two decades later, the church erected a new brick building on the north end of the block, across Mulberry from Lydia. Because the church was squeezed in, with the large Franklin School taking up the entire east side of the block, and the proposed new Federal Building going in to the south, on the church's old site, church officials probably wanted Lydia's lot for parking or storage.

CHAPTER THREE

Lucy Petway Holcombe Pickens

"The brave may fall but can never surrender."

. . . Lucy Pickens

They called her Lady Lucy and "our fleur-de-lys de Texas." Even her critics acknowledged her beauty and grace, her social and political acumen. She dazzled czars and presidents, was the only American woman ever pictured on Confederate currency, and she grew up near the banks of Texas' Red River.

VIRGINIA BACKGROUND

Lucy Petway Holcombe was born in LaGrange, Tennessee[1], on June 11, 1832, the second of five children of Beverly Lafayette and Eugenia Dorothea Hunt Holcombe. Through her father, she descended from an old Virginia family which had settled in Prince Edward County. Her great-grandfather was a veteran of the French and Indian War and

Lucy in her widow's weeds, circa 1870.

(Courtesy Harrison County Historical Museum, Marshall, Texas)

a trustee of what is now Hampden-Sydney College; four of his sons served in the American Revolution including Lucy's grandfather, James Philemon Holcombe Jr. He was with the Marquis de Lafayette at Yorktown and, in memory of this comrade, named his youngest son—Lucy's father—Beverly Lafayette Holcombe.[2]

Beverly (1806-1864) was born at "The Oaks" in Amelia County, where the family had moved a few years earlier to raise tobacco and thoroughbred racing horses. His mother, Lucy Maria Anderson Holcombe, descended from a Russian nobleman who emigrated to Virginia and from a maid of honor at the Hapsburg Court of Austria who claimed Marie Antoinette among her relations.

Lucy Maria was the organizational talent behind the Holcombes' Amelia operation. But even her abilities could not counteract liberal spending and soil depleted by tobacco; in 1829 she and Philemon packed up their estate, son Beverly, and daughters Fannie and Amanda, with their families, and moved to LaGrange in Fayette County, Tennessee.

Beverly, a tall, muscular, blue-eyed blonde, married Eugenia Dorothea Hunt the following year, and the couple set up housekeeping at "Woodstock," a 900-acre plantation. Their first child, Anna Eliza, was born in 1830, and Lucy in 1832, followed by John Theodore (1834), Martha Maria (1836), and Philemon Eugene (1837).

EUGENIA HOLCOMBE

Lucy's relationship with her mother proved crucial to her psychological development and later actions, so it is important to understand Eugenia Holcombe. Born near Petersburg, Virginia, in 1811, she was the daughter of John and Rhoda Petway Hunt. Her mother and sisters died when Eugenia was a toddler; her father remarried but that wife, too, died. When

Eugenia was four, John married again. About 1825, the family moved to Alabama and, a few years later, to Fayette County, Tennessee, where Eugenia met Beverly Holcombe.

In the diary she kept from 1839 to 1866, Eugenia recalled that she had "never felt a mothers [sic] love or kindness" and that the only affection she received as a child came from John Hunt, whom she adored, calling him "my earthly all . . . my best of fathers, an idol of mine." A naive girl with poor health, she was also deeply religious. As a result of all these factors, she submerged herself in her husband and children; and only after Beverly died did she admit that she had "clung to him as the Ivy to the Oak."

She fretted over the family's health and spiritual well-being, prodding the boys toward a career in ministry and adjuring the girls to "labor with their own hands[,] giving the proceeds to the missionary cause."[3] Martha's death at the age of three intensified her fears. Remembering her own loveless childhood, Eugenia lavished affection on all the children and considered them "sufficient compensation for all my sufferings" in giving birth to them.[4] They responded by being very deferential to her wishes.

But it was with Lucy that she shared an especially strong bond, "my sweet Lucy" who, Eugenia boasted, is "so strangely devoted to me, her father thinks she will die if she is ever separated from me. . . ."[5] Lucy was seven when her sister Martha died, old enough to grieve herself and to be troubled by the depth of her mother's despair. Perhaps it was this episode that forged the bond between them, perhaps it was always there. But that it lasted for years is evident in Lucy's extant letters home from Russia (1858-1860), in one of which she told her sister Anna that "Mother really must not expect me to love my children as much as her . . . because it is not in me and I cant [sic]."[6]

As a child, Lucy would not stay away from home—and mother—more than a few days. She finally left LaGrange at the age of fourteen when she and Anna, after graduating from a local school, went to Bethlehem, Pennsylvania to study for two years at the "quiet and excellent Moravian Institute, on the beautiful laurel-covered banks of the romantic Lehigh."[7] She was popular with the other students there and demonstrated "superior" scholastic ability and intelligence.

MOVING TO TEXAS

Woodstock, the family's LaGrange home, was a productive operation and, about the time Lucy was in Pennsylvania, Beverly Holcombe felt financially comfortable enough to co-sign a note for a friend going into business. But the enterprise failed and Beverly had to sell his estate, which had been the collateral for the loan. Eugenia referred to the disaster in her diary: ". . . [*our*] riches have taken to themselves wings and flown away. . . ."

As did so many others in this period, Beverly looked west to the cheap lands of Texas to start over. In Harrison County, he bought acreage near Caddo Lake for a cotton operation and property on a hilltop in the new town of Marshall where he began building "Wyalucing," a two-story brick structure with enveloping porches.[8] In May 1850, when Eugenia and the children arrived, the house was still under construction.

Until repayment of his debt by Beverly's Tennessee friend let him complete Wyalucing later that year, the family lived in a Marshall boardinghouse. To Eugenia's delight, her husband helped organize the First Presbyterian Church of Marshall "in our room" at the hotel. And in the spring after they moved into Wyalucing, Lucy made her debut at a garden party on the pine and magnolia-filled grounds: an occasion remembered for years since it marked the first Marshall appearance of iced tea.

A YOUNG WOMAN

Now Lucy began to flourish, a beautiful young woman with "classic features, titian hair, pansy eyes, and graceful figure." A slender 5'5", Lucy enhanced her appearance by ordering her clothes (mostly Worth originals) from New York to produce an effect that was nothing short of stunning to the young men—and the old ones, too. Those who knew her recalled her attractive and commanding speaking voice and the way she "floated over a ball-room like a thistle."

Life in Marshall for the lovely Holcombe sisters was enlivened with frequent trips: New Orleans for the winter social season and summers in the mountains of White Sulphur Springs, Virginia, where Eugenia fled to escape the Texas heat. And everywhere they went, Lucy was the center of attention. At a ball in New Orleans, she dropped one of her satin shoes; it was retrieved by a young man who filled it with wine and toasted her as "the belle of the South."[9]

In June 1853 Lucy and another Marshall girl stopped in Shreveport, Louisiana on their way to New York for the World's Fair. The Marshall newspaper reported that the "young gentlemen of Shreveport" gave a ball in their honor which was "the most brilliant assemblage ever convened in our sister city." And the entire Mississippi legislature adjourned in her honor after an 1850 trip to visit Governor John A. Quitman and his family.

How did Eugenia view her daughter's triumphs? She confided to her diary that she was often asked if she was not proud of her girls. "Proud of them, no, pride I feel is too sinful a passion to mingle in my secret throughts of my precious darlings, but I am thankful. . . ."[10]

FREEING CUBA

One of these jaunts would prove to be a fateful one for Lucy. Probably through John Quitman's influence, she had become interested in the Southern movement urging the U.S. to purchase Cuba from Spain.[11] In either Mississippi or New Orleans, she met and fell in love with a young man who shared her feelings to the point of enlisting in the "Cuban Junta." He has been identified as William Crittendon of Kentucky, but that is probably inaccurate. Whoever he was, the young man visited Lucy in Marshall before leaving on an ill-fated expedition to Cuba in August 1851. There the Lopez forces were defeated, and Lopez, Crittendon, and several other Americans—including Lucy's unknown lover—were imprisoned, then executed by Spanish authorities.

Lucy's response to this devastating loss was to write a novel under the pseudonym of H. M. Hardiman that recounted Spanish atrocities to Cubans. *The Free Flag of Cuba, or the Martyrdom of Lopez: A Tale of the Liberating Expedition of 1851* was published in New York in 1855 and dedicated to the "hero and patriot" John Quitman.

In the preface, dated September 1854, Lucy writes that the fame of publishing a book "would be worthless to me, since there is not one who would smile and call it beautiful . . . I am utterly alone. The only kindred blood I ever knew, stains the green shore of Cuba . . . which has robbed me of all that made life beautiful."

The Free Flag of Cuba is the story of Genevieve Clifton, a wealthy young Louisiana woman, her Yankee friend, auburn-haired Mabel Royal—who bears more than a passing resemblance in appearance and character to Lucy herself—Genevieve's beau Ralph Dudley, and her neighbor Eugene de France, with whom Mabel falls in love. Lucy describes Ralph, the hero of the story and presumably modeled after her own lover, as six feet tall, a model soldier with regal brow, dark brown hair, large hazel eyes, a Grecian nose and square chin, and small, white hands which told of his noble birth.

Both Ralph and Eugene go off to Cuba with Lopez, despite Genevieve's protests and with Mabel's encouragement. (William Crittendon makes only a fleeting appearance in the novel, leading one to the conclusion that he is not Lucy's real lover.) Before leaving, Ralph instructs a servant that, in the event of his death, a small cabinet, its contents never described, be taken to Mrs. Clifton for Genevieve. In reality, Lucy's lover did just that, leaving her a hand-carved casket filled with engravings, which remained in the family until it was sold in the 1950s.

But it is Eugene, not Ralph, who dies in Cuba. And it is likely Lucy speaking through Mabel, when she hears of his death: "My heart is hard and cold, like a rock . . . I have no tears; they are frozen."

In the end, fickle and irresponsible Ralph, who has lost his fortune to the Cuban cause, flees to California for three years before returning to marry Genevieve. In a double wedding, Mabel marries Stuart Raymond, another freedom fighting friend. As the omnipotent author, Lucy expounds on her views of marriage. "A marriage night! It is always one of mirth and gladness, but to me there is a sadness inexpressible in this sealing of destinies; this stepping into a new world, whose regions are yet unexplored; one which imagination and hope have filled with the beautiful flowers of unchanging love. . . ."[12]

Her lover's death spurred Lucy Holcombe to new social heights and ambitions. A descendant wrote that "with almost reckless abandon, she sought the gaiety of today with no thought of tomorrow . . . [and] resolved . . . to move in higher circles among men of power and pursuit."[13]

She also continued her writing with "literary contributions" to *Harper's Magazine* and to the *Memphis Eagle and Enquirer*.

FRANCIS PICKENS

Anna, elder of the "beautiful and accomplished sisters," had married Elkanah Greer in 1851, and now it was Lucy who traveled with Eugenia. In the summer of 1856, they went as usual to White Sulphur Springs, where Lucy "was the queen of every gathering" and attracted "wooers . . . by the score." But it would be a "gallant son of South Carolina" who succeeded that summer "where so many others met defeat."[14] A gallant son who was fifty years old, twice widowed, with three daughters already married and the remaining two girls accompanying him on this trip.

Francis Wilkinson Pickens was of an old and prominent South Carolina family.[15] Born in 1807, he attended South Carolina College and read law in Edgefield with Eldred Simkins. After being admitted to the bar in 1828, Francis followed the fast track, marrying Simkins' daughter Margaret Eliza (1808-1842) and becoming his law partner. In 1832 he entered the political field—that bastion of the South Carolina aristocracy—and was elected to the state legislature, where he was embroiled in the Nullification controversy.

Two years later he won the seat in the U.S. House of Representatives which Eldred Simkins had once held. Francis did well there, chairing two important committees, since he was a protege and kinsman of John C. Calhoun.[16] In his more than eight years in the House, he made a name for himself as an outspoken supporter of states' rights and slavery. One of his early speeches predicted the war that was to come: "Everything proclaims that, sooner or later, we shall have to meet . . . or abandon our country to become a black colony, and seek for ourselves a refuge in the wilderness of the West.

Francis Wilkinson Pickens, circa 1862.

(Courtesy of South Caroliniana Library, University of South Carolina)

It is in vain to avoid the contest." With Calhoun's support Francis was even nominated as Speaker of the House but lost the bid to trickery by a South Carolina rival.

In 1843 Francis was elected to the South Carolina Senate. But he fell out with Calhoun over the Mexican War and other issues and was forced into a temporary retirement in 1846. Four years later he emerged to run for governor but was defeated. Francis chaired the state Democratic conventions of both 1852 and 1856, and drafted the party's first ordinance favoring secession. But he also grew more conservative in his opinions and came to believe that South Carolina could not secede and stand alone without the other Southern states, an opinion he would later reverse.

In 1857, while he was courting Lucy by mail, Francis once again ran for Congress but lost the Senate seat. He wrote her pettishly that his victory had been expected by most people but, in the end, "it was necessary to put down aristocracy in the state. . . ."[17]

Francis' personal life had been as turbulent as his political career. With his first wife, Margaret Eliza, he had seven children; four daughters survived. He then married Marion Antoinette Dearing (1824-1853) of Georgia, who bore Francis another daughter before she, too, died.[18] He had traveled to White Sulphur with his two youngest daughters to "take the waters" when Lucy Holcombe swept him off his feet.

From "Edgewood," his plantation near Edgefield[19], he wrote her long letters on the political problems facing the country and interspersed them with passionate declarations: ". . . I love you madly, wildly, blindly. . . ." He feared she didn't return his feelings and felt contempt for him, and so he reminded her that "even the strongest men of the earth have been humbled and overwhelmed by deep devotion to those they love."[20]

Roy Meredith described Lucy's suitor in *Storm over Sumter*. "A portly man of medium height, Pickens managed to make an imposing appearance despite watery eyes and broad, flabby features. He had a pompous manner . . . Yet even those who laughed at his pretensions . . . could not deny that he was a determined man and a master of intrigue . . . rash and impulsive, his zeal [*was*] often stronger than his discretion . . . an experienced and professional diplomat, skilled in legal subleties and expediency . . . kind and hospitable by nature, but he was driven by a hunger for personal glory. . . ."

MARRIAGE

What prompted the beautiful and charming Lucy, who had more than her share of suitors, to finally accept such a man and one old enough to be her father? "May-December" marriages were not uncommon and no one but Lucy, of course, can know her reasons; but it would appear that true love died for her in Cuba.

And Francis Pickens offered her an entree to the world of power and ambition that she now wanted. He was wealthy—owning six plantations and more than four hundred slaves—was recognized in political circles, and was both capable and desirous of achieving even higher office.

So Lucy offered him a choice. She would marry him *if* he secured a diplomatic post in Europe.

That must have presented Francis with a real dilemma. He had earlier declined posts as U.S. Minister to England and, later, France[21] because he was at loggerheads with the government over federal tariffs. His feelings toward Washington could scarcely have changed since then, given the tensions between North and South; but his desire for Lucy won out. He approached President James Buchanan, who rewarded him with the minister's legation in St. Petersburg, Russia, the glittering capital of Czar Alexander II.

In the nearly two years of their courtship and engagement, Lucy studied both French and Russian and began preparing "a suitably elaborate wardrobe." She married Francis at Wyalucing on April 26, 1858, just a few weeks short of her twenty-sixth birthday; the Holcombe slaves watched through the windows while guests and family from throughout the South thronged the house and enjoyed a wedding supper on the grounds that lasted all night. The editor of the *Texas Republican* was much taken with Lucy's new husband, who was "plain and unassuming in his manners, earnest and lively in his conversation . . . [*and*] . . . possesses . . . practical common sense."[22]

The Pickenses left for South Carolina the next morning and Eugenia Holcombe sobbed in her diary: "My precious darling Lucy[,] so long my companion[,] is married and nearly broken my poor heart."

Francis took Lucy home to Edgewood, which he had built for his first wife in 1829. Shaded by magnolias and hickories, the long white frame house fronted onto a covered gallery and had two rear wings. It was surrounded by gardens laid out in the English style and filled with bronze statuary. Inside Edgewood were spacious rooms, mahogany furniture, fine paintings, and an extensive library. The stables and kennels housed pedigreed horses and dogs for riding and fox hunting: Francis loved to entertain.

More than eighty slaves ensured the smooth operation of the house and the cotton plantation. And Lucy herself brought two more to add to their number. Tom and Lucinda were Wyalucing slaves given her by Beverly Holcombe as a wedding gift.

"Edgewood" was built in 1829 and was moved to Aiken in the 1930s. It is now used by the University of South Carolina at Aiken.

(Courtesy Public Information Office, University of South Carolina, Aiken)

OFF TO EUROPE

The newlyweds stayed at Edgewood only a few days before leaving for Russia with an entourage that included Francis' daughters Rebecca and Jennie, the slaves Tom and Lucinda, and Adele, Lucy's French maid. En route to catch their steamer in New York, the Pickenses stopped in Washington to pay their respects to President Buchanan and to attend a White House ball; Francis also received a briefing from the State Department.

Eugenia's diary entry noted, "She is gone, To Russia and I am inconsolable."

The family sailed for Liverpool on May 28 aboard the *Persia*,[23] and Lucy wrote an account of their first few months which was published in the *Memphis Eagle and Enquirer*. "Her reflections," declared the editor, "evince sound sense, correct judgement, and nice discrimination, but are more to be admired for the evidence which they afford of the loveliness of her character and of the affection which she cherishes for her native land and of friends which it contains."[24]

England proved something of a disappointment to Lucy for it looked like Pennsylvania. She was pleased with the wildflowers but thought the wild peach hedges of her "own dear South" prettier than England's famous hawthorne hedges. She also speedily pronounced her distaste of London's Hyde Park and Fenton Hotel ("the gloomiest place in the world") and the family moved to Morley's with rooms overlooking Trafalgar Square.

She awoke there on June 11, her twenty-sixth birthday, to find Francis' gift: a basket of fresh fruit and a bouquet of flowers. Hidden in the petals was a jewelry case containing wrought gold earrings, a bracelet and pin, all enameled with bunches of violets, and a diamond in each violet.

Before departing London, Francis was presented to Queen Victoria. Lucy was happy to leave, for "however great the comfort of an English home, nothing is more barren . . . than an English hotel."

Then it was on to enchanting France and Paris, "the lovely capital of fairy land and pleasure." Though she raved about Paris for the newspaper, Lucy confided in a letter to her mother that "my stay in Paris was not very pleasant for it was nothing but dresses and bills and etc and you know how uncongenial all that is to me." That didn't prevent her boasting publicly about being presented to Emperor Napoleon III in a blue silk glacé ballgown, with a lace train looped up with diamond sprigs, and more diamonds on her neck and arm.

With her new Paris gowns, a bad case of homesickness for mother and Texas, and—though she may not have known it—suffering from morning sickness, Lucy arrived in St.

Petersburg on July 6 after a stop in Berlin. Already she had written Eugenia that "the longer I am from home, the more ardently I long and pine for its simplicity and endearments." She went on to assure her mother: ". . . as God is my judge[,] no one steps into my heart before you or beside you. You are my first and dearest love. . . ." Francis may have been tiring of Lucy's longings for home; she joked in the same letter that "Mr. Pickens says if I loved heaven one third as well as I do home, I would go up to heaven without dying like the prophet of old."[25]

RUSSIA AND THE CZAR

Until they could settle into the American legation on the Neva River near the Imperial Palace, Lucy and Francis took rooms at the Hotel de Russia. She was stunned by St. Petersburg's baroque architecture and the gilded domes of the churches, the bearded men and their "singular costumes," and the "confused sounds of a language" studied but never heard in its native setting.

The royal court was then at Peterhof, the summer palace thirty miles from St. Petersburg, and there "His Excellency, Monsieur Pickens, Ambassador of America, Madame the Ambassadress, and Mademoiselle" (Rebecca) made their first bows to the Czar and his Czarina, Maria. Francis had already presented his credentials, but Lucy had refused to attend that event "as it was Sunday." She was pleased that the royal couple spoke English and were "very fond of America and Americans, and I think it will be very pleasant for me in this respect."

Lucy established herself as the center of male attention on this very first visit. Dressed in white silk and tulle, she sat so as to show a daring glimpse of her feet—on a cushion "after the Russian fashion"—while she listened to "the kindly-meant English" of two Russian noblemen. When the English

Attache and several others joined the group, they became "rather merry for court etiquette," Lucy's euphemism for fashionable flirting. Francis broke up this pleasantry by taking her for a drive through the Peterhof grounds.

The palace and attendant court ceremony dazzled Lucy: ". . . I am looking with all the wonder and delight of a child on this magnificence, which is so new to my republican eyes. . . . "

Her observations on Russia's people for the Memphis paper were remarkably egocentric. "The lower classes here are very ignorant; and yet the higher classes are well informed, fine looking, and remarkably cordial and kind. They have manners more like the planters of the South than any people I have met with in Europe."

RUSSIA'S NEW STAR

Lucy was now at the zenith of her beauty. "She possessed a slender, exquisitely rounded figure and moved with patrician grace and authority. Her features were as clear cut as an intaglio, and her eyes, which, in repose were fawnlike in their softness, could flash when she was aroused. Her hair, which fell almost to her feet, was like skeins of molten gold."[26] *Success* magazine later described her as "a rose in the diplomatic garden."

Her vivacity, intelligence, and unaffected American manners brought her the friendship of the imperial couple, Alexander and Maria.[27] Francis wrote Eugenia proudly that the Czar had singled out his wife on several occasions, conversing with her privately in French, a sign of favor "not known before to happen to a foreigner, at least lately."

As her pregnancy advanced through the winter of 1858-1859, Francis grew anxious, and Lucy herself wavered between fear that the baby would look more like "a Muscovite Don Cossack than an honest American child" and certainty that it would be ugly because of her constant grief and homesickness. Morning sickness plagued her and she became "very fat" but continued to socialize during the day. To the doctor's surprise, she insisted she would nurse the baby herself rather than hiring a wetnurse and resuming her social whirl after the birth.

Lucy by now had become such a favorite with the Czar and Czarina that they invited the Pickenses to move into an apartment at the Imperial Palace in St. Petersburg to await the birth. Czarina Maria even appointed herself the baby's godmother, a rare honor, and insisted that the birthing would follow court precedure with royal witnesses.

What Lucy thought of that is not known. In any event, on the night of March 14, 1859, she quietly gave birth to a daughter in her own apartments with the aid of an American doctor. The child's sex may have been a disappointment to Francis, who was hoping to finally have a healthy son, but the Empress ordered the guards to fire a salute and the band to play.

She then set about planning a christening to be held in the palace chapel and attended by the Russian nobility and by foreign diplomats in the capital. The baby was named Eugenia Frances Dorothea, and the Czarina added Olga Neva to the name, then decreed that the child would be known as "Douschka," or Little Darling, which was indeed the name she bore the rest of her life. Maria and Alexander gifted the baby with diamonds and her mother with more jewelry.

AN UNHAPPY AMBASSADRESS

The year following Douschka's birth found Lucy increasingly unhappy in Russia.

She took Jennie to Germany to enroll in school and apparently hoped to return to Texas for a visit afterwards; Eugenia Holcombe was ill again and Lucy fretted over her

mother's condition. She planned a recuperative trip to Rome
or England and looked forward to having the house to herself
and to being alone with her mother. Even leaving Douschka
didn't trouble her—"I could do [*her*] no actual good if she was
ill"—and the child had her nurse, her father, and a doctor.

But Francis failed, or refused, to see the depth of her
misery and so would not allow the trip. In a letter to Anna,
Lucy raved about men in general and her own husband in
particular. "But my dear sister, the *best* of men . . . are selfish
and incapable of sacrifice . . . [*If he had let me go home*], I would
have felt bound to him forever, and could never have done
enough to repay him. I think in my gratitude . . . I would even
have consented to live at Edgewood in the midst of all the
children, grandchildren, and relations of No. 1 and No. 2 etc.[28]
but he did not and therefore I owe him nothing. He (like all
other men) loves his own comfort and happiness better than
mine."

Several times in the same letter Lucy begged Anna not to
judge her harshly for she could not understand the situation
Lucy was in. "There are unpleasant things connected with my
married life which have annoyed me. . . ."

One of those annoyances was her stepdaughter. In St.
Petersburg that October, Rebecca married Francis' private secretary, John Bacon, a relationship Lucy feared would not
prosper and one which she tried to prevent. The two women
did not get along; though Lucy felt she had performed her
duty to all her husband's children "to the utmost of my ability,"
she also didn't hesitate to describe Rebecca in a private letter
as the most uncongenial companion she'd ever had.[29]

The irregular letters she received from home, and their
apparent lack of interest in her life and activities, were another aggravation. At one point, she chided her brother John
Theodore that Douschka was "barely alluded to" by anyone;

she sent photographs home of the baby, but no one commented on them.

Lucy wavered between love for her daughter and a refusal to "put almost my soul into her being as Col. P. has done." The child's dark hair (which later lightened to a red more akin to her mother's titian color) seemed strange to Lucy; but as Douschka was "only a Pickens" and not a Holcombe, she decided it wasn't important. When Douschka was thirteen months old, Lucy acknowledged that others found her beautiful and "something wonderful," but she herself was primarily pleased that her daughter was "lady like and intelligent and inclined to be obedient." She could refer to her "fairy queen" and at the same time warn Eugenia not to "expect to see anything as pretty as [*Anna's child*] Bev."

Lucy recuperated slowly from Douschka's birth and continued to be unwell for at least a year. And Francis' spending habits irked her. He was quite capable of buying his mother-in-law a $400 shawl or Lucy a $40 handkerchief and then refusing to pay the duties to ship her presents back to Texas.

But what really rankled her was "the miserable emptiness of European society." Clothes and rank were of value; anyone advancing ideas met with "a kind of well-bred disgust," and women without a fortune or title received "no deference." Lucy was appalled at this lifestyle and forced herself to continue French and singing lessons and to attend the opera so as "not to lose what little energy and cultivation I have." She didn't particularly enjoy St. Petersburg's social round, except for Court balls, and complained that several nights in overheated rooms made her "look as yellow and haggard as any Russian woman."

RUMBLINGS OF WAR

By December of 1859, when she wrote the above letter, events in the United States had begun to seriously trouble Francis. The Democratic party, to which he had devoted years, was splintering under the same pressures that were also sundering the nation: slavery and states' rights. For Francis, "the sovereignity of the States was not an abstraction or a theory—it was a creed, a religion[30];" John Brown's raid on Harper's Ferry (October 16, 1859) and its repercussions alarmed Francis. Still, he was uncertain whether to resign his mission early and return home.

Lucy apparently expected him to do just that and may even have urged such a course for her own reasons; she confidently informed Anna in late December that they would return in the spring of 1860, as soon as the weather made a trans-Atlantic crossing feasible. But events would hold the Pickenses in Russia for months to come.

That did not stop Francis from thinking about and planning for the future. In February he hinted strongly to President Buchanan that he, Francis, was the ideal Democratic candidate to run for president that year: a Southerner, yet one who loved the Union. But it was Stephen Douglas who emerged as the front-runner in the following weeks. Douglas' campaign manager recognized Francis' political clout and privately offered him the vice presidency if he would promise to deliver South Carolina's vote to Douglas at the nominating convention.[31] But Francis would not support Douglas.

And Lucy continued to dislike Russian society, feeling that it had left its mark on her. "You will doubtless find me changed in many respects," she wrote Anna in April (1860). "I am no longer handsome, tho' I pass for a great beauty at Court." She was repelled by the courtiers who thronged around her simply because she was the only foreign minister's wife with whom the Czar danced. She alluded to "incidents" of lapsed virtue on her part, though it is difficult to tell if she meant actual lapses or rumored ones. Francis, she wrote, "loves me more for my dignity and goodness, than for my beauty and intellect," and because she had conducted herself with "prudence." (Apparently she had reconciled with him after their quarrel the preceding summer.)

As the spring of 1860 progressed, Lucy began planning their return to America, projected for September. Because of her continuing poor health, she wished to first travel through the warmer climate of Southern Europe and regain her strength, a plan with which Francis apparently acquiesced. In the meantime, they continued to entertain at the Legation with dinners featuring Southern cuisine and to attend Court festivities.

And there were more gifts from the Imperial couple. Among the items given Lucy by Alexander and Maria were marble busts of her and Francis commissioned by the Czar (now at the University of South Carolina), a medallion bearing Alexander's likeness, oil portraits of him and Maria, a diamond suite and ring, a pearl necklace, and a number of silver serving pieces including a three-foot solid silver tureen.

In late July or early August of 1860, Lucy left St. Petersburg with Douschka, the slave Lucinda, and the baby's nurse and endured a rough crossing down the Baltic Sea to Germany, where they picked up Jennie and went on to the spa at Schawlbach. Lucy drank and bathed in the waters, read, walked, and enjoyed this quiet interlude after the gaiety and tensions of Russia. Not even news of agricultural disasters in Texas and South Carolina could dampen her buoyant spirits, though she did complain that it would "interfere" with purchases she wanted to make in Europe. "But I know Col. P. will give me the very last cent of his ability."[32]

Lucy's only worry was the Atlantic crossing. Douschka had not yet been baptized, Lucy desiring to have "dear Mr.

Dunlap" in Marshall perform the ceremony. But what if their steamer capsized and the child died unshriven? She decided to have Douschka christened in England before they departed on the *Adriatic* on October 24.

Sometime after Lucy left for Germany, Francis resigned his position as Minister to Russia. Several sources state that he was recalled "by popular demand of the people of South Carolina" to run for governor, or even that he had already been elected before leaving Europe; but neither is correct. More likely is that his correspondents advised Francis that South Carolina was close to secession—which he opposed, believing the state could not stand alone—and that he hastened home to try and stop any precipitous action. He was mortified to learn, while traveling to London to catch the steamer, that Europe was laughing at South Carolina's pretension in thinking of establishing itself as a separate sovereign nation.[33]

SECESSION!

The Pickenses landed in New York and hurried south, stopped briefly in Washington to settle affairs with the State Department, and arrived home in the midst of the fury and screaming rhetoric of the presidential campaign. South Carolinians were practically foaming at the mouth over the thought of the "gorilla" Abraham Lincoln winning the election. Francis, who was not opposed to secession if *all* of the South did so together, urged moderation but was overwhelmed by the radicalism that swept the state after Lincoln did indeed win, and he reversed his stand: "If need be, [*we must*] cover the state with ruin, conflagration and blood rather than submit."

South Carolina's governor was selected by the Legislature rather than by the people, and that body met in mid-December. Francis' strongest opponent was Robert Barnwell

Rhett, a former co-operationist turned ardent secessionist. Too radical to satisfy the majority, Rhett finally dropped out and Francis won by a bare margin on the seventh ballot, elected by men who prayed that his uncontroversial past would bring harmony.

Characterized by some historians as "bold and clear in mind," by others as "a man of ideas but not action," even Francis knew his personality lacked elements that would prove crucial now: "I believe it my destiny to be disliked by all who knew me well," he wrote Lucy.[34]

His first task was to lead his state out of the Union.
On December 20, 1860, South Carolina seceded.[35]

FORT SUMTER

Francis needed to take possession of the federal military installations in Charleston, principally Forts Moultrie and Sumter in the harbor. He demanded that President Buchanan surrender the forts. However, during the night of December 26, the new federal commander in Charleston, Major Robert Anderson, moved his forces from Moultrie to a more defensible position in Fort Sumter.[36]

His maneuver enraged the secession convention, which had already declared that any U.S. attempt to fortify their installations would be regarded as an act of war; members criticized Francis for not having seized the forts already. Now he moved to do so and took control of all the evacuated properties. And when *The Star of the West* arrived on January 9, 1861, to provision Sumter, Francis authorized the harbor batteries to fire—the first salvo in a war that would split the nation and cost over half a million lives.

But Francis Pickens did not want to be the man who started a war. He played for time until the opening of the convention in Montgomery, Alabama, on February 4, 1861, which would create the Confederate States of America. He was undoubtedly relieved when that new government assumed responsibility for the forts.

In the meantime, Lucy had taken Douschka home to Marshall to visit. The *Texas Republican* noted that the governor's lady was "immensely popular with the officers of the South Carolina army. She rather fancies military affairs and makes regular inspections of the forts and camp(s), where she is always received with enthusiasm." She was, the editor noted, "the same as of yore," neither her appearance nor her manners changed by her experiences and exalted position. When Lucy hurried back to South Carolina at the end of March, Eugenia remarked sourly in her diary that "poor Lucy deceived herself with promises of being with us that will never be fulfilled."

Lucy's return found her making her first appearance in the pages of another journal, that kept by Mary Boykin Chesnut, who quickly perceived in Lucy a formidable social rival. Writing of a party on April 2, Mary scorned the gentleman who begged Lucy for the violets she wore in her breast-pin. "She is a consummate actress, and he well up in the part of male flirt. So it was well done." Mary added that Lucy was "silly and affected, looking love into the eyes of the men at every glance." These comments (though made by a rival), taken with those in the Marshall newspaper regarding the military and Lucy's own vague allusions to misdeeds in Russia, lead the reader to wonder if she was simply indulging in the fashionable flirting expected of a Southern woman or if Lucy actually carried on affairs. There is no hard evidence of indiscretions, only rumor and innuendo.

Then came the morning of April 12. Was Lucy present when firing began on Fort Sumter? Several accounts state that either Douschka or Lucy herself set the match to the fuse of the first cannon, but that honor actually went to a statesman who was present. Another says mother and daughter watched the cannonade from a nearby rooftop, which is more likely.

LUCY'S LEGION

Soon after Sumter, Lucy sold a number of the Czar's gifts to outfit seven companies of infantry and one of cavalry with arms, uniforms, and equipment. For the Lucy Holcombe Legion, she designed a blue silk flag with gold fringe, emblazoned with both the palmetto and crescent of South Carolina and the lone star of Texas. At the presentation of the flag, she exhorted the men to "remember the seige of the Alamo, that spartan struggle whose bloody glory fills every woman's breast with that generous sympathy and honest admiration which the brave alone can give. . . ." Commanded by Colonel P. F. Stevens, superintendent of The Citadel, the legion operated under the motto Lucy gave them: The brave may fall but can never surrender.[37]

Lucy turned with zest to her role as First Lady of South Carolina, entertaining the officers and statesmen that thronged around the governor. On one occasion a group of politicians came to Edgewood to see Francis, but he had left. Lucy kept them waiting an hour while she prepared herself but so charmed the gentlemen when she did arrive that they stayed nearly three days.

Gene Stovall, who wrote of her after her death, declared that she "attracted about her a coterie of distinguished men . . . wielded a subtle, potent influence . . . [*Francis*] consulted her regarding matters of state. She unraveled many knotty problems, and thus rendered the Governor invaluable assistance."[38] Even Mary Chesnut acknowledged that Lucy was "young, lovely, clever" and "a host in herself" who would help Francis outwit his political adversaries.[39]

By now, he had many of those. W. G. Simms pronounced Francis an ass who drove away all decent counselors, a vain man susceptible to flattery. Lack of confidence in Francis' abilities led the convention to create a new government for South Carolina late in 1861: an Executive Cabinet consisting of the governor and four others which limited him to only one of five deciding votes. Francis was incensed, as was Lucy, and even Mary Chesnut felt the convention had gone too far. Her already shaky relationship with Lucy deteriorated at this point, as her husband, James Chesnut, was a member of the new Cabinet. Lucy showed her displeasure by refusing to rise and greet the Chesnuts at a reception soon afterwards.

Mary delighted in recounting an evening when Lucy made one of her few faux pas. "In her slow, graceful, impressive way, her beautiful eyes eloquent with feeling, she inveighed [*to General Cooper*] against Mr. [*Jefferson*] Davis' wickedness in always sending men born at the North to command at Charleston." While Cooper uncomfortably twitched his neckcloth, someone told Lucy the general was a New York native, a revelation Lucy greeted in "sudden silence."[40]

Mary's diary paints a picture of Lucy as gay and charming, a woman who relished clever conversation and jokes, and one who didn't hesitate to indulge in a little backstabbing if it served her purpose. Mary was amused by Lucy's reception for General Wade Hampton (June 1862) when she embarrassed "poor Wade" with her fluttering attentions and the ostentation of the evening: servants in Russian court livery, champagne and tea served in a Russian samovar. But while she reluctantly honored clever Lucy, Mary was not so polite about Francis, referring to him as Pickens the 1st and "a noisy old horsefly doing nothing."

QUEEN OF THE CONFEDERACY

As First Lady, Lucy received one of her greatest honors. The Confederacy's one dollar paper bill issued in the summer of 1862 bore her likeness, probably at the instigation of C. G. Menninger, Secretary of the Treasury, who was an admirer of hers. In December, when the Treasury issued its $100 bill, the portrait in the center was to have been of Mrs. Jefferson Davis. Instead it carried a profile view of Lucy, said to have been made from Czar Alexander's bust of her. A fairly poor likeness of her, in it Lucy wears a wreath of flowers in her hair and a dress with a lace collar. The same bill was reissued in April 1863 and February 1864—both dates *after* Francis' term as governor, indicating her continued popularity and her unofficial status as "Queen of the Confederacy." She was the only woman pictured on Confederate currency.

BACK TO EDGEWOOD

When Francis' term as governor expired in December 1862, the family returned to Edgewood, where he devoted himself to running the plantation. Early in 1865 General William Tecumseh Sherman and his troops left Georgia, burning and proceeded into South Carolina, the hated birthplace of secession. Several sources recount his visit to the beautiful Lucy and his subsequent sparing of Edgewood; none of them mention Francis, who was still quite alive. Whether legend or fact, it is true that Edgewood survived the war intact.

Intact but impoverished. Francis was forced to borrow $13,900 from Lucy, money she raised "by sale of her own private property . . . in New York[,] August 1866." Likely, she sold more of the Czar's gifts to finance her husband. He still owed her at the time of his death and made provisions in his will for the estate to repay her.

After the war, Francis emerged from his seclusion to attend the state constitutional convention and urge its members to accept President Johnston's reconstruction plans. And he attempted unsuccessfully to get a pardon for his wartime actions.

Francis Pickens died at Edgewood on January 25, 1869. The night before, knowing that death was near, he summoned the Negroes to the house and they gathered outside his bedroom window. He implored them to stand by Lucy and Douschka, then died as the moon rose. Edgewood's former slaves carried him to his grave in the plantation cemetery.

Now Lucy was a widow at the age of thirty-six. Francis had named her his executrix and left her Edgewood with all its furnishings and another nearby tract of land. Her brother John Theodore Holcombe, a Confederate veteran and bachelor, came from Texas to help Lucy manage Edgewood and the other plantations Francis had owned in South Carolina and Mississippi.[41] She opened her home to a number of relatives and friends left penniless by the war and donated a large sum to the state to help defray its war debt. Lucy also continued her studies, spending part of each day in Francis' immense library.

THE BERRY BROWN GIRL

Just a child, Douschka, her father's "darling little Eugenia," received four plantations through Francis' will, which Lucy was to sell if necessary to educate the girl "in a pious and most Lady-like manner." His devotion to the daughter "very dear to my heart" shines through in the will. Francis feared it would be difficult to sell the land because of the "now straightened [sic] conditions of my resources," an apparent reference to the poverty left him by the war. Sale of the lands would have helped ease the estate's burden. But, he wrote, he cared more for Eugenia's proper upbringing than any property.[42]

An outstanding and daring horsewoman at an early age, Douschka soon matured into an excellent manager. At eighteen she instituted a new plan which paid the Negroes a bonus, based on the success of the season, in addition to salary; it helped Edgewood return to profitability much sooner than other plantations. Douschka was loved and well known in Edgefield County, having inherited her mother's beauty and charm.

In 1876, as a young woman of seventeen, she put that charm to work. South Carolina was still under reconstruction rule, and General Wade Hampton was running for governor. But in Edgefield, near the Pickens home, carpetbaggers incited an "uprising" of former slaves which threatened to spread across the state. Douschka led a contingent of Hampton's "Red Shirts" (estimated at 1,500) to disperse them. For this action, she was known as the "Joan of Arc of the South."

In 1881 Douschka married Dr. George Dugas (1853-1903) of Augusta, Georgia. (Francis' biographer Francis B. Simkins declared it an unhappy relationship that Lucy pushed her into.) Among the wedding gifts was a sterling tea service from her old playmate in St. Petersburg, now Czar Alexander III. Douschka and George had three children: Lucy Francis, Louis Alexander (who died at fourteen), and Adrienne Dorothea.

Disliking city life, Douschka often returned to Edgewood, and she died there on August 18, 1893, after a brief illness. Edgewood Negroes carried her coffin, lined with white velvet and topped with white flowers, to the cemetery as they had her father's, while Civil War veterans marched alongside. Even Douschka's hunting dogs joined in, adding their chorus of wails and barks.

Lucy poured out her sorrow in a eulogy published in the *Edgefield Chronicle*. Sitting by Douschka's grave made Lucy recall the days when she "sat by her alabaster cradle in the proud Russian capital where she was born among kings and princes. . . ." Douschka, she recounted, was a loving and giving person, who asked nothing and gave much.[43]

MR. WASHINGTON'S HOUSE

In 1866 Lucy had been appointed vice regent from South Carolina of the Mount Vernon Ladies' Association. Founded in 1853 by another South Carolinian, Ann Pamela Cunningham, the Association strove to preserve the Virginia home of George Washington. (And it still operates the mansion today.)

Each participating state was assigned a room to furnish, and in 1884 Lucy undertook a major fundraising campaign to restore South Carolina's "very dilapidated" room. She appealed to Charleston women to prevent "the work begun so nobly by women [*from ending*] in failure through their neglect!"

But her contemporary on the Ladies' Association Board, Mrs. Lorenzo Sweat of Maine, later recalled that the Civil War had been Lucy Pickens' real passion. "The imaginary kingdom, which to many was only an ill-considered political experiment, was to her a glorious reality, a faith, a religion, and she gave it a loyalty that only strengthened as it became helpless."[44]

After Douschka's death, Lucy rarely left Edgewood except for Mount Vernon business, the annual meeting of the United Daughters of the Confederacy, and an occasional visit to Marshall. Those must have been sad trips for her, for her mother, Eugenia, and sister Anna were reduced to running Wyalucing as a boardinghouse. Lucy gave her share of the house to her siblings.

Another project to fill her time was the erection of a Confederate monument in Edgefield, but that was not completed before her death.

LUCY'S DEATH

Lucy Pickens died at Edgewood of a cerebral embolism on August 8, 1899. A few days later, her longtime maid and former slave Lucinda also died.

"Since the death of my dutiful and devoted daughter Douschka," she had written in her 1893 will, "her little children constitute the remaining objects of my solicitude; to make provision for their education, and comfortable support, is the controlling desire of my heart." To her granddaughters Lucy Frances Pickens Dugas and Adrienne Dorothea Rebecca Dugas, Lucy left all her personal estate. The girls and grandson Louis, who had not then died, were to share all her real estate.

Lucy also remembered her "faithful brother" J. T. H. Holcombe, leaving him "land enough for a two-horse farm—not to exceed seventy acres. . . ."

Her inventory takes up fifteen handwritten pages and includes $895 of silver, $2,360 of jewelry, and household furnishings of $1,040. Among the items listed are two marble busts (presumably those commissioned by the Czar of Russia), portraits of the Czar and Czarina valued at $2, one lot of sea shells, an ice cream freezer, two mules named Kate and Nell, bronze statues in the front yard, a copy of the Declaration of Independence (no value), and a library containing an astounding 766 volumes.[45] The $800 diamond ring and $750 diamond earrings are probably those given her by the Czar, for they are the most valuable pieces on the inventory.[46]

Her friends on the Mount Vernon Board remembered her fondly: "Mrs. Lucy H. Pickens is one never to be forgotten; her presence shed brightness and sunshine . . . but later in life came to her the heavy clouds of sorrow which enshrouded her . . . But hers was not a weak character; she realized the responsibilities devolving upon her [*i.e., the care of her grandchildren*] and roused herself to energy . . . But, alas! her last heavy blow was more than her shattered heart could bear. . . ."[47] This last is probably a reference to the death of her grandson Louis at age fourteen.

Other memorials referred to her love of flowers and the devotion of her former slaves, most of whom remained at Edgewood.

AFTERWORD

Eulalie Salley, an early Aiken, South Carolina land developer and suffragette, bought Edgewood some years after Lucy's death. In 1930 she had it dismantled and moved to Aiken. Today the Pickens-Salley House belongs to the University of South Carolina at Aiken. Francis' Edgefield law office was donated to the County Historical Society in 1950. East Hill, home of Francis' son-in-law M. C. Butler, is also extant.

And in 1985 the South Carolina State Museum finally acquired the only known surviving pair of plates used to print the Lucy Pickens $100 bill. It had been taken from Columbia as a Civil War souvenir by a Michigan soldier.

Confederate $100 bill with portrait of Lucy Pickens.

(Courtesy of South Caroliniana Library, University of South Carolina)

Notes—Chapter Three

1   Eugenia Dorothea Holcombe, Lucy's mother, was born near Petersburg, Virginia. Lucy herself, in a published memorial after her daughter's death, referred to Douschka's "proud Virginia mother," but that may simply reflect pride in her heritage.

2   The eldest Holcombe son, Thomas Anderson, was a lawyer in Lynchburg, Va. and known as the Father of Temperance in Virginia. The third son, William James, gave up his Lynchburg medical practice to become a Methodist preacher and abolitionist. Sarah married Edward Ambler, whose plantation covered the site of Jamestown; her children married into the Washington, Tazewell, and Carter families as well as the Napoleons of America, the Murats. Beverly actually met the Marquis for whom he was named in 1824 when Lafayette visited Richmond on his American tour: the French general presented the young man with a pipe, which became a family heirloom.

3   Diary entries of July 21, 1840; December 21, 1839; and undated entry, circa winter 1841. From typewritten copy in collection of Harrison County Historical Museum.

4   *Ibid.*, December 21, 1839.

5   *Ibid.*

6   *Leaves from a Family Album* by Jack Thorndyke Greer, page 82, undated letter circa 1859.

7   *The Free Flag of Cuba*, 52.

8   "Wyalucing" is an Eastern Indian word meaning "home of the friendless," an apparent reference to Beverly Holcombe's generous nature. The name may have been bestowed by Anna and Lucy, for there was a Wyalusing near their school in Pennsylvania. During the Civil War, the house was the headquarters of the Trans-Mississippi Agency of the Confederate Post Office Department. The

family sold it in 1880 to trustees of Bishop College; it was razed in 1962 after Bishop moved to Dallas.

9   "Only Texas Girl Ever Pictured on Money," *Dallas Morning News*, May 19, 1929.

10 Eugenia Holcombe diary, January 1850.

11 Cubans who wanted annexation by the United States organized filibuster expeditions under General Narciso Lopez, 1849-1851, which were headquartered out of New Orleans. Quitman was closely involved with the movement.

12 *The Free Flag of Cuba*, 197.

13 Franklin Holcombe, "Lucy Holcome Pickens," *Harrison County Historical Herald*, September 1966.

14 Eulogy on Mrs. Pickens by Belle Walsh, *The News and Courier*, Charleston, South Carolina, August 9, 1899.

15 Grandfather Andrew Pickens (1739-1817) served in the American Revolution and in the U.S. Congress; he married John C. Calhoun's niece. Francis' father, Andrew, was governor of South Carolina 1817-1819.

16 Calhoun's daughter Anna Maria lived with Francis and Eliza while attending school in Edgefield, and his son James Edward married Eliza's sister.

17 Letter of December 6, 1857, quoted in *James Henry Hammond and the Old South* by Drew Gilpin Faust, 340.

18 Francis' children by his first two marriages: Andrew, died 1832, age 2; Eliza, married J. S. Coles in 1853; Frances, died 1838, age 7 months; Jennie, married Mitchell Whaley, died 1865, age 19; Maria, married M. C. Butler (U.S. Senator from South Carolina 1877-1895) in 1858; Rebecca, married John C. Bacon (appointed U.S. Minister to Columbia 1872, U.S. Minister to Uruguay and Paraguay 1885) in 1859; and Susan, married J. N. Lipscomb in 1848.

19 Edgefield also had other Texas connections: it was the home of James Bonham of Alamo fame and of early Texas Indian commissioner Pierce Butler.

20   Quoted in "The Woman Called Lucy," by Kathleen Lewis, in *The State Magazine*.

21   The author of a *Ladies Home Journal* article wrote that Francis boasted of having recently declined the London post, and that Lucy would have said "yes" sooner if he hadn't.

22   *Texas Republican*, May 1, 1858.

23   *Ibid.* Belle Walsh wrote Lucy was not ready when sailing time arrived. Francis tried to hasten her but Lucy refused. The captain himself came to check and was so charmed "by this bewitching young passenger," that he delayed departure for three hours. Lucy was "accustomed to rule [*and*] she never allowed the scepter to pass from her hand; but the iron rod was always wreathed in flowers."

24   Following excerpts are from typewritten copy in Harrison County Historical Museum.

25   Letter from Lucy to Eugenia Holcombe, July 2, 1858, quoted in *Leaves from a Family Album*, 73.

26   Unattributed typescript article by Gene O. Stovall, "Lucy Holcombe Pickens, Queen of the Confederacy." And unattributed newspaper article, "Wyalucing at Marshall was Landmark—Was Childhood Home of Girl later known as Confederacy Queen," by Robert M. Hayes.

27   Lucinda received several proposals of marriage from fascinated Russians. After their return to South Carolina, she was known to the other slaves as "The Duchess."

28   This was Lucy's unflattering reference to Francis' first two wives. Her willingness to stay at Edgewood out of gratitude was no light matter to her; in the same letter she told Anna that Francis had promised her they would live in Texas after their return from Russia.

29   Undated letter to Anna from St. Petersburg, quoted in Greer, 81-83.

30   Leroy F. Youmas, *A Sketch of the Life and Services of Francis W. Pickens of South Carolina*, 7.

31 Steven A. Channing, *Crisis of Fear: Secession in South Carolina*, 86-87.

32 Letter to Eugenia Holcombe, August 17, 1860, quoted in Greer, 95-96.

33 Channing, *op. cit.*, 201-202.

34 Letter of February 23, 1860, quoted in *The Confederate Governors*, edited by W. Buck Yearns, 164.

35 The Ordinance was passed in the State House in Columbia, the capital, but was signed several days later in Charleston, where legislators and the Pickenses had fled to avoid a smallpox epidemic. During Lucy's reign as First Lady, there was no Executive Mansion; governors rented or owned homes. Much of the action during Francis' tenure centered at Edgewood, where Lucy's "batter cake parties" were famous.

36 Elizabeth Boatwright Coker, who claimed to be a frequent visitor at Edgewood, later wrote her memoirs, thinly disguised as a novel. In it, she attended a dinner and ball given at the house just prior to Anderson's move. Mrs. Coker described Lucy wearing her Russian diamonds and the dining room table laden with Italian linens, gold bordered Sevres plates, Bohemian crystal goblets, and the famous silver tureen. She recalled that a number of people had begged Francis to postpone the dinner because of the possibility that Anderson would make some move, but he refused to do so because "beautiful Lucy needed *excitement*." Coker's account, though interesting, is rendered very suspect by her insistence that everyone present was drinking champagne when the sound of cannon fire from Sumter swept the room: Edgewood is located hundreds of miles from Charleston on the western border of the state. Even if she was referring to a dinner at the Charleston house, all historic accounts agree that Anderson accomplished his move in silence.

37   The Lucy Holcombe Legion fought at Second Manassas, Kingston, Vicksburg, and Petersburg, surrendering after the Battle of the Crater.

38   Undated, unattributed typescript copy, Harrison County Historical Museum.

39   Mary Boykin Chesnut diary entries for January 9, 1862 and February 11, 1862.

40   *Ibid.*, March 20, 1862.

41   John served in Richardson's Company of Ford's 2nd Regiment, Texas Mounted Rangers. Later he was ADC to his brother-in-law General Elkanah Greer. He died in 1907, still unmarried, and was buried in Edgefield.

42   Francis directed Lucy to give his daughters Maria and Rebecca $500 of silver tableware each, and the same for Susan's daughters. He noted that he had recently given Rebecca and grandson Francis land in Mississippi. Appended to his will is a note that he had given 132 slaves and "other things" to his four older daughters.

43   Typescript in collection of Harrison County Historical Museum.

44   *Minutes of the Council of the Mount Vernon Ladies' Association of the Union*, May 1900, 17.

45   The Pickens library included congressional documents, a *History of Russia*, Irving's *Life of Washington*, Walpole, Julius Caesar, Tennyson, Gibbon's *Rise and Fall of the Roman Empire*, histories of many countries, Shelley, Browning, Byron, Shakespeare, *Gulliver's Travels*, works in French, and a fair number of "miscellaneous novels."

46   That document also spells out the rooms in Edgewood: Parlor, dining room, adjacent pantry, Major Kirkland's room (a Confederate veteran who lost a leg in the war), Dr. Dugas' room (Lucy's son-in-law), Lucy' bedroom, Magnolia room, nursery, washroom, kitchen, hall, garret, and library.

47   Minutes of the Council of the Mount Vernon Ladies' Association, *op. cit.*, 9.

CHAPTER FOUR

Olive Ann Oatman Fairchild

"May God grant that *my* experience
may never be yours."

. . . Olive Ann Oatman

Death, captivity, starvation, and slavery.

To those of us in the safe, comfortable twentieth century, it is the stuff of movie and television Western dramas. To her, it was reality. Her contemporaries believed she must emerge from this ordeal brutalized and crazy, a sideshow freak, but she remained "more delicate and courteous than those who rushed to gawk at her." And with the courage to stand before the gawkers and tell her tale.

A WANDERING CHILDHOOD

Olive Ann's early history is sketchy, for the primary focus of historians has been on her years in Indian captivity. She was born in September of 1837 somewhere in Illinois, probably in Laharpe. Her father, Royse Oatman (circa 1810-1851), was from Vermont; as a young man, he joined his parents who had previously moved to Laharpe. He married New York-bred, eighteen-year-old Mary Ann Sperry (circa 1811-1851), and they moved to a farm outside town. Their first child, Lucy, was born in 1833, followed by Lorenzo in 1836 and Olive in 1837.

By that time, Royse had brought his family back to live in town, where he opened a mercantile business. But the financial crash of 1837 ruined him, and, after Olive's birth, the Oatmans moved to the Cumberland Valley in distant Pennsylvania. There Mary Ann gave birth to her namesake daughter (1843), Royse Jr. (1845), and another daughter known only as C. A. (1846). But Oatman's "love for the free life of the Western prairies . . . drew him back" to a log cabin near Fulton, Illinois in 1846.[1] The seventh of their children, a son, was born there.

Then Royse the wanderer fell under the influence of James Collins Brewster. "Leader of a Mormon sect at Independence, Missouri, [*Brewster*] had had a vision that he was destined to establish a new Zion on the lower Colorado River in New Mexico Territory."[2] His advertisement for pilgrims to follow him into the wilderness led Royse to sell the Fulton farm for $1,500, gather his seven children and pregnant wife, and meet Brewster and more than forty others in the summer of 1850. Twenty wagons left Independence on August 10 to travel the Santa Fe Trail, bound for Bashan, the site on the Colorado divinely revealed to Brewster.

Along the way, dissension began to split the party, even to the point of disagreement over their destination. Should they follow Brewster's dream or go on to California? Near Las Vegas, New Mexico, the train divided after Brewster announced he would establish his colony there on Socorro Peak. Royse Oatman led the remaining twenty people and eight wagons towards California. But in the mountains of New

Mexico and Arizona, stock died, water and food ran short, and more livestock was stolen by Apaches. Some of the travelers decided to stay in Tucson; the Oatman, Wilder, and Kelley families pushed on toward the Pima Village (near present-day Maricopa Wells, Arizona).

By early February of 1851, when they reached the Village, their situation had become even more desperate. The Wilders and Kelleys decided to stay awhile, but Royse relied on the account of entomologist Dr. John L. LeConte, who reported seeing no Indians for 200 miles. Others warned Royse not to proceed, but Oatman "was of an obstinate & contrary disposition and would take advice from no one."[3]

In the worst decision he would ever make, he elected to go on alone with one wagon and his family toward Fort Yuma (modern Yuma, on the Arizona-California border).

The Gila Trail they were now following proved to be either a muddy bog or deep sand; at every hill, the family unloaded the wagon so the animals could labor to pull it up. It was backbreaking work that had to be repeated over and over again. On February 15, on the Gila River, Dr. LeConte caught up with them and agreed to carry a request for assistance to the commander at Fort Yuma, still more than a hundred miles distant. To Major S. P. Heintzelman, Royse wrote that he hadn't enough livestock to get through and, without help, "I am confident we must perrish [sic]."

Two days later, however, before he could reach Yuma, LeConte himself was set upon by Indians and robbed of his animals. Leaving a note on a tree to warn the Oatmans, he set out on foot. They never found his message.

By February 17, the Oatmans were still eighty miles from Fort Yuma and bogged down in a sand island in the rain-swollen Gila River, where they spent the night (somewhere near modern Agua Caliente, Arizona). With the river surging up almost to their campfire, and the wind whistling in the cold desert night, the older Oatman children spent the night in sleepless conversation about their situation. They each devised a plan about what they would do in case of an Indian attack. And it was Olive who stoutly informed her siblings that she would kill herself before she'd be taken as a captive.

The next morning the family worked the wagon loose, only to face a "steep declivity" of 200 feet. Again they unloaded the wagon and pushed it up onto the plateau. Royse Oatman now began exhibiting signs of severe stress that were evident even to the children. "At one time," Olive wrote, "during the severest part of the toil and efforts of that day to make the summit of that hill, my father suddenly sank down upon a stone near the wagon, and exclaimed, 'Mother, mother, in the name of God, I know that something dreadful is about to happen!' "

Working into the night to reload their goods, the family was eating a sparse meal when Olive spotted Indian riders, who proved to be Yavapais when they reached the camp.[4] Royse Oatman "had been among them [*i.e., Indians*] much in the Western states [*i.e., the prairie area around Iowa*]" and "it had long been his pride and boast that he could manage the Indians" by treating them leniently. Still, Olive recalled, "his wonted coolness and fearlessness" had left him now, the result, she believed, of his growing fears. He greeted the men in Spanish, and they smoked a pipe together. But when the warriors asked for food, Royse told them there was none and then finally gave them some bread when the men became surly. Then, while the family resumed their loading, the Indians went off to talk amongst themselves.

Suddenly, "as a clap of thunder from a clear sky," they turned and fell on the Oatmans with "a <u>fiendish yell</u> & tigers bound," felling Lorenzo and smashing Royse's skull with war clubs. Then they killed both his wife, Mary Ann, and the youngest child, whom she was holding in her arms. In quick succession, Lucy, Royse Jr., and C.A. were also clubbed to death.

As soon as the attack began, several warriors struck Olive and seized her and little Mary Ann (thirteen and seven years old), restraining the girls when they tried to help their family. Olive fainted at the grisly sight, only to be aroused by the tears of Mary Ann.

After the attack, the Yavapais looted the wagon and the dead bodies, then force-marched the two barefoot and captive girls north across 250 miles of desert and mountains, a route that took them west of the future site of Phoenix and through land that even today is barren, rocky, and home to few.

For three days and nights, the Oatman girls traveled with their captors with little food or rest, their feet bleeding. When Mary Ann fell and could not rise again, though beaten, one warrior finally slung her over his shoulder and carried her. At last they reached the Yavapai village near modern Congress, Arizona.

By the time John LeConte's message reached the fort, the Oatmans had been dead several days. An army reconnaissance party turned up nothing. Western newspapers sharply criticized Yuma's commander, Major Heintzelman, for his actions following the massacre, but he contended that the attack had taken place on Mexican soil, out of his jurisdiction, and that Royse Oatman had practically invited it by making "an incautious display of a quantity of Indian goods."[5]

LORENZO

What the sisters didn't know was that one other family member had actually survived the massacre near the Gila River. Left for dead by the Yavapais, older brother Lorenzo, then fourteen years old, had started back toward the Pima

Village after the Indians left.[6] Staggering blindly and suffering recurring blackouts from the blow to his head, he traveled several days before meeting two friendly Maricopa Indians who fed him and helped him on his way. At the Village, he found the Kelleys and Wilders with whom the Oatmans had traveled earlier; they sent out a party to bury Lorenzo's dead family and to confirm that Olive and Mary Ann were missing.

Convinced he could do nothing more there to find his sisters, Lorenzo went on to Fort Yuma where he lived with a Dr. Hewitt and later moved to San Francisco. He made regular attempts to launch an expedition to find Olive and Mary Ann but was thwarted by the gold fever which absorbed all manpower and attention.

LIFE AS A SLAVE

The impoverished Yavapais with whom Olive and Mary Ann now found themselves lived in primitive huts built into the rocky hillside, "holes in the ground," as Olive described them.[7] Dressed only partially, if at all, in skins and bark, the tribesmen were a walking nightmare to the two young girls.

On their arrival in the village, cold and their clothes badly torn by the rigors of their journey, Olive and Mary Ann were thrown onto a pile of wood while the Yavapais—"fierce, laughing, whooping wretches"—danced around them, spitting at them, screaming and taunting the children all night long.

"The next day," Olive recalled, "they showed [us] how to dig roots & kept us at it."

It was the beginning of months of horror. Even in her later memoirs, Olive could barely bring herself to describe their life: "I can not dwell upon particulars—we were kept for one year at perpetual drudgery . . . I do not think, during this first year[,] we had a single day of rest."

Within days, the girls' clothes fell apart and they were forced to adopt the Yavapai bark skirt. Taunted by the Indian children, and beaten for any perceived transgression, they foraged endlessly for food, fuel, and water for their masters and themselves. None was easy to find in this desert; scattered sage bushes provided the only fuel, and water was collected from holes in the rocks after a rain. All had to be carried back to the village on the children's backs. Their captors "seemed to create necessities of labor, that they might gratify themselves by taxing us to the utmost, and even took unwarrented delight in whipping us on beyond our strength." Mary Ann fell ill under this treatment, but the Yavapais ignored her "with all of the heartlessness of a dog."

As the girls became more conversant in their new language, the Yavapais quizzed them endlessly about the white man's world, only to laugh at the stupidity of their answers. How could such things be? they asked.

TO CALIFORNIA

A year after the horror on the Gila River, the girls were purchased by visiting Mojaves for two horses, three blankets, beads, and some food. Espaniola, the Mojave chief who now owned them, marched them for eleven days northwestward to their new home in a green valley on the Colorado River (between present-day Needles and Black Canyon, California).

Though the sisters were required to do much the same work as they had for the Yavapais, their lot had improved markedly, for Espaniola, his wife, and their seventeen-year old daughter Topeka treated them "in every respect as his own children." They were each given a blanket and seeds of their own to plant in a garden plot, though they quickly wearied of the "mesquite mush" the Mojaves made from ground up, boiled mesquite seeds.

But despite the more relaxed atmosphere, Olive and Mary Ann were still slaves and they were marked as such: their chins and upper arms were tattooed with the "Chief's mark." A sharp stick was used to prick the skin with small regular holes into which the Mojaves rubbed a powdered blue stone and an herb to dye the tattoos blue. Five straight lines ran from their lower lip to the bottom of their chin, with four small triangles at each corner; on each arm was a single straight line. The marks were indelible—Olive's were still visible the day she died.

The tattooing was part of a purification ceremony that eased captives into the life of the village and assured them a pleasant afterlife. The sisters were then given Mojave names; Olive's was Aliutman but Mary Ann's is unrecorded.

FAMINE

Life in the Mojave village was indolent. Their gardens watered themselves with periodic inundations of the Colorado River, and no one bothered to plant more than needed for immediate use. But in the second year of the Oatmans' captivity (autumn 1853), there was no overflow and, consequently, no crops of melons and beans. And soon, as the drought continued, even the supply of mesquite seeds dried up.

Mary Ann began to fail once more, yet even so, she and Olive were forced to spend "whole days in search of roots & seeds with out getting as much as we could hold in our hands." When Mary grew too weak to move from her blanket, Olive went alone, frantically seeking food to keep her sister—her only link to her former life—alive. "I traveled whole days together in search of the eggs of blackbirds for Mary Ann." But what little she found was often taken from her to feed starving Mojave children, and the girls often went for days at a time with nothing to eat. Espaniola's wife and daughter, according to Olive, wanted to do more for Mary Ann but were unable to. And they wept "from the heart and aloud" as they watched the ten-year-old girl become ever thinner and more sunken. Others were not so charitable, wanting to kill Mary Ann to force Olive back to work. And Olive herself raged that her sister was suffering because the Mojaves were too lazy to look ahead.

The girls sang hymns, and Mary Ann spoke often of joining her dead family, releasing Olive from the burden she had become. After days of suffering, Mary Ann died, "as sinks the innocent infant to sleep in its mother's arms."

Olive was devastated but determined to bury her sister properly. Though Mojave custom was to burn the dead, her captors allowed Olive to bury Mary Ann in their garden plot—"the first and only grave in all that valley"—and to stand by her grave singing the few hymns she remembered. Then she gave up, expecting to die herself of starvation: "This was the only time in which, without any reserve, I really hoped to die."

But Espaniola's wife, Aespaneo, secretly ground up precious corn and made a gruel to sustain Olive until the early spring of 1854 brought rain and fish to a nearby lake. Now she was left alive, but alone, among the Mojave.

YEARS ALONE

Olive contemplated escape but didn't know how to reach the closest white settlement. Espaniola's family had come to care for her and told her she could leave but refused to take her themselves, fearing they would be punished for holding her captive.

Matters worsened when the tribe went to war against the Cocopah. Then Olive learned another Mojave custom: for each warrior killed in battle, a captive was sacrificed. For months she waited to learn her fate, but the war party returned triumphant and without a single loss. "I buried my face in my hands," she later recalled, "and silently thanked God." But any desire that Olive had to run away was dashed when she saw the fate of a captive Cocopah girl who did escape but was caught. The Mojaves crucified her, then spent hours shooting arrows into the girl. And they forced Olive to watch. She decided then that her best course was conciliation and abjection.

Life with Espaniola's family was as pleasant as possible under the circumstances. "There were some few for whom I began to feel a degree of attachment . . . Time seemed to take a more rapid flight; I could hardly wake up to the reality of so long a captivity among savages, and really imagined myself happy for short periods."

Many writers and historians have questioned whether Olive was sexually abused by or married to any of the warriors, but she always and emphatically denied that. "To the honor of these savages, let it be said that they never offered the least unchaste abuse of me," she declared, a statement corroborated by famed ethnologist/anthropologist A. L. Kroeber, whose studies showed that the Mojaves did not sexually molest female captives. And despite the later rumor that she bore two children, there is no record in the Bureau of Indian Affairs of anyone—either Yavapai or Mojave—claiming descent from her.

RESCUE!

Lorenzo Oatman had never given up hope of finding his sisters. From his new home near Los Angeles, he wrote angry letters to newspapers, petitioned Congress when California's governor refused to help him, and followed every rumor of Indian captives he heard.[8]

The *Los Angeles Star* had taken up his cause, and the paper's editorials demanding action made their way to Fort Yuma and a carpenter named Henry Grinnell. Meanwhile the Mojaves were growing exasperated with Olive's "constant weeping" over the death of her sister, so "they allowed the fact of her still being with them to transpire through a Yuma Indian."[9] This Indian, Francisco, crept into Fort Yuma in January of 1856 and contacted Henry Grinnell, whom he knew. Grinnell told him of the furor raised by the *Star* which had renewed interest in the girls' fate.

With the blessing of the fort commander, Lt. Col. Martin Burke, and a letter of safe passage, Francisco returned to the Mojaves with a horse, blankets, and beads to ransom Olive Oatman.

But the Mojave council was now unsure of what to do. They confined Olive to Espaniola's hut for three days while they debated the matter, their sudden fear of army reprisals overriding their desire for the ransom. At last they summoned the eighteen-year-old Olive to the council session, but only after painting her with "a dun, dingy color, unlike that of any race I ever saw" to disguise her pale skin and ordering her to speak only gibberish to Francisco.

With wonder, she read the note Francisco carried from Martin Burke, stating that it was "desirable she should come to this post, or send her reasons why she does not wish to come." Olive read it aloud to the council and, fearful its message would not be sufficient, made up an additional sentence saying that the "Americans would send a large army and destroy the Yumas and Mohaves, with all the Indians they could find" unless she returned with Francisco. "I never expect to address so attentive an audience again," she recalled humorously of her imaginative efforts to secure her freedom.

The council continued to argue, with Espaniola stating sadly, "Well, I would like to raise this girl. We traveled far to buy her. We like her." His conclusion summed up the fears that now preyed on the Mojaves: "And we want to make friends [through her]. When those who come by us know how we treat her, they will treat us well, too."[10] Some warriors suggested killing Olive to eliminate the blame the army would surely place on the Mojaves for her capture. But those who argued for returning her to her people eventually won out, with the stipulation that Espaniola's daughter Topeka accompany Olive to Fort Yuma.

But her leavetaking was not without sorrow. "Ancious [sic] as I was to regain my liberty, yet I could not leave the wilde [sic] mountain home, without a struggle. Every stream and mountain park & shaded glen I was as familiar with, as with the dooryard of my childhood home." She especially hated leaving Mary Ann's tiny grave.

For nine days Olive and her companions—Topeka, Francisco, another Mohave, and a Mexican captive whom Francisco thought was Mary Ann—traveled down the Colorado to Fort Yuma. The only items Olive took with her from her servitude were the bark skirt she was wearing and a handful of the mesquite seeds she had spent years gathering.

On the opposite side of the river from Fort Yuma, the party halted while Henry Grinnell came across to greet Olive. He later recalled that she sat on the ground, her hands covering her tattooed face, and cried. The carpenter helped her wash and Olive changed her bark skirt for a calico dress he had borrowed from one of the officer's wives.

Thus, on the morning of February 28, 1858, six years and ten days since she had been captured on the Gila River, Olive Ann Oatman entered Fort Yuma and returned to the white world.

MEETING LORENZO

Olive had forgotten much of her English, as was evidenced by Lt. Col. Burke's comment that she answered every question "yes," regardless of what it was. He examined her about her years with the Indians, and she told him forthrightly that the Apaches [*i.e., Yavapais*] beat her but the Mojaves treated her and Mary Ann "very well."

And Burke stunned her by telling her that Lorenzo was still alive. He had read of her rescue in the *Los Angeles Star* and hastened to Fort Yuma, arriving only a few weeks later. Neither recognized the other after the passage of six years: they were children when the attack took place and had now matured into adults. Brother and sister were so overcome at their meeting that they sat quietly, unable to speak, for an hour.

PUBLIC RESPONSE

The California press led the way in recounting to the world every detail of Olive's ordeal and exciting rescue, which displaced murders, political shenanigans, and Central American escapades from the front page. And everyone had suggestions on how to help her. The San Francisco paper expressed the "hope that some of our philanthropic San Francisco ladies will offer their services to either provide a home for her, or use their influence in procuring her admission to the Orphan Asylum."[11] A family in San Diego did offer her a home with the opportunity "to resume that position in society which five years of savage bondage has deprived her."[12] The state legislature passed a bill to appropriate her $1,500, much to the public's approval; but she likely never received it.

Olive's readjustment to her old world and lifestyle progressed rapidly. The *Star* noted at the end of March that she was "fast recovering her English, reads readily, and sews like a mantua-maker." Almost incredulously, the reporter described her "lady-like deportment . . . pleasing manners . . . [*and*] amiable disposition." Olive was "more delicate and courteous than those who rushed to gawk at her." No doubt the reporter, like the rest of America, expected her to be a wild animal after the savagery she had endured.

In April, as soon as she had recovered enough, Lorenzo and Olive returned to Los Angeles, riding with a military wagon train. As they departed Fort Yuma, she promised Musk Melon, a Mojave who had traveled there with her, that she would tell everyone about the Mojave and how she had lived with them. On reaching the city, they stayed at the Thompson Willow Grove Inn in El Monte, owned by Ira Thompson, who had been part of the wagon train to Arizona.

The *Star*, which had supported Lorenzo's rescue attempts, pulled off a coup by snaring the first official interview with Olive for its April 19, 1856 issue, devoting two columns on the front page to the story. "Her timidity and want of confidence prevented her from giving the details unassisted," wrote the *Star* reporter. But he was pleased to add that though "her faculties have been somewhat impaired by her way of life . . . her friends assured us that in the short time she has been among them she has made very perceptible progress."

The article described her life among the Indians and the tattoos on her face and arms, and noted her attachment to Aespaneo who, when Olive left, "cried a day and a night as if she were losing her own child." The young woman's studies consumed much of her time now, reported the *Star*; "she converses with propriety, but as one acting under a strong constraint; and she has not forgotten the instructions of her childhood."[13]

ROYAL STRATTON

In June 1856 the siblings moved to Phoenix in Jackson County of Oregon's Rogue River Valley where a cousin, Harrison (or Harvey) B. Oatman, farmed and operated a stage station. He had heard of Olive's rescue and had come south to claim his kin. Ira Thompson was more than a little miffed, writing the *Star* an acrimonious letter that asked why Oatman hadn't come to care for Lorenzo years ago.

In Oregon they met a thirty-year-old Yreka minister named Royal Byron Stratton, to whom Olive dictated her memoirs. *The Captivity of the Oatman Girls* was published in San Francisco in 1857 at Lorenzo's expense (he borrowed the money) and sold out a first printing of 5,000 copies in only two weeks. Within two years, the book went through several editions and sold an amazing 30,000 copies; the proceeds allowed Olive and Lorenzo to return to California in 1857 to study for six months at the University of the Pacific in Santa Clara.

In a copy of the book intended for an aunt, Olive inscribed a poem that included these lines:

> "I cannot! How can I,
> Express to you here;
> Of the sorrow and grief,
> That still lingers near;
> It seames (sic) to have molded
> And fashioned my heart,
> And casts a dark cloud
> Ore my bright hopes of youth."[14]

But *The Captivity of the Oatman Girls* was more than just a bestseller. It was one of the few accounts of Indian captivity in the Southwest to actually be published, and, as such, it acquainted thousands of Americans with the horrors of these ordeals and also with the previously unknown lifestyles of these tribes.[15]

ON THE LECTURE CIRCUIT

In 1858 Olive decided—or was persuaded—to go on the lecture circuit to promote Stratton's book. With the Stratton family, she and Lorenzo sailed from San Francisco to New York City on the fifth of March, arriving on the twenty-sixth. While there, they also released a new revised edition of Stratton's book.

The *New York Times* hastened to interview this "modest, intelligent young woman . . . [*who*] has evidently suffered greatly from the hardships she has been compelled to undergo. . . ." In describing her tattoos for the readers, the reporter declared that "this savage embellishment does not materially enhance the personal charms of the lady, but it is an indelible evidence of the scenes she has undergone."[16] Such a snide comment may have been what caused Olive to begin wearing a veil in public, if she had not already done so. Lorenzo, the *Times* more charitably likened to "a fair specimen of a Western man."

For her lectures, which opened in New York City that May, Olive prepared handwritten notes. "Neither the position of public speaking nor the facts that I am to relate," she told audiences at the beginning of her speech, "are in harmony with my own feelings, for my nature intuitively shrinks from both. But I yeald [sic] to what I conceive to be the opening of providence & the stern voice of duty."

The poster advertising her lecture featured an illustration of Olive's tattooed face and the horrific scene in which the Yavapai war party attacked the Oatman family. She would tell, it promised, of "her Wonderful Adventures, Extreme Sufferings, and Hair-Breadth Escapes" as well as describe the

The only known photograph of Olive, taken
circa 1859 while she was on the lecture circuit.

(Courtesy Red River Historical Museum, Sherman, Texas)

terrain of the West and the "Manners and Customs of the Savage Indians." And "a book, narrating the entire of their perils and sufferings will be for Sale at the Lecture."[17]

Reviews of her program were laudatory: "the audience listened with breathless interest, and all were deeply affected!" reported the *New York Times*. The *Evansville Enquirer* adjured its readers to attend "for she is doubtless well worthy the sympathy of our citizens." And the *Terra Haute* (Indiana) *News* predicted that Olive "will have crowds to hear her wherever she goes." Though no itinerary exists of her lecture schedule, it has been determined that she appeared in cities in New York, Indiana, and Ohio from the time of her first engagement in New York City through the end of 1859. The Reverend Edward J. Pettid, an Arizona priest who studied Olive extensively, wrote that she continued to lecture regularly until 1865, when she married.

What modern readers may not understand is the courage it took for a woman to stand on a public platform and speak in 1858, especially when the topic was of such an extremely personal and horrifying nature. This Olive did despite her own shyness, for her programs helped raise money for church work and provided the funds for her to continue her education.

These lectures were among the few occasions when she appeared without a veil to hide her scarred face.

When not traveling on the lecture circuit, Olive lived with the Stratton family in Albany, New York. Lorenzo meanwhile had moved back to Illinois (Whitesides County), where he lived with and worked as laborer for a farming family and eventually married; he died in 1901 and was buried in Red Cloud, Nebraska.

In 1864 Olive had one last encounter with her former captors. Learning that an unidentified Mojave chief would be among an Indian delegation visiting New York City that

February, she traveled there to meet him. He proved to be Espaniola's son, Irataba, who had succeeded him as chief. "We met as friends[,] giving the left hand in friendship . . ." and talked in Mojave. From Irataba, Olive learned that Topeka was still alive but continued to mourn the loss of her "pail faced" friend and hoped she would return.

JOHN FAIRCHILD

Sometime in 1865 Olive visited her Sperry relatives in Monroe County, New York and may also have given a lecture there. During her stay, she met thirty-five-year-old John Brant Fairchild and fell in love.[18] They married in Rochester that November.

Fairchild was born in New York in 1830, the son of John Hare and Elizabeth Hagar Fairchild, but little more is known of his youth.[19] He apparently went to California at an early age to make his fortune in the Gold Rush. In 1850 he appeared on the California census in Placerville, El Dorado County, working as a gold miner; at least one brother accompanied him but was killed by Indians. How successful John was as a miner is not recorded.

But what he did recognize was that miners have to eat, and he quickly got in the business of driving cattle herds to California from Missouri and Texas. In August 1854, for example, John and brothers Rodney and Homer started from Texas with a cattle herd. On the twenty-first, they were attacked in the Sonoran Mountains of Mexico by Indians who killed Rodney, ransacked the wagons, and stole 200 head of cattle. The survivors made it back to California.[20]

Several sources from Sherman, Texas, name John as "Major" Fairchild and state that he was a Confederate officer during the Civil War. Confederate service records do list several John and J. B. Fairchilds, but it is impossible to determine if any are the right man.

John had made and lost several fortunes before he met Olive Oatman. In his later years he was described as "a distinguished, handsome, impressive man with a beard . . ." and as "a man of grim determination." That may explain the persistent story that, after their marriage, John bought every copy of Royal Stratton's book he could find and burned them, presumably to protect his new wife's privacy.[21]

TO TEXAS

After John and Olive married, they settled in Detroit, Michigan, where he had family, and lived there about seven years. In 1872 they moved again to Sherman, Texas, just south of the Red River in Grayson County. John was likely drawn there because of the boom that resulted from the coming of the railroads to North Texas, for Sherman was quickly becoming the financial and cultural center of the region.

He immediately plunged into the business life of the growing town by opening the City Bank of Sherman, serving as president and a member of the board of directors, positions he would hold for well over a decade.

He also began buying and selling real estate. More than two dozen deeds are recorded in his name between 1873 and 1904, including outright deeds, deeds of trusts, and note assumptions. Most of the land was in Sherman, where John became one of the largest real estate owners in the city; but some of his property was in Whitesboro, a town on the western edge of Grayson County. Among the transactions there was John and Olive's sale of land to the trustees of the Shiloh Baptist Institute, an important early school in the area.

John reinvested his fortune in other Sherman enterprises, too. He owned stock in Commercial National Bank (where he met longtime friend William R. Brents), and in Greiner-Kelly Drug Company, a major pharmaceutical firm headquartered in Dallas. He proudly listed himself as a "capitalist" in the Sherman City Directory and did business with some of Texas' foremost men, including cattleman, land developer, and hotelier Jot Gunter, who lived near the Fairchilds for a time before moving to San Antonio. John was "public spirited" and "could always be counted on to do his full part in any enterprise in the city."[22]

The Fairchilds lived first between Pecan and Houston Streets and later built a large, two-story home on the northwest corner of South Travis and West Moore Streets, in one of Sherman's finer neighborhoods; it was razed after their deaths and another house built on the site. The couple were also very active in St. Stephen's Episcopal Church and were likely among its organizing congregation in 1872.

MAMIE

Olive devoted herself to her home and charity work, particularly with orphans. William Brents' daughter Katharine was a frequent visitor to the Fairchild home when she was a child and later recalled that Olive "helped many people in her quiet way," a hint that she also may have dispensed some of John's fortune to those in financial straits. Katharine was much struck by this woman, who was "very shy and retiring, probably due to the blue tatoo around her mouth . . . She was very slender and walked with great dignity . . . The fact is that I thought that she had the face of an angel."[23]

After years of marriage, John and Olive had had no child. It is uncertain whether the starvation and hardship she endured at a vulnerable age precluded her from becoming pregnant.

Sometime in 1875 Olive solved this dilemma by taking a Sherman-born baby, Sarah Catharine Leonard, into her home. Sarah had been born in February of 1874 and how her mother and Olive met, if at all, is unknown. Was Sarah one of the orphans that Olive worked with? Probably, for the legal document of March 15, 1876, in which she and John adopted the infant, does not name a birth mother.[24]

They gave her a new name, Mary Elizabeth, but called the child Mamie. She grew up in the house at Travis and Moore and attended St. Joseph's Academy, the Catholic school two blocks away which opened in 1877.[25]

With her family about her, and work to occupy her, Olive lived her remaining years quietly and, one hopes, peacefully. She died at home of a heart attack on March 20, 1903 at the age of sixty-five and was buried in Sherman's West Hill Cemetery. John followed her four years later, after he collapsed one night in Mamie's presence.[26] In 1969 Olive's gravesite was honored with a marker from the Texas Historical Commission, the first of its type placed in Grayson County.

And it is said that, to the end of her days, Olive kept by her the jar of mesquite seeds she carried from the Mojave village.

Notes—Chapter Four

1 *New York Times*, May 4, 1858, 5.

2 Howard H. Peckham, *Captured by Indians: True Tales of Pioneer Survivors*, 195-196.

3 Letter of Major S. P. Heintzelman, quoted in Alice Bay Maloney's "Some Oatman Documents," *California Historical Society Quarterly*, Volume 21, 109.

4 Though often referred to as Apaches, the "generic" Southwest Indian, these Indians were probably Yavapais. Olive herself insisted they were Pimoles on their way to Fort Yuma. The village to which they took her was south of the modern Yavapai Reservation, which lends more credence to their identification as Yavapais.

5 Maloney, *op. cit.*, 108. Legally, Heintzelman was correct about his jurisdiction, for the Gadsden Purchase had not then been completed and that portion of Arizona did still belong to Mexico. In hindsight, Olive later wondered if Royse Oatman had actually found John LeConte's message warning of Indian danger and hidden it from the family to keep them from worrying.

6 Lynn Galvin writes that Lorenzo was rendered unconscious by the blow to his head. ("Olive Ann Oatman—An Indian Captive Returned," unpublished manuscipt.) But Robert Benjamin Smith ("Apache Captives' Ordeal," *Wild West*, June 1993) disagrees. "Lorenzo had been temporarily paralyzed . . . but remained conscious throughout the attack; he heard his two sisters screaming as they were dragged away, and he felt the Apache rifle through his pockets." The final word must come from Lorenzo himself who wrote, in *The Captivity of the Oatman Girls*, that he regained consciousness soon after being struck and heard the screams of his family as they were attacked.

7   These and all other quotes of Olive's, unless otherwise identified, are from *The Captivity of the Oatman Girls* by Royal B. Stratton, first published in 1857, or from her Lecture Notes in the collection of the Arizona Historical Society.

8   One of these rumors, late in 1855, declared that both girls were alive and married to Mojave chiefs.

9   *Los Angeles Star*, March 29, 1856.

10 From A. L. Kroeber's article, "Olive Oatman's Return," quoted in Lynn Galvin, *op. cit.*

11 *San Francisco Daily Herald*, March 11, 1856. Quoted in William B. Rice, "The Captivity of Olive Oatman: A Newspaper Account," *California Historical Society Quarterly*, 98.

12 *Ibid.*

13 Interview quoted in Rice, *op. cit.*, 100-104.

14 Original in San Francisco's Sutro Library, quoted in Lynn Galvin, *op. cit.*

15 The Indians, of course, would make the point that no whites would have been captured if they had honored their treaties and stayed off tribal lands.

16 *New York Times*, May 4, 1858, 5. Even the friendly *Los Angeles Star* described her face as disfigured.

17 Copy of poster in collection of Red River Historical Museum, Sherman, Texas.

18 *Harper's Magazine* of November 1864, however, reported Olive and Lorenzo living in Rochester when she met John. And Edward Pettid wrote that John was "first attracted to her when he saw her as a young woman going to school with little children."

19 Interestingly, John's family also had its share of brushes with Indians, experiences which may have helped him cope with the traumas Olive surely suffered. His grandfather, Benjamin Fairchild, was captured by Mohawks as a youth and taken to Canada; a brother found him and

brought him back to New York. Benjamin later returned to Canada as an Indian interpreter.

Benjamin's son John (1798-1886) and wife Elizabeth (1803-1891) had seven children: Rodney Ward (182?-1854); John Brant; Benjamin Homer (1828-1893); Peter Hare, killed by Indians during the California Gold Rush; Azuba Hagar (1833-1850); Mary Hare (1838-1926), married to Leverett Clark Hargar; Martha Amanda (1840-1911); James Hagar (1842-?); and Elizabeth Jane (1844-1925), married to George Dallas Humphrey.

20 John Fairchild's obituary in the *Denison* (Texas) *Daily Herald*, April 25, 1907.
Early Fairchilds in America and Their Descendants by Jean Fairchild Gilmore.
"A Cattle Drive from Texas to California: The Diary of M. H. Erskine, 1854" by Walter S. Sanderlin (editor), *Southwestern Historical Quarterly*.

21 That story originated with Mrs. Katharine Brents Collie of Sherman, whose father was a close friend of John and Olive's. As a child, Mrs. Collie often visited in the Fairchild home.

John's efforts to destroy Stratton's book were foiled in 1909—after both he and Olive were dead—when a new abridged edition of *The Captivity of the Oatman Girls* was published in Oregon. Still another was published in San Francisco in 1935; it carried an introduction by Southwest historian Hubert Howe Bancroft that claimed Olive died in a New York insane asylum in 1877. According to Lynn Galvin, daughter Mamie Fairchild had a copy of the second edition.

22 *Denison Daily Herald*, April 25, 1907.
23 Rev. Edward J. Pettid, "The Oatman Story," *Arizona Highways*, November 1968.
24 Though written in 1876, this document was not filed until June 2, 1896. (Grayson County Deed Book 114, page

593) Edward Pettid wrote that Mamie was born February 8, 1873.

25 St. Joseph's still operates, though under the name today of St. Mary's.

26 John Fairchild's estate was valued at $28,900 and included real etate in Sherman and Detroit, stocks, notes and judgements due him, and household furnishings. He left his sisters Mary, Martha, and Elizabeth, all living in Detroit, $500 each; the residue of the estate went to Mamie, who was also his executrix. She continued to live in the house until she married Alister MacKay Laing in 1908 and left Sherman.

CHAPTER FIVE

Lucy Ann Thornton Kidd-Key

"We need more courageous women."

. . . Lucy Kidd-Key

"I have an abiding faith in the sanity of women."

Guided by that belief, Lucy Ann Kidd-Key dedicated herself for nearly forty years to the education of young women. The world in which she began her work was not very tolerant of her goals; and it took all of the Southern charm that Lucy possessed in abundance, as well as innate executive skills and a strong dash of practicality, to prove that world wrong.

FAMILY HISTORY

Lucy was born in Salvisa, Kentucky, near Lexington, on November 15, 1839, the second of three children of Willis Strother and Esther Stevens Thornton. Through her father, she descended from the Strothers, who first settled in Virginia in the late seventeenth century. Lucy's great-great-grandfather, William, moved the family to Kentucky after the Revolu-

Lucy, circa 1895.

(Courtesy Red River Historical Museum, Sherman, Texas)

tionary War. Susanna Strother Hawkins Coleman, William's youngest child, was the first to bestow the name of Lucy on one of her daughters; and it is from her that Lucy Thornton descended.[1]

Her mother, Esther Thornton, the daughter of a Huguenot refugee to South Carolina, was "a most excellent and devoutly pious woman," from whom Lucy was said to have "inherited much of her womanly winsomeness."[2] Between the two families, Lucy could claim kinship to many of the South's leading figures, including Jefferson Davis, John Marshall, James Madison, and Patrick Henry. That lineage would be important to her in later years, creating a socially impeccable background and a mystique that helped give her entree to money and the best families.

As a young girl, Lucy attended the Reverend Stuart Robinson's Institute in Georgetown, Kentucky, on the Elkhorn River north of Lexington. There she specialized in literature and history, an early indication of the interests that would guide her later career. In 1856 her life took its first turn when she married Dr. Henry Byrd Kidd and moved to Yazoo City, Mississippi.

LIFE IN MISSISSIPPI

Kidd, born in Kentucky circa 1820, was a widower. Sometime in the mid-1840s he had settled at Manchester, as Yazoo City was then called, and in 1846 he married Rebecca E. Wright of Virginia. He quickly established himself as one of the area's "most eminent and active physicians" and began amassing money and property. By 1850 his holdings were valued at more than three thousand dollars and included lots in town and farming property outside it. But he fell victim to the 1853 yellow fever epidemic that swept the area. Rebecca nursed her husband through the worst of the fever, then died of it herself. (Rebecca bore him no children.)

The frontier city to which Henry brought Lucy Thornton as a bride three years later was on the Yazoo River about forty-five miles northeast of Vicksburg and a major cotton shipping point for the Mississippi Delta. It was surrounded by large cotton plantations, including that belonging to Jefferson Davis; and later newspaper accounts of Lucy's life stated that Henry Kidd also owned an estate and many slaves. But his name does not appear on either census slave schedule.[3]

In addition to his medical practice, Henry had a half interest in a pharmacy with his brother-in-law, Dr. W. Y. Gadberry, who had married Lucy's older sister Sarah and moved to Yazoo City also. By 1860 Henry's estate was valued at $11,000, roughly half in real estate that included several lots in the city's business district, and half personal.

Lucy lived a wealthy, well-ordered life, was active in the Methodist Church, and soon bore Sarah (1858) and Henry Jr. (1860). Her now widowed mother, Esther Thornton, also lived with the young family.

Then came Civil War and hard times. In the lean winter of 1865-1866 that followed the war, with no credit available, Federal troops occupying the city, and the region's farming system in shambles, Henry tried to keep the family afloat by selling land. Family legend says that Lucy also helped stretch their money during this period by baking pies and selling them to the troops.[4]

But by 1870 Henry still had not recovered his prewar financial status, exacerbated by the birth of two more children: Price in 1863 (who would live only ten years) and Edwin in 1870. Moreover, Henry's health began to fail. In 1874, convinced he had not long to live, Henry Kidd made his will, bequeathing his entire estate to Lucy, his executrix. But he rallied and lived another three years before dying on September 11, 1877, leaving Lucy a thirty-eight-year-old widow with three children and a mountain of debts.

WIDOWHOOD

Within two weeks of Henry's death, Lucy had begun to take action, filing suit in Yazoo County Chancery Court against a widow and her three children for nonpayment of $1,500 in notes due on land she and her late husband had bought from the Kidds in 1876. In October the court ruled in Lucy's favor.

According to a descendant, she also began a campaign to retrieve bad debts owed the Kidd-Gadberry pharmacy. She stationed a Negro servant outside the door to watch for customers who had large unpaid charges, then accosted them about the monies owed. By these methods, and by selling land she had inherited from Henry, Lucy began to again build up the family finances. But not long after his father's death in 1877, her oldest son, Henry Jr., died while attending medical school in Kentucky.

Probably one of the few happy times for Lucy in this period was Sarah's marriage in 1878 to Joseph H. Holt, a lawyer and justice of the peace. Unfortunately, that happiness, too, was shortlived, for Holt died several years later, leaving Sarah with a young son.

WHITWORTH COLLEGE

When the family finances were stable once more, Lucy began to look for a secure investment for her money. She learned of Whitworth College in Brookhaven, Mississippi, a girls school opened in 1858 by the Reverend Milton J. Whitworth, a Methodist minister. Possibly the connection was made through Charles B. Galloway, a rising star in the Methodist hierarchy. Lucy and Galloway had met years earlier when he came to Yazoo City to serve his first pastorate and boarded with the Kidds.

Lucy bought an interest in Whitworth[5] and moved to Brookhaven with her family about a year after Henry's death to become the "Proprietress of the Boarding Department." What happened to her investment is a bit murky. Family members claim she lost her money in a questionable transaction with Whitworth's president, who had not, they say, the authority to make a contract with her. The daughter of her closest friend later wrote only that she lost it "due to misplaced trust in a personally ambitious friend who failed to substantiate her rightful claims and just dues."[6]

Lucy used her ten years at Whitworth to good advantage and may have developed some of her own later educational principles from the example of Whitworth's president, Dr. H. F. Johnson. Hired in 1867, Johnson guided the college for twenty years through one of its biggest periods of expansion.

It was at Whitworth that Lucy met a fellow teacher who would become her closest friend, Maggie Hill.[7] In many long talks over the years, they developed their own ideas about the education of young women, based on an understanding and appreciation of the fine arts. It was their belief that "education for girls must always give a large share of those things that enrich the personal life, that rightly motivate action and fix right standards of living in the home. To do these things is the special mission of arts in education."[8]

As the years of her tenure at Whitworth passed, Lucy's reputation grew; Mississippi governor Robert Lowry, speaking there in 1882, publicly praised her. By this time, Whitworth was the South's largest college for women and featured an exceptional music department—all fodder for Lucy's future plans.

In 1887 President Johnson died and was succeeded by Dr. L. T. Fitzhugh. And, hundreds of miles away, events were happening that would again change the course of Lucy's life.

NORTH TEXAS FEMALE COLLEGE

In 1870 the Sherman Male and Female Academy was established in the North Texas town of Sherman. On four acres of land along Post Oak Creek, trustees built a two-story frame structure crowned with a cupola and opened for business.

A year later the school and its property were deeded to the North Texas Conference of the Methodist Episcopal Church, South. The new management converted it to a school for women named North Texas Female College and transferred all the boys to another school.

The new college had its ups and downs, mostly downs. Between 1870 and 1887 there were at least six presidents, and the trustees incurred thousands of dollars in debt to provide facilities for the ever growing number of students. Of its $15,000 valuation in 1885, $11,000 of that was indebtedness to cover mortgages. The church finally decided the school was a losing proposition and closed it in 1887.

For a year, the buildings sat empty, and weeds and sunflowers took over the grounds. Then Charles Galloway, by now the youngest bishop in the Methodist Church, suggested that the North Texas Conference take a look at his old friend, Lucy Ann Kidd.

TO SHERMAN

In April of 1888 Lucy traveled to Sherman to interview with the college's board of trustees. She broke the first of many rules when she politely refused to go to the board but, instead, required the gentlemen to visit her at her suite in the Binkley Hotel. They went and came away impressed by this diminutive, blue-eyed woman in the widow's weeds, with excellent credentials in the educational field and, best of all, they thought, money to invest in their college.

What Lucy never let them know was that she actually had less than $10,000, hardly enough to rebuild a college.[9]

The trustees offered and she accepted a contract by which she would assume control of the school for ten years. It was understood between them "that a great many improvements are to be made and the buildings to be put in shape for use in September." Newspaper coverage of this event noted that Lucy was "a Christian lady in every way calculated to fully meet the requirements made of her" and that the college trustees had been very impressed by Lucy's letters of recommendation from Bishop Galloway and from the governor and lieutenant governor of Mississippi.[10]

Her first action after signing the contract was to telegraph Maggie Hill, just returned from Europe, and offer her a position as presiding teacher. Her salary would be seventy-five dollars per month, but only, Lucy added, if the school made money. She then returned to Brookhaven to put her own affairs in order before the move.[11]

Her son Edwin, then eighteen, withdrew from the University of Mississippi to accompany her and become the college secretary and financial agent. Sarah, who had studied music in New Orleans, New York, and Paris, also planned to make the trek west to teach voice for her mother.

Lucy then set about enticing four other of Whitworth's best teachers to come with her. The *Brookhaven News* reported their departures: "Surely Mrs. Kidd has displayed fine executive ability in her wise selections. She feels that money is not to be taken into consideration in the organization of her faculty."[12]

Lucy returned to Sherman early in July 1888 with her family, servants, and enough furniture to outfit the school, and with her money sewn into her lingerie so that no one would guess her true financial status.

She then took to the road, traveling across Texas and the Indian Territory (now Oklahoma) in the heat of summer to attend church sessions and camp meetings, drumming up money and students. In later years she would entertain "her girls" with tales of those days, of the wolves that howled at night outside lonely cabins—"I would cover up my head with a quilt and shudder," she told them—and of dirty, exhausting journeys on horseback or by stagecoach. Helen Norfleet, a student in the Class of 1910 and later a renowned musician and teacher herself, recalled her favorite story about the five-foot-tall Lucy: "Once she traveled all night by coach and, arriving at the tent meeting, took her seat quietly inside. The ground under the tent was covered with straw and was, apparently, innocent enough, but when the brother in charge called on 'Sister Kidd' to address the congregation and the little woman rose, she found herself sinking deeper and deeper with every step, until by the time she reached the front she was up to her knees in sand." Mrs. Kidd, Helen wrote, chuckled about the impression she must have made on the congregation "with her less than four feet of visible height."[13]

At another revival, Lucy was preceded by a minister who informed the audience that music and instruments such as the fiddle were tools of the Devil, a hard act to follow when one of Lucy's pitches was the opportunity to study music. Her job was gargantuan, for not everyone appreciated the usefulness of the accomplishments and skills she was selling.

Still, North Texas Female College reopened in September 1888 with 100 students, among them Marie Lowry, daughter of the governor of Mississippi (who had recommended Lucy for the position in Sherman).

BUILDING A CAMPUS

Now that she had fulfilled the first clause of the contract by opening on time, Lucy turned her attention to rehabilitating the college's physical plant. She later said that calling the facility she came to in 1888 a college was pretentious indeed, in view of "its scant physical equipment." There were only two buildings: a brick chapel and the two-story frame structure that housed classrooms. Post Oak Creek, which ran through the four-acre campus, frequently flooded the property; in rainy weather, mud ran down the hill and into the front door of the main building. Lucy quickly hired a landscape expert from Mississippi to begin improving the neglected and poorly drained grounds.

In 1889, at the close of her first successful year, she personally purchased four lots for $850 to begin the expansion of the campus. Annie Nugent Hall, a three-story frame dormitory, was begun later that year on the new property and completed in 1890; it was named for the daughter of Colonel William L. Nugent, a member of the Whitworth College Board of Trustees who gave Lucy her first major gift: $10,000.

This was only the first of more than a dozen buildings Lucy would erect during her twenty-eight years as president. The chapel was enlarged in 1893 and renamed Julia Halsell Hall in honor of the woman who assumed "payment of the entire bonded indebtedness" of the college that year. Lois Thompson Dining Hall was erected in 1897 for $11,000. Nugent Hall itself would burn in 1903, a serious financial loss for Lucy who personally owned the building; it was replaced the following year with Annie Green Dormitory. Binkley Hall, built in 1911, was named for Lucy's second financial agent, the Reverend J. M. Binkley of Sherman. Of the $7,000 raised to construct that building, she personally donated $1,500.

The original main building of North Texas Female College,
built 1880 and later renamed Julia Halsell Hall.

(Courtesy Red River Historical Museum, Sherman, Texas)

There was also Leona Kimbley Hall, six cottages for the
faculty and her family, and an infirmary. By 1892 the ever-in-
novative Lucy had installed telephones and electricity. The
school had incandescent lights, zinc bathtubs, and running
water; and the kitchen was equipped to produce hundreds of
meals on a daily basis, as well as six-course treats on Friday
nights.[14] The school was the first in Texas to hire a nurse
whose sole duty was to attend the students.

The library grew steadily year by year: 500 "well selected
volumes" in 1892, 700 by 1896, and 1,000 books in 1898. The
science laboratories were stocked with the newest equipment,

including a $700 refracting telescope; both it and the labs were still the only ones in a Southern women's college in 1909.

"Paradise Cottage," Lucy's home adjacent to the college.

(Courtesy Red River Historical Museum, Sherman, Texas)

JOSEPH KEY

But in the midst of all this construction and planning and innovation, Lucy found time to fall in love. On April 5, 1892, her old friend Charles Galloway married her to Joseph Staunton Key, also a bishop of the Methodist Church.

Born in Georgia in 1829, Key was himself the son of a Methodist minister, Caleb Witt Key, whose family included Francis Scott Key, author of "The Star-Spangled Banner." After graduating from Emory College, Joseph entered the ministry and, two years later, married Susie McIntosh Snider. Joseph and Susie had three children before she died in 1891, including Dr. Howard Key, who later became president of Memphis Woman's College.

In 1886, in Richmond, Virginia, Joseph was elected a bishop of the Methodist Episcopal Church, South; also elected that day was Charles B. Galloway, at thirty-seven the youngest in church history. Key spent much of his subsequent career traveling as a missionary across the South and to Mexico, China, and Japan, where he amassed a rich collection of Oriental artifacts. He also became known as the "father of the Epworth League in Texas," because of the deep interest he took in that church organization.[15] Key was founder of Fort Worth's Polytechnic College (Methodist) and served as president of the board of trustees from 1890 to 1906.

By the time he married Lucy and moved to Sherman, a year after Susie's death, Joseph Key was already considered "the most loved and revered man of the Methodist church."[16] His gentle humor and love for young people attracted Lucy's "girls," many of whom had snapshots of him in their college Memory Books. And it certainly could not have hurt Lucy's cause, when soliciting the church and church members for funds, to be married to a Methodist bishop.

What to do about her new name, however, posed Lucy a puzzle, for the many people she came in contact with professionally knew her as Mrs. Kidd. Her solution was socially audacious in 1892: she hyphenated her name to Kidd-Key. That this was highly unusual and confusing can be seen in the records of her own college, where her name appears both hyphenated, and not, for years.

PHILOSOPHY OF TEACHING

Lucy's philosophy of education for women was unorthodox for her time and was a curious mixture of the traditional and the practical. She urged her girls to always remember they were women and that their "divine prerogative" was to "be womanly."[17] Yet her own experience made her leaven that rosy view with a strong dash of common sense.

She expounded some of her beliefs in a 1913 interview with the *Fort Worth Record*. "Home means more than anything else," she said. "I cling to the old traditions of the South regarding women . . . I do not oppose women's suffrage, but I do not approve of the actions of such women as Carrie Nation and Emmeline Parkhurst . . . Neither do I approve of the clinging vine sort of a woman." But she added quickly: "If a woman has brains, *and they all have*, let them think for themselves and not twine themselves helplessly about a man. We need more courageous women." (author's italics)[18]

But perhaps her most telling words are found in a college catalog from about 1909 in which she explained why girls should be educated. "Competition in social and professional and business life grows sharper and more severe," Lucy wrote. "The fact that some parents educate their daughters makes it imperative that all must do likewise . . . Your daughter needs the means of taking care of herself more than she needs anything else . . . you will pass away, and if you leave her nothing but wealth, in the chances of fortune she may lose it; but if she be well educated, she has resources that cannot be taken from her."

Lucy's personal answer to being "womanly" and an executive at the same time led her to fine fashions and gentle graces, and to fill her home with lace and flowers. She was particularly fond of dresses with trains, "lovely trailing things that swept graciously about her," and that, with an erect posture, made her appear taller than her five feet.[19]

And the keys to her character—romantic, tough, efficient—can be found in recollections of her students and in newspaper articles about her. "Mrs. Key never admitted that anything she wanted to do was impossible," recalled Kitty Crawford. "She never admitted that she was old. . . ." Jennie Hill Barry wrote of conversations she heard as a young girl between her mother and Lucy. "When you have no money,"

Lucy would tell Maggie, "always do something which will prevent the public's having the slightest suspicion of your poverty. Evidence of poverty will always defeat you."[20]

When Annie Nugent Hall and the president's house burned one December night in 1903, Lucy remained "outwardly calm," calming hysterical students and ordering the faculty into fire brigades. That despite the fact that the fire represented a personal loss of at least $25,000, with less than half insured, reported the *Sherman Daily Register*. Only once did she come close to breaking down, when her voice trembled during the next day's press conference.

A Boston newspaper, writing about this "great woman educator of the South," called her "a queen." She "is a thoroughbred to the end of her fingertips, and would grace a throne. Mrs. Key is one of the great souls who should live forever. Humanity needs her."[21]

MARY NASH COLLEGE

During the critical early years of North Texas Female College's life, Lucy faced stiff competition that was literally across the street: Mary Nash College.

Founded in 1877, Mary Nash College was especially proud of its conservatory of music. From a four-room cottage, the campus grew to four elegant buildings over the years. But its troubles began when founders Jesse Nash, and then Mary, died. The Nashes' son served as president after his parents died, but he was forced to close the college in 1901 after a severe smallpox epidemic broke out among the students.

Four years later Lucy fulfilled a longheld dream when she personally purchased the property and its buildings for $15,500. The Nash buildings were incorporated into the North Texas campus: Alamo, a brick study hall; a frame gymnasium which Lucy renovated; and Senior, or Cammie Starnes, Hall.

KIDD-KEY CONSERVATORY OF MUSIC

The fourth Nash building became the centerpiece of Lucy's greatest achievement: the Kidd-Key Conservatory of Music. From the beginning of her career at North Texas College, she had made music a dominant course of study and insisted on only the finest faculty. In 1891 she hired Pierre Douillet, a Russian pianist who had studied in Vienna under Rubenstein and Liszt, and who made his American debut at Steinway Hall.

But Lucy wanted more. She sought, and received, financial backing from "several influential men of the Southwest," including Wilson N. Jones, governor of the Choctaw Nation and later benefactor of the Sherman hospital that still bears his name, to create a world-class conservatory.[22] It was operated separately from but cooperatively with North Texas College, with Lucy as president of both. The four Mary Nash buildings, owned by Lucy personally, housed the conservatory, which is considered the first major one in Texas.

Lucy's next coup came in 1897, when she lured Harold von Mickwitz to Sherman to become director of the conservatory, succeeding Pierre Douillet. Born in Finland in 1859, von Mickwitz debuted at thirteen with the Finland Philharmonic Orchestra. He studied in Russia under the famed pianist Paderewski and played concerts across Europe before conductor Victor Herbert recommended him to Lucy.[23]

With the name of von Mickwitz as a draw, Lucy recruited other top notch musicians and singers that, over the years, included composer Frank Renard; Pettis Pipes, who came to Kidd-Key in 1904 and taught piano until the college closed; and violinist Carl Venth, later hired as director of Dallas' first professional symphony orchestra. Louis Versel, a Swiss-born voice teacher and composer, married Lucy's daughter Sarah Holt in 1911; together they ran the Voice Department. Sarah frequently recommended or engaged teachers for her mother and trained "many of the leading singers and voice teachers in the Southwest, a number of whom attained vocational prominence."[24]

To the auditorium at the college, Lucy brought renowned orchestras and singers of the day, such as Victor Herbert, Campanini, and the United States Marine Band. In 1903 she engaged the Chicago Symphony Orchestra—but only on the condition that they allow thirteen-year-old student Louise Love to play a piano solo. Students and faculty of the conservatory gave regular recitals which were open to the public. Glee clubs from Texas A&M and The University of Texas appeared on the Kidd-Key stage as did traveling companies like Ben Greet's Woodland Players, performing Shakespeare. About 1902 Lucy organized the Sherman Spring Music Festival to further showcase the talents of her voice students. In 1906 the Chicago Symphony returned to play in concert at the Festival.

The Kidd-Key Orchestra provided accompaniment for many of the college's events; it and the Oratorio Society were popular performers every year at the Texas State Fair. The orchestra also played benefit performances: the students gained experience, and the college reaped positive publicity benefits.

Most piano students had an instrument in their rooms, and the size of the conservatory's piano orders were legendary in the business. In 1892 Lucy could afford only thirty instruments; but as the school's fame and attendance grew, so did the number of pianos, to 120 by 1910. Family members and longtime Sherman residents recall vividly the sound of dozens of pianos and compositions floating on the evening air as the girls practiced. Frequent excursions to Dallas exposed students to additional opera and symphony performances.

Lucy's pride in the conservatory can be seen clearly in the college catalog: ". . . this is the only conservatory in the South, in my opinion, prepared to develop a finished artist on the piano."[25]

Her passion for music and the arts, and her firm belief in their educational importance, led her to personally provide scholarships for promising students. In one recruiting letter, she stated her position: "In some cases where the girl has reduced means I will give the Literary education free of charge." To other needy students she gave jobs as office help and tutors.

In addition to its Mistress of English Literature Course and the Classical Course, the school also offered bachelor degrees in painting and music. The *Sherman Daily Democrat* would later note that "Mrs. Key was the first educator to bring artist teachers of the highest standing to the Southwest."[26] Lucy herself summed up her philosophy more pungently in 1892: "It has at last dawned upon the American mind that too little attention is paid to drawing and painting, and that the study of art is one of the most important of all studies."[27]

When Mary Nash College closed, Lucy promptly hired Eva Fowler, its longtime art instructor, and she remained with North Texas for several decades. Another of Lucy's early instructors was Mary O. Norris, hired in 1897 after completing a commission with the State of Arkansas to paint several portraits for the capitol in Little Rock.

EUROPEAN TRAVELS

To secure the best faculty for her conservatory, Lucy looked to the leading musical centers of the day: New York, Paris, Vienna, and London. Sarah did some recruiting for her mother, but Lucy employed the top conservatory faculty herself. Hans Rischard, for example, was hired after she heard him perform in Dallas.[28] During the summer, Lucy escaped the Texas heat to travel north, seeking new students and donors, looking into the musical scene and new artists of New York and Chicago.

In 1911, when her personal finances at last permitted it, she made her first venture abroad. She found "the unchanging ever changing ocean most fascinating and very restful," she wrote her students. Sarah and Louis Versel traveled with her, as did Maggie Hill Barry; the Versels would visit his family, then continue on to Paris to spend the summer studying. Lucy and Maggie planned "to take in" the Munich Music Festival. But even Lucy's passion for music had limits; ". . . one of Wagner's operas will be enough for me," she wrote. She would leave Maggie there "and go on to Oberammergau so that I can give you some idea of the Passion Play."[29]

She enjoyed that trip so much that she returned the next year, spending three months in Germany and Holland. She reported that she "greatly admired the orderliness and efficiency of the Germans as a people."

Understanding that travel had a broadening and educational effect, Lucy also arranged for her girls to spend summers in Europe under the direction of a faculty member. These trips continued until World War I put an end to them late in 1914.

CAMPUS LIFE

The list of rules for the students at North Texas College was short, to the point, and typically Victorian, with one main principle: "Every pupil is required to conduct herself in a lady-like manner . . . We wish no pupils here that *must be watched.*" Parents also received instructions. It was better to write "encouraging letters" than to visit; if their daughter was sick enough to need them, they would be notified. "Let us be frank with one another," Lucy wrote in the catalog, "send your daughters to school to learn, rather than to graduate. . . ."[30]

Students were not to dress extravagantly. "They are not in society, nor have they any need for the follies of fashionable life." Simple clothing was the rule on campus, and uniforms in town; every girl had a white dress for receptions, recitals, and graduation.

All students, except Jewesses, attended church. The girls could correspond only with family members and were not allowed to open accounts in town. Boys were entertained to tea on Sunday afternoons in the college parlours, but only with a chaperone present.

One of the girls' favorite traditions was the annual Washington's Birthday reception. As early as 1880 the custom began of marking February 22 with a celebration, but Lucy elevated it to an art form. The college reception rooms in Lois Thompson Hall were decorated lavishly with flowers, greens, and ribbons and opened to the public. Students considered it an honor to be selected by Lucy to impersonate the costumed historical figures; and boys from Sherman's Austin College, male faculty, and local dignitaries were pressed into service to escort them. General and Mrs. Washington always greeted the guests, while Mr. and Mrs. Thomas Jefferson, General and Mrs. Lafayette, and Lord and Lady Fairfax, among others, received in subsequent rooms.[31] Lucy herself awaited them in her private apartments where beaten biscuits, cakes, and Waldorf salad were served. Alumnae and important guests from Texas and elsewhere carried away an indelible impression of Southern hospitality and culture.

The tradition best remembered by townspeople was "the string." Girls who needed to do errands marched into town two by two, with a chaperone at the head of the line and another at the end. Recollections differ from that point. Some girls recall that the group did errands *en masse*: if one went into the drugstore, they all did. Others remember that the students went their separate ways once in town, but were not allowed into the men's side of department stores or to talk to the "soda jerks." The Austin College boys loved the string and would station themselves at various spots around town to watch. The girls would have dressed up for them, but Lucy required her students to wear their uniforms of navy blue wool anytime they were in Sherman.

Another chance for students of the two colleges to get together came at the annual spelling bee held between the Austin College and North Texas juniors. The girls usually won and reported mockingly in their school literary journal, *The Key*, that the boys missed such simple words as "cedar."

There were also tennis and basketball teams, music and social clubs, and wonderful marble-topped dressers in the dorm rooms on which to cool surreptitiously cooked fudge. Photographs in treasured Memory Books show that Lucy's girls weren't too different from any others, sneaking forbidden cigarettes, filling the frames of their mirrors with pictures of boys, flaunting suffragette banners on the walls—and gossiping. When Sarah Holt Versel had her face "enameled" one summer while in Paris, the students remembered it for years.

On special occasions, they made excursions via the "Interurban" to Woodlake, an amusement park between Sherman and Denison, and attended "moving picture parties."

Calisthenics were an important and innovative part of the routine, taught by both the Swiss and German methods. In 1903, to raise money for the Texas exhibit at the St. Louis World's Fair, Lucy had the students drill for the Texas Bankers Association meeting in Sherman. At commencement, on a specially built and spotlighted platform behind the Main Building, groups of students drilled in intense competition over costumes and awards. Shortly before she died in 1916, Lucy, "with her usual progressive spirit," installed a skating rink in the gym "in order that the young ladies may have the fine physical benefits to be derived from such wholesome exercise." And with her usual eye to marketing, she also made the rink available to Sherman residents.[32]

In the fall of 1908 the junior and senior students enjoyed a new experience. The kitchen staff went on strike and Lucy hired the upperclass girls to take their places; by mutual consent, their wages went toward the New Building Fund. "Mrs. Key thought of it, of course," reported one student. "Does she ever fail to think of anything which will give her girls pleasure? The girls considered it quite fun enough to wash dishes, and set tables, with no thought of any reward save to bring the New Building a step nearer realization. . . ." The hired staff soon realized that Lucy had circumvented them and offered to come back, but she refused to take them for several days. And the students "shrieked with glee" when they learned that Lucy, in return for their help, would give a dinner for them at Sherman's elegant Binkley Hotel—a high treat.[33]

One favorite college landmark was not a building or statue, but a man. Lem Davis, her "colored" servant, had come to Sherman with Lucy in 1888 to supervise the college's custodial and grounds crews. It was he who made the rounds of the dorms on cold winter mornings to light the stoves. When Lucy traveled around Sherman or on short trips, Lem dressed in livery and drove her personal carriage; and he was also Joseph Key's body servant. But he is best remembered by the students as "the college bell." With his bugle, Lem "blew" the girls awake in the morning at 6:30, signalled meals, and, at night, warned of lights out.

GRADUATES

North Texas graduates were sought after in artistic and teaching circles, and several became well known in their field.

Mary Winn Smoots of Sherman was a humorist who wrote the popular tales of Aunt Lucindy and Uncle Jeems Rainwater. In 1907 she established *The Texas Woman*, the first woman's newspaper in the state. Oklahoma-born Mary

McDougal was a poet and writer, also; her play, *Birth*, was the basis of the movie *Life Begins*. Louise Pace King, from Corsicana, organized the Texas Federation of Women's Clubs. Electra Waggoner Biggs, heiress to the Waggoner oil and ranching empire, later became a sought-after sculptor but was best loved by the North Texas girls for her charity while a student there: sharing boxes from home and buying white evening dresses and graduation flowers for her less fortunate classmates.

Evorie Dillingham was principal of Sherman's Jefferson Elementary School for nearly forty years. There she organized the first physical education classes and the first school cafeteria program in Texas public schools.

Helen and Catharine Norfleet were conservatory graduates, specializing in the piano and violin, respectively. With their brother, they formed the Norfleet Trio. The sisters later established the Norfleet School in New York and a summer music camp in New Hampshire. Maggie Hill Barry's daughter, Jennie, was also a graduate. After studying in New York and Paris, she headed the Fine Arts Department of Greenbrier College for Women in West Virginia and was a popular concert singer.

LUCY'S DEATH

North Texas College's peak enrollment came in 1912, with more than five hundred students from fourteen states and Canada. But the golden years, the decades when even President Teddy Roosevelt pronounced North Texas "the only finishing school west of the Mississippi," began to fade with the outbreak of World War I. With social and financial conditions changing almost daily, the number of girls who could afford—and who wanted—such an education fell. In 1915 Lucy was forced to pay faculty salaries herself because of a $10,000 shortfall; but she refused to consider closing the school for the duration of the war, knowing it would take years to recover. She also had to ask for credit from many of the local businesses she patronized.

Early in 1916 she went on the attack, publishing "a history" of the college in the *Sherman Daily Democrat* that was, in reality, a succinct and pointed reminder to the community of what she and North Texas had done for them. She figured annual average receipts of $110,000 and estimated that the students spent about $100,000 in town: a total of more than $3.7 million over the twenty-eight years she had been president. "From these figures," she wrote, "you must see that the school is a paying investment commercially. . . ." She listed some local contractors and lumber dealers who had received construction jobs on campus and many of the prominent local people who had made gifts.

She then proceeded to what some considered the heart of the matter: just how much of the college she personally owned, an issue that had first arisen in 1903 when Annie Nugent Hall and the president's house burned. Over the years, Grayson County deed records show that Lucy had bought most of the land surrounding the original four-acre campus and that she had taken out several mortgages to pay for construction of new buildings. But in 1905 she and Joseph Key had sold to the college and the Methodist Church a part of her holdings that included one dormitory. Annie Green, Lois Thompson, Julia Halsell, Binkley, and Colonial Halls, she wrote, were now "the exclusive property of the North Texas Conference." She then went on to make a somewhat obscure promise and a direct request that reflected her marketing skills. "My control of the school only lasts until such time as I may think it necessary for the good of the institution . . . Give us your support in making a greater school *and a greater Sherman*." (author's italics)[34]

Now Lucy was facing even more formidable obstacles than those she had conquered in 1888. Southern Methodist University opened in Dallas in 1915, siphoning off church support that had once gone to North Texas. State schools became more numerous and were less expensive. The rigid social standards that had ruled Lucy and North Texas for so long were less attractive to young ladies who were experiencing the world's first global war and the passing of the Victorian era. They wanted to go into the business world, not fulfill Lucy's precept that "their great mission in life is to make the home happy and comfortable for their husbands and sons."[35]

With her health affected by these setbacks, Lucy made plans to convert North Texas to a junior college in order to stay competitive. She, Edwin, and Maggie also outlined a course of action for Lucy's retirement or death, since she was now in her mid-seventies.

The Class of 1916 was the last to receive a full degree from the college; the next year North Texas became an accredited junior (two-year) college. Lucy lived only long enough to see the first week of it, for she died peacefully on September 13, 1916 in her apartment in Lois Thompson Hall. The *Sherman Daily Democrat* reported that she had spent the summer, as usual, in the north and was "stricken on the return trip home." A Dallas paper added that she had suffered a "nervous breakdown."

During the funeral service at Travis Street Methodist Church, every business in Sherman closed; hundreds of people poured into town to pay their respects to "one of the South's leading educators." The active pallbearers were faculty members, but the honorary ones were drawn from Sherman's leading citizens: Mayor Thomas U. Cole, nurseryman Clarence C. Mayhew (whose wife, Cammie Starnes, was a major donor to the college), Judge H. O. Head, banker C. B. Dorchester, cotton entrepreneur Nathaniel B. Birge, and hardware dealer C. A. Sanford, among them. Lucy was buried in West Hill Cemetery and her body transferred to the mausoleum when it was completed several years later.

Her will left everything to be divided equally between her two surviving children, Edwin and Sarah, and included her college holdings such as the former Mary Nash property. An inventory filed in November shows an estate valued at $41,150, with $25,000 of that being the "Four Buildings known as Kidd Key Conservatory." One hundred and ten pianos for the music school ($5,000) were also listed as was property in South Texas at Aransas Pass and Crystal City (total of $2,150).

LIFE AFTER LUCY

The plan she had carefully formulated months earlier now went into effect. Edwin became president and Sarah[36] vice president, while Maggie Barry[37] was one of two associate principals.

To the home nursing and bookkeeping courses Lucy had started earlier, the college now added home economics, shorthand, and typing in response to the increased labor market for women since the outbreak of the war. A swimming pool and classes in playground instruction and public school drawing were attempts to keep in step with modern times. And in 1919 the college rechartered with a new name: Kidd-Key College and Conservatory, in honor of Lucy.

The Methodist Church, in the meantime, took its own steps to settle the "crisis" brought on by Lucy's death and the issue of Kidd-Key's ownership. The City of Sherman and the Chamber of Commerce worked with the church on the matter, so eager were they to retain a first-class college and the business it brought to the area.

In 1920, the same year that Bishop Joseph Key died at the age of 91, the Methodist Church purchased all of Lucy's interests from her heirs and consolidated them with its own. Edwin and Sarah agreed to the sale "on the condition that the name of Kidd-Key should be perpetuated in forever [*by*] calling the college Kidd-Key as a memorial to the indefatigable woman who had raised it from obscurity to renown and put herself, her possessions, and her influence into it."[38] For less than $50,000, the church purchased seven buildings and their furnishings, and more than one hundred pianos.

In 1924 Edwin stepped down as president and was replaced by Dr. E. L. Spurlock, who had been the college's business manager and traveling representative since 1903. He served four years before retiring in ill health, and college officials then coaxed Edwin into returning. He did so reluctantly, happy with his farm north of Sherman and his community interests that included serving on the board of Merchants & Planters Bank. But he did, guided by personal financial interests and his desire to keep his mother's dream alive.

The next seven years were an unending struggle. Under Spurlock's administration, the college had let a contract for a $69,000 administration building and auditorium that was to be a memorial to Lucy; but only one portion was completed. Desperate to counteract the stranglehold the Depression had left on the school's finances, Edwin explored a joint program with Austin College, which had its own money problems. From 1930 to 1935, the two schools shared classes and faculty by bussing the students from one campus to the other.

Edwin also set up a similar program with Sherman Business College so students could take secretarial courses. He attempted to refurbish the conservatory by ordering forty-one Baldwin pianos, one of the largest orders ever made by a southern school. New faculty, such as Pettis Pipes' protege Bomar Cramer, were hired, and the lyceum schedule and college recitals continued in full force. The dorms and halls were remodeled and refurnished, and several thousand dollars went to landscaping.

But none of Edwin's efforts helped stop Kidd-Key's downward spiral, impelled by debts, lack of endowment, and competition from state-supported schools. By 1933 enrollment had dropped to 165. The North Texas Conference of the Methodist Church, wishing to put more money into such new institutions as Southern Methodist and San Marcos, recommended that Kidd-Key, Texas Woman's College, Wesley, and Weatherford "be abandoned" to the cities where they were located. They offered to sell the Sherman campus to Edwin Kidd, who refused, and then tried to sell one of the larger buildings to Grayson County for a new courthouse to replace the one burned by a riot in 1930.

At the end of the 1934-1935 term, Kidd-Key closed and students transferred to Southern Methodist to complete their degree work. The dormitories were converted to apartments managed by Edwin and his wife Cecile[39], and a relief office and WPA surplus commodity warehouse were opened in the Conservatory.

In the late spring of 1937 the City of Sherman purchased the western part of the campus and its buildings, which included the yet-to-be-completed administration building and auditorium. The older Kidd-Key buildings were razed and, with public works administration funds, the city finished construction of the auditorium building for city offices. Today they are still housed in that structure.

Over the next few years all the remaining Kidd-Key buildings were demolished. The only physical remnants of the once elegant campus that Lucy Kidd-Key built are a statue of Athena and a cast iron fountain which formerly stood in front of Lois Thompson Hall and are now on the southeast side of the Municipal Building. There is also a Texas Historical Marker at the site, erected in 1967, and a plaque dedicated to Lucy inside the Municipal Building.

As for Lucy herself, her legacy was best summed up by orator Thomas Nelson Page, after her death: "She has filled practically every position that needed to be filled in the institution . . . She was mistress, manager, nurse, counselor, seamstress, teacher, housekeeper, slave, all at once. What she really was is known only to God."[40]

Notes—Chapter Five

1   William's daughter Sarah married Colonel Richard Taylor there and was the mother of General, later President, Zachary Taylor. Her granddaughter, child of Zachary Taylor, married Jefferson Davis.

Lucy's father, Willis, descended from Susanna's first marriage to Captain Moses Hawkins; two of his brothers worked for their cousin Zachary Taylor as overseer of his Louisiana plantation.

2   R. G. Mood and C. W. Dennis, editors, "Minutes of the Fiftieth Annual Session of the North Texas Annual Conference of the Methodist Episcopal Church, South," 106.

3   Lucy's sister and her husband did own slaves and a cotton operation, which may account for the confusion.

4   Deed records of Yazoo County, Mississippi.
Interview with Edwin Worthley, Dallas, Texas: August 29, 1993.

5   At this time, private colleges such as Whitworth were operated similarly to businesses: one could buy and sell an interest in them. The president, moreover, was usually expected to be a major investor and to personally pay for the building of college structures for which there was otherwise no funding.

6   It would appear that she became anxious for money in 1880 and early 1881, for there are a half dozen or more land sales during that time. In August 1882 Lucy also entered into an interesting arrangement with her sister Sarah Gadberry, to whom Lucy had loaned money a year earlier. Now Sarah secured the payment of those notes by giving Lucy a deed of trust on "the Sessions Place," near Yazoo City. Sarah agreed to work the farm and bring in and ship a cotton crop. Lucy in return placed her three nieces at Whitworth.

Jennie Hill Barry, "Kidd-Key—Early Days," unpublished

manuscript in Kidd-Key Collection of Southern Methodist University, Dallas, Texas, 2.

7 Maggie Hill was born in Palo Alto, Mississippi and educated in Macon, Mississippi and at Tuscaloosa Female College. She received her M.A. from Murfreesboro Institute in Tennessee. After studying music in Boston and abroad, she returned to Murfreesboro to teach and then became principal of a school in Macon. At Whitworth she headed the literary department and taught modern languages. She taught at North Texas Female College for three years and, in 1891, married Mississippi congressman Frederick George Barry. He died shortly after their daughter Jennie was born, and Maggie returned to Sherman as head of the English Department.

8 Letter by Maggie Barry to *Dallas Morning News*, reprinted in *Sherman Democrat* (Sherman, Texas), January 24, 1916.

9 Barry, *op. cit.*, 3-4.
Worthley, *op. cit.*

10 *Sherman Democrat*, April 11, 1888.

11 At commencement, Bishop Charles Galloway presented Lucy with a gold watch on behalf of the Whitworth students "as a token of their appreciation and love." Lucy was "much affected by this token of esteem." (*Yazoo City Herald*, June 29, 1888)

12 *Brookhaven News* (Brookhaven, Mississippi), May 16, 1888.

13 Annie Laurie Connelly, "The History of Kidd-Key College, Sherman, Grayson County, Texas," 86.
The Key, November 1917, 4.

14 Menu from October 4, 1907: Oyster stew a la royal, Waldorf salad, mixed pickles, loin of veal a la mode, macaroni a la napolitaine, french peas in cream, sweet potato souffle, Parker House rolls, brick cream, assorted cakes, Edam cheese, water crackers, cafe noir.

15 *Sherman Daily Democrat*, February 17, 1916.

16 *Ibid.*, April 6, 1920, 1.

17 Unidentified clipping (probably from the *Texas Advocate*) and dated June 27, 1914; in Kidd-Key Collection of Southern Methodist University.

18 "Kidd-Key Girls Honor their Preceptress," *Fort Worth Record*, April 20, 1913.

19 Undated clipping from *Dallas News* in Kidd-Key Collection of Southern Methodist University.

20 Connelly, *op. cit.*, 87.
Barry, *op. cit.*, 10.

21 Johnson, Frank W., *A History of Texas and Texans*, Volume III, 1541-1542.

22 *Sherman Democrat*, September 19, 1946, Section 8, 6.

23 Harold von Mickwitz left Kidd-Key Conservatory in 1905 but returned from 1908 to 1912. (Church officials were staggered at the salary Lucy paid him in 1910: $3,000.) He taught at Southern Methodist University from 1916 to 1918 and later in Chicago and New York. When he died, Kidd-Key ex-students erected a monument at his grave in Finland.

24 *Sherman Democrat*, December 2, 1926.

25 "Catalog of North Texas College and Kidd-Key Conservatory," (1908-1909), 3.

26 *Sherman Daily Democrat*, September 4, 1916, 1.

27 "Catalog of North Texas Female College and Conservatory of Music—Sherman, Texas—Term of 1892-1893," 28.

28 Rischard was director of the Conservatory, 1915-1928.

29 Unidentified clipping titled "In Mid Ocean—Steamer Hanover, July 15," in Kidd-Key Collection of Southern Methodist University.

30 "Catalog of North Texas College and Kidd-Key Conservatory," (1908-1909), 34.

31 In a strange mixture possible only in the South, General and Mrs. Robert E. Lee also joined the Revolutionary War and colonial personages.

32 *Sherman Daily Democrat*, March 4, 1916, 6.

33 Jane Foss Anderson (editor-in-chief), *Kidd-Key Journal* (November 1, 1908), 5, 14-15.

34 *Sherman Daily Democrat*, February 17, 1916, 6.

35 *Fort Worth Record*, *op. cit.*

36 Sarah Holt Versel continued to head Kidd-Key Conservatory's Voice Department until her death on December 1, 1926. She was survived by her second husband, Louis Versel, and by her son, Joseph Holt Jr.

37 Two years after Lucy's death, Maggie left Sherman to teach at Texas A&M in College Station. In her twenty-five years there, Maggie Barry became known for her work with women's organizations through the Texas Extension Service. She founded the state's home demonstration clubs "to mobilize farm women in support of rural education" and wrote several books, including *The Land and Its Use*. She never lost her belief in the fine arts as a tool to teach ethics and build character.

38 Connelly, *op. cit.*, 42.

39 In 1898 Edwin had married Alabama native Cecile Stollenwerck, a North Texas graduate; their only child, Lucy Kidd Worthley, still lives in the Sherman-Denison area. After Kidd-Key closed, Edwin ran for the Texas Senate but lost. He died in 1963 and, like Sarah and Lucy, is buried in the Sherman Mausoleum.

40 Undated clipping from Dallas News in Kidd-Key Collection at Southern Methodist University, re Lucy Kidd-Key's death.

C H A P T E R   S I X

Ela Hockaday

"Cornerstones of the Hockaday School: character,
courtesy, scholarship and athletics."

. . . Ela Hockaday

She had a dream. A dream that young women needed a
different kind of education to prepare them for the new world
of the twentieth century, a place where science, not the rigid
morality of the past, would be the guiding force. Yet she also
knew that world would want—indeed would need—the sof-
tening wrought by culture and the beauty found in nature.
That was woman's role.

So with one foot in the Victorian era and the other planted
firmly in a new century, Ela Hockaday spent her life changing
the lives of the thousands of girls who would follow her.

FROM VIRGINIA TO TEXAS

Ela's family background can be traced to England's early
eleventh century when, in the reign of Ethelred the Unready,

the Anglo-Saxons attempted to drive out the hated Danes. They celebrated what would prove to be their short-lived victory with a "hock day," or holiday, on the second Tuesday after Easter. One grateful family commemorated the event by taking that as their name.

By the sixteenth century, the Hockadays were located primarily in Southampton and in Wales; William was the first to make his way, about 1636, across the ocean to Virginia. Of those who stayed in England, one descendant was writer Joseph Addison (*Sir Roger de Coverly*).

Thomas Hart Benton Hockaday, Ela's father, was born in Lynchburg, Virginia in 1835 and presumably named for the fire-eating senator from Missouri, Thomas Hart Benton. (The painter of that same name was not born until 1889.) His parents died when he was twelve, so Thomas and his sister Emma moved to Spring Hill in Maury County, Tennessee to live with a cousin, Presbyterian minister Fred Thompson.[1] Classically educated, Thomas became fluent in Greek, Hebrew, and Latin to the point that he preferred reading the Bible, especially the New Testament, in the Greek. Under Thompson's influence, he also joined the Presbyterian Church and was a steadfast member for the rest of his life, rising to the position of elder.

On January 12, 1858, Thomas married Maria Elizabeth "Lizzie" Kerr (born in Tennessee, January 23, 1838) and their first child, Frederick Thompson, was named in honor of the man who had raised his father. The family then moved to Helena, Arkansas on the Mississippi River south of Memphis, where Thomas operated a school with strict discipline and the highest standards. That quality attracted the attention of emigrants from Giles County, Tennessee who had settled the Texas frontier on the North Sulphur River in eastern Lamar County. They offered Thomas $1,000 to join them and open a school on the Sulphur.

In 1859 he, Lizzie, and Fred journeyed south to a new life in Texas and opened the Giles Academy—named for the settlers' Tennessee home—three miles east of Pecan Gap, almost on the Lamar/Fannin County line.[2] Known for rapping his misbehaving students on the knuckles with a ruler, Thomas emphasized reading, writing, math, and English in his curriculum. And though stern, he also had a dry sense of humor which endeared him to most of his students.

When the Civil War broke out, Thomas enlisted as an ordinance officer in Company D of the 6th Texas Cavalry, leaving Lizzie, Fred, and new baby Emma Blanche to live with Lizzie's parents, Major and Mrs. G. W. Kerr, who had previously moved to McKinney (Collin County).[3] Thomas returned home at least once—Edgar Park was born in 1864—and appears to have escaped the war relatively unscathed.

THE FANNIN HOMEPLACE

After the war, Thomas returned to teaching at the Giles Academy. In 1868 he bought 286.5 acres near the school to build his homeplace, a white L-shaped, frame building with a partial second story.[4] Soon after, in 1870, he retired from education to farm his land by progressive methods and operate a cotton gin, which he built near the house. Four more children followed the first three: Clarence Brown in 1868, Jimmie Williamson in 1870, Albert Shepperson in 1873, and the last, Ela, on March 12, 1875.

Her name was entered in the family Bible as Eliza but, for some reason, the "i" and "z" were later marked out. The vestige of that earlier name remained in the long "e" with which the family pronounced Ela.

Growing up on the Pecan Gap farm, Ela was particularly close to her older brother Brown. The boys helped out with the farm and the gin operation, but there was still plenty of time for play and to fish for perch in the gin's pond. Being Thomas Hockaday's children, however, meant strict attendance at the Presbyterian Church and a good basic education.[5] Ela developed an early interest in nature here that she sustained the rest of her life.

A shy young girl, Ela was no doubt devastated when Lizzie Hockaday died in 1881 just ten days short of her forty-third birthday. Older sister Emma had married Bonham lawyer Brown Spurlock Johnson the year before. A happy, vibrant woman with a hearty laugh, "Sissy," as Ela called her, now took her six-year-old sister home and raised her in Bonham with her own brood of four children. Of her, Ela later said, Emma "gave me the love and understanding which children need. The determination of my father was tempered by her sympathy. Whatever in my heart is warm with compassion and human feeling springs from her gentle influence."[6]

Thomas and the boys stayed on the farm, looked after by a negro housekeeper and, later, by Brown's wife Minnie.[7]

Ela attended the Bonham public schools and then enrolled in the North Texas Normal College in Denton (now the University of North Texas). Her choice of a teaching career was the direct and natural result of her father's and Emma's influences. And her successful college sojourn in Denton would prove to be crucial, for it was North Texas' president, Menter B. Terrill, who would eventually direct her to Dallas.

TO SHERMAN

By the time Ela graduated, Thomas Hockaday had married again to a Corsicana woman named Missouri B. Bird whom the children called Miss Sue. He had sold all but the eighty-acre homestead of the Fannin County farm and moved to Ladonia. (He would die and be buried there in 1918.)

Ela, a fresh-faced young woman with a plain hairstyle from which curls insisted on escaping, took her first job teaching at the Sunshine School in Ladonia to be near her family. Her nephew Olin, the family historian, treasures one special memory of her standing in the door of that one-room school ringing a handbell to call the students in. Like Thomas Hockaday, Ela taught the classics and tolerated no disruptions of her classroom.

She had many beaux in Ladonia, but Ela was busy with other interests. With her cousin Helen Kerr, she attended summer school for additional credits and indulged her strong interest in nature. Emma saw to it that her little sister had cultural treats and was not above asking her brothers for money to pay for them. When Ela would protest that she had no time, Emma would cajole her: "Ela, think of the *refinement* you will acquire from this trip!"[8]

In 1898 Ela moved west to adjoining Grayson County and began teaching fifth grade in Sherman's Jefferson Elementary School, located across from Austin College. Her reputation as a woman who could handle headstrong students, particularly boys, won her the job. She boarded in private homes and was one of seven teachers in the school, a position she held until about 1903 when she was promoted to principal.

Ela introduced manual training into the Sherman schools in an attempt to interest her unruly students in other studies. The *Sherman Register* complimented the school system on the program, which had first met with much criticism. "The child who was formerly idling and gave a great deal of his time to the study and practice of mischief, is now deeply engrossed in the manual training work, [*and*] is gaining a taste for the general studies of the school room. . . ."[9]

Her second innovation was music. A Sherman store offered an upright piano to the school showing "the greatest cultural development," and Ela worked her heart out to help

Ela at the beginning of her educational career.
(Courtesy The Hockaday School, Dallas, Texas)

Jefferson win it. She must have been gratified when some of her students later entered local piano contests as a result of her efforts.

But life in Sherman was not all work. She made friends with philanthropist Cammie Starnes, and the two women traveled together to St. Louis for the 1904 World's Fair and to the cool heights of Manitou Springs, Colorado for summer vacations.[10]

MOVING ON

Ela remained at Jefferson as principal for several years, but furthering her education was important to her. Thomas Hockaday's obituary stated that Ela was a graduate of Sherman's Kidd-Key College; there is no documentary evidence of that, but it is quite likely she took some classes there, particularly given her friend Cammie Starnes' association with the college. At some point, Ela also added post-graduate work at the University of Chicago and Columbia Teachers College to her schedule, possibly resigning from Jefferson in order to do so full time. Olin Hockaday writes that she was studying at Columbia when her sister Emma died suddenly of pneumonia in Durant, Oklahoma on December 22, 1905.[11]

Heartbroken, Ela returned to Texas and decided to stay in the region. She moved to Durant to head the Department of Biological Sciences at Oklahoma State Normal School (now Southeastern Oklahoma State University).[12] There she met the woman who would be her lifelong friend and teaching partner, Sarah Basima Trent, head of the English Department. About a year later, the two transferred together to Chickasha and took positions on the faculty of Oklahoma College for Women (now the University of Sciences and Arts of Oklahoma).

Oklahoma was then undergoing the turmoil of young statehood after nearly a century as a federal territory, and controversy surrounded every aspect of its government, including education. Ela and Sarah endured the politics only a short time before deciding to chuck it at the end of the 1912-1913 school term and spend their lives farming. They bought forty acres of land near Falfurrias in deep south Texas (between Kingsville and Laredo), sank a pump, and started irrigating their crops of melons and tomatoes.

It was a grand idea, but one summer was enough to convince them that teaching wasn't so bad, after all.

Ela was increasingly restless with a feeling that she was simply "lying fallow." Years later, she would tell her students, "From some welling up within me, I suddenly knew that I had to be about a different type of living if there were to be any satisfaction with myself, that I should be found when the time came, and that whatever the nature of the task that lay ahead of me I should find the strength to do it."[13]

AN OFFER IN DALLAS

To their north, events were happening that would end Ela and Sarah's farming career forever. Early in September 1913, a group of parents in wealthy East Dallas met to discuss their need for a girl's college preparatory school—not just another "finishing" school.[14] They sought advice from Menter B. Terrill, the former president of North Texas Normal College and then head of the Terrill School for Boys in Dallas (today's St. Mark's School). Terrill didn't hesitate. He knew only one woman capable of delivering what the parents wanted—Ela Hockaday. She had, he said, "the quickest, most incisive mind in comprehending that he had ever taught."[15]

Ela went to Dallas to visit the school committee and ended by accepting their offer to become headmistress. To her, it was the chance to fulfill a dream, one she'd had for years—to fill the gaps in education and knowledge that too many girls' schools left.

And 1913 was a propitious time to start such an undertaking. The world was changing, the Victorian era and morality that had governed lives for so long fading under the onslaught of ever-new technology and social conditions. Women were marching in the streets for suffrage, joining the work force in growing numbers, and shedding their cumbersome clothes for more practical ones. They were looking ahead and wanted the tools necessary to make their way in the twentieth century.

Ela knew this and, indeed, could be considered a "new" woman herself, for she had chosen career over husband and family. But into this progressive philosophy she also incorporated several basic beliefs that she felt continued to be important; some might have considered them hopelessly Victorian and outdated, but Ela held strongly to them.

The first was that "woman's chief service, that of motherhood and homemaker," could complement the increasingly popular scientific approach. A woman could have a home and a career, too, if she wished, but she needed to know how to do both well. Thus Ela would teach her girls the correct way to pour tea in addition to algebra. Second, there was no reason to ignore beauty simply because one chose a modern lifestyle. And an appreciation of beauty meant that one could find it in whatever form it might take, from a flower to an intricately carved wooden cupboard. Graceful living was the mark of the truly cultured person. Lastly, Ela felt that character and courtesy went hand in hand with scholarship and athletics to build a well-rounded young woman.

When Ela got through with them, Hockaday women would go forth to conquer their new world, *and* they would do it with white gloves and impeccable manners.

THE HOUSE ON HASKELL

With these parameters long since worked out in her mind, Ela accepted the committee's challenge on September 21, 1913. Her first action was to telegraph Sarah Trent to come to Dallas: "Come at once, I am starting my school on Monday." And then she set to work.

She had one week to open a school.

Ela spent the weekend with H. H. Adams, Ruth Bower Lindsley, and Sarah, driving around East Dallas, a lovely section of town with tree-lined streets and large, elegant homes, once a separate governmental entity that had merged with Dallas in 1889. They finally located a simple, two-story grey house at 1206 North Haskell Avenue, just off Live Oak, and spent the next frenetic days papering, painting, and cleaning.[16]

On September 25, Ela opened Miss Hockaday's School for Girls with ten students, some maps, and two Webster's dictionaries. Tuition was $250 per year. She and Sarah taught all the classes: English, history, Latin, German, and French. Ela's always-neat desk sat in the study hall squarely in front of the bookcase, because of space, and she had to move her chair whenever students needed a book. The room was heated with a potbellied wood stove, next to which slept the doorman's dog.

The house "had no elegance," recalled student Genevieve Hudson, who later taught there, "it was just an old, renovated frame house. . . ." But in true Southern tradition, Henry, the Negro doorman, opened the front door and bowed the students in every morning. It was their first lesson in deportment.

And while the building had "no elegance," the school had a proper crest, modeled on the Hockaday family crest: a shield bearing six fleurs-de-lis and topped by a unicorn. The motto was the family's, also; *Virtus Scientia* meant virtue and knowledge, the principles by which Thomas Hockaday and his daughter lived.

Ela ran her school by what she called the Four Cornerstones: Character, Scholarship, Courtesy, and Athletics. "She believed, as did her father, that education should not end in the classroom—that its ultimate aim was the building of character . . . [*She believed*] that a cultivated, well disciplined mind, together with high cultural, moral, and spiritual values, constituted the most valuable attributes of education."[17]

To promote equality, all students wore a uniform, with no makeup or jewelry allowed. (The only exception was the later, upper-class Hockaday ring, which Ela had designed and produced by Tiffany's.) The girls rose when a teacher or any other adult entered the room, had their skirts measured to ensure they were a full three yards around the hem, and took turns conducting the informal chapel service that began each day.

Fresh flowers and linens gave the house an elegant air, in keeping with Ela's artistic nature. But she regularly treated the girls with rough-and-tumble hayrides to White Rock Lake for wiener roasts. She also encouraged their sense of community service. When World War I broke out shortly after the school opened, Hockaday students crocheted "cootie belts"— to be impregnated with insecticide—for the soldiers. They also sponsored poor families and gave Christmas parties for orphans.

"Hockadaisies" quickly started a number of traditions: Founder's Day observances that fell on Ela's birthday, the Courtesy Cap awarded for exemplary behavior, and wide-brimmed picture hats and white organdy dresses from Neiman-Marcus for graduation, among them.

The girls loved Sarah Trent but were in awe of the tall, distinguished Ela. "If you were in the corridor or study hall you felt the presence and looked up and here was Miss Hockaday," said Genevieve Hudson. "You forgot your name, you forgot everything . . . She was electric, absolutely electric, and had the uncanny ability to materialize when least wanted (thanks to rubber-soled shoes)."[18]

The school prospered and grew rapidly. Ela added a Boarding Department the second year, and Mary Miriam Meredith Morgan came the next year to run it. Well traveled and diplomatic, Morgan supervised the two houses at the corner of Live Oak, which soon housed 100 boarders as the reputation of the Hockaday School grew. By 1917 all the lower grades had been added so that a girl could attend from first grade through high school. And still the students continued to come in even greater numbers. Only five years after opening her school on Haskell, Ela knew it was time to move and expand.

The first Hockaday school, at the corner of Live Oak and Haskell.

(Courtesy The Hockaday School, Dallas, Texas)

THE CARUTH FARM

The thirty-acre Walter Caruth farm, "Bosque Bonita," was then at the very end of Dallas' Greenville Avenue (near the modern intersection with Belmont), an unpaved street serviced by a nearby Dinkie streetcar line.[19] Ela sold stock in the school to finance the purchase of eight acres of the farm and in doing so, said Genevieve Hudson, nearly lost control to an unidentified party who tried to buy all available stock. A friend and attorney saved Ela and her school, but "this put some steel in her soul and . . . she made up her mind that she would never again be in a position of being able to be hurt the same way. . . ."[20]

Groundbreaking for the new campus was literally in the middle of a just-harvested cornfield and a thunderstorm on a hot summer night in 1918. More rains delayed construction, and it was not until October of the next year that staff and students made "The Move." That same year Ela and the trustees incorporated with capital stock of $80,000—a far cry from the first hand-to-mouth year when income was a mere $2,300. Ela owned the majority of the stock, which never paid dividends but, instead, rolled back all proceeds into the operation of the school.

Walter and Anna Caruth's farmhouse was relocated to become a residence hall for older students and named Trent Hall, in honor of Sarah. The elegant Georgian-style Main Building which Ela built stood in the center of a campus that also included a swimming pool, playhouse, music practice house, and chemistry building.[21]

For a few years, Ela, Sarah Trent, Miriam Morgan, and several others all lived together in one residence. About 1921 Ela built her first and only home on one side of the campus near Trent House. "The Cottage" was a white brick building that she filled over the ensuing years with flowers, plants, and the finest antiques: Hepplewhite furniture, bone china, and

Oriental rugs.[22] The house "was not particularly large," recalled Margot Holt Gill, "but every nook and cranny was full of something." An invitation to dine or take tea at The Cottage induced nervous fits in both students and teachers but came to be a mark of the highest standing in Dallas society.

Ela saw the student visits as opportunities to continue learning; she would "entertain" the girls by talking of the treasures in her home and of her farflung travels. Even the way in which she spoke was carefully planned with "vocabulary that would cause us to reach a bit," explained Gill. Mary Frances Yancey described these sessions years later: "To have her students excel academically was not enough. Miss Hockaday wanted her girls to know how to serve tea, to speak on her feet, to lead chapel, to know a Lowestoft plate and a fine oil painting."[23]

A DALLAS INSTITUTION

As Texas prospered after World War I, so did Hockaday. Its student body represented a real cross-section of the state, from daughters of wealthy Dallasites to those of West Texas ranchers and oil wildcatters. And the school fully lived up to its original goal of being college preparatory: Hockaday sent more of its graduates to college than any other school in the West. In 1920 Ela asked the forty-five women who had already graduated to form an Alumnae Association, which remains vitally strong and active today.

Ela attracted some of Texas' most dynamic figures to her board of trustees, including Herbert Marcus, a founder of Neiman-Marcus; Karl Hoblitzelle, who built his fortune on vaudeville acts and later motion picture theaters; Texas Instruments co-founder Eugene McDermott; Toddie Lee Wynne Sr.; and Jake Hamon. That progressive leaders such as these respected and helped her is a tribute to Ela's vision and perseverance.

She insisted on the finest teachers, too, many of whom were recognized by and served on national education committees such as those reading college entrance exams.

With a strong belief in the educational value of travel, Ela began the first "Travel Classes" to Europe in 1928, where senior girls studied as long as eight months. Hockaday was one of the first schools to give credit for study abroad. Ela regularly went to Europe herself, often traveling with Miriam Morgan and bringing home more wonderful purchases for The Cottage.

She had an unerring eye for the best and invested heavily in European china and silver during the Depression there, when many old families sold off their treasures. Those collections helped sustain her during her own lean times, when she would dispose of prime items; and more than one Hockaday graduate was gifted with a piece of Ela's antique silver when she married.

Not even the Great Depression stopped Ela Hockaday. In fact, she decided it was a good time to expand and opened a Junior College (1931). "She went to see the leading people in Dallas," Genevieve Hudson recalled, "and said, 'I must have this building and you must help me. It's your responsibility as much as mine to have this Junior College here.' . . . Even the most prominent businessman would just have to say, 'Yes, Miss Hockaday.' "[24] Sarah Trent was the first dean of the Junior College, built on the original site of the Caruth farmhouse, where business skills—typing and shorthand—were as important a part of the curriculum as psychology and literature.

In 1932 she followed the Junior College with a kindergarten and, five years later, the Music Institute.[25] Hockaday's Fine Arts course was one of only two offered in Dallas; the other was at Southern Methodist University.

Ela's cool and collected facade convinced many people that the school was experiencing no financial difficulties, even in the depths of the Depression. That it didn't was thanks to the economies she and her cousin, business manager Ruth Kerr, practiced. Ela "had this tremendous ability to improvise. No matter what the problem was she could improvise a solution. She had tremendous ingenuity."[26] Thriftiness, staggered payment plans, and students working off their tuitions in various offices helped pull Hockaday through.

MISS HOCKADAY

This ambitious, persevering, always-looking-forward Ela is the woman most people remember. "She was tall and commanding in appearance, somewhat like a general, with iron grey hair and piercing blue eyes." (Retail giant Stanley Marcus carried the image even further by calling her "the perfect casting for the Virgin Queen.") Ela's favorite pep talk to the girls—delivered every year—was "The Message to Garcia," which used the example of Cuba's fight for independence to urge them "that we were not to flinch in the face of adversity but to carry through to the successful conclusion of our mission in life."[27]

But family and friends looked past the public austere image to the shy, caring woman behind it. She "made me feel," wrote one niece, "that the stars were the limit, and each one had to or could reach them if the effort were concentrated." She had a strong sense of what was just and right and never failed to credit others—faculty, students, donors—for Hockaday's success.

And remembering what Emma Hockaday Johnson had done for her, Ela raised her deceased sister's two daughters, Elizabeth and Ruth, the latter of whom graduated from her school in 1918.

Ela had a flair for life that she exhibited in everything from her soft and simple but well-made clothes to the way she traveled. Her maid Exie and chauffeur Sam traveled with her to meetings such as the National Association of Principals of Schools for Girls. She would sweep into the hotel as if she owned it, Exie following behind with her lap robe and sable coat and Sam carrying the suitcases. "There was no other headmistress in the country who cut such a swath as she did," said Genevieve Hudson admiringly.[28]

She wanted only the best for her girls. To the Greenville campus came some of the world's luminaries: both Franklin and Eleanor Roosevelt[29], conductor Andre Previn, actor/dancer Ray Bolger, Sir Thomas Beecham, and Edward Teller, among them. Gertrude Stein and her secretary, Alice B. Toklas, stayed a week and fell in love with cornbread, Stein enjoying long walks with Ela; in turn, they hosted Hockaday Travel Classes visiting Paris.

No money ever changed hands, but very few refused the honor of speaking at Hockaday. It was "not like the rest of America," said French teacher Lucette Moulin, "[but] . . . a little island of civilization."[30]

In 1940 Austin College in Sherman, just across the street from Jefferson School where Ela had taught so many years earlier, recognized that civilizing effect by awarding Ela an honorary Doctorate of Letters.

CHANGES ON THE WAY

When World War II began to affect every aspect of life in America, Ela called on, and expected, her girls to become involved, just as they had in another war more than twenty years earlier. There were Red Cross blood drives, trips home sacrificed to make space on trains for servicemen, and dance invitations to British pilots training in Terrell, Texas. The Music Institute staged a performance of *I Pagliacci* to raise money for the Red Cross, with Hockaday students taking many of the parts.

By 1941 Hockaday had grown to a student body of 450 with 83 faculty and staff members, and a million dollar campus. No endowment or tax money supported the school, just tuitions and Ela's constant fundraising.

But she knew that the school could not continue to grow and thrive as the privately owned institution it had been since 1919; it was too dependent on her personally. With advice from trustee Herbert Marcus, she began her planning even as the war broke out in Europe and finalized it in 1942, calling in all the stock, including her own, and turning Hockaday over to the alumnae and the citizens of Dallas, with authority to be vested in the board of trustees. This made it nonprofit and publicly owned and represented a significant financial gift on Ela's part. Harriet Olmstead Weber, then president of the Alumnae Association, later commented that Ela "was brave to do it because she no longer could control [*the school*] once she had given it to us."[31]

The official changeover ceremony took place on a rainy May 13 as part of the twenty-third reunion of the Alumnae Association. Dr. Homer P. Rainey, president of the University of Texas, spoke along with Southern Methodist University president Dr. Umphrey Lee, Dallas mayor Woodall Rogers, trustees, and alumnae. All extolled Ela and her years of work.

RETIREMENT

Ela continued as headmistress for four more years, despite her age. But in 1946, at seventy-one, she finally decided to retire after thirty-three years of building and directing the school that bore her name.[32] In her last address to the students and faculty as president, Ela reflected on the school's history at the Greenville site, from the days when it held only

"Johnson grass and dead cornstalks" to the landscaped and impressive campus of 1946. Of her career and what it had meant to her, she said, "Everything God has given me of wisdom, love, ability, and energy I have poured into this school. I feel that He has richly blessed me in allowing me to do this work and giving me the strength to see it through . . . It is not given to everyone to spend his life doing work in which he believes, nor is it given to everyone to see the results of his efforts in so tangible and gratifying a way as I see the results of mine."

And what was her greatest achievement? To "have seen very delicate, frail little fairy-like six-year-old beings," she said, "grow into clear-eyed, forward looking, magnificent women, sympathetic and helpful mothers, and honest, public-spirited citizens."[33]

She visited the school only rarely after her retirement, though freedom from office work enabled her to "give more personal counsel and encouragement" to the students. She did keep up her traditional New Year's Eve parties for the faculty. And tea parties at The Cottage continued to intimidate another generation of Hockaday girls. Anne Schoellkopf Coke vividly remembers the experience: "On arrival, the class, the intelligence, the privilege of the place was obvious even to us babies. There was a refinement of color, of fabric or paneling, of paintings, of furniture, of bibelots—nothing overpowering, no pretentiousness whatsoever, but just beautiful. . . ." Ela, she said, "exuded a kind of serenity . . . yet you would never have fantasized sitting on her lap. She was a 'lady' but not a 'grande dame'. . . ."[34] Watching over the progress of the tea party would be Ela's servants, Exie and Sam, dressed, Anne said, like servants "in the movies featuring the 'high life.' "

Other students realized they were looking at a phenomenon, "an anomaly in her own era, when self-directed women were not generally prized." Hockaday staff member Hortense Trage allowed that, while Ela had little sense of humor, "her way with men from whom she wanted some favor was something to see." She demanded—and received—excellence, even when she was no longer directing the operations of her beloved school.[35]

Ela did agree to chair a building committee to develop a site near Belt Line Road slated to be given to the school by alumnae, a campaign actually begun the spring before her retirement with a $100,000 pledge from trustee Herbert Marcus for a Music and Arts Building. But that site did not work out and plans to move the campus were dropped.

She preferred to spend her days in volunteer and club work or at one of her other properties. Green Gate Farm (near Mockingbird and the railroad track) was the frequent site of faculty bingo parties, and the South Texas property she had bought with Sarah Trent remained a favorite summering place. Most important to her was her church work; she had joined First Presbyterian when she moved to Dallas in 1913 and was active in its women's circles. But Ela also maintained membership in other Dallas organizations: the Woman's Club, Garden Club, the Stanford Literary Club, and the Texas Philosophical Society.

According to the *Dallas Times Herald*, Ela helped her post-retirement finances in a manner she'd been doing for years, but on a grander scale. She opened a gift shop at The Cottage to sell gifts such as English china and silver that she'd collected on her trips abroad. To each piece of merchandise, reported the *Herald*, "she attached a frilly white bow, printed in green with 'Miss Hockaday.' "[36]

LAST DAYS

Early in 1956 Ela began making her final plans as meticulously as she had all her others, directing nephew Olin Hockaday to meet her at the funeral home to select a casket and arrange the details of her funeral. On February 12 she complained of a severe headache and numbness in her right hand but felt well enough by the end of the week to visit the beauty shop and sit for her portrait. But on February 23 she collapsed in her bathroom and burned her arm on a gas heater and was taken to Baylor Hospital. She died there on March 26 of cerebral arterial thrombosis.

Her body lay in state at The Cottage until the funeral at First Presbyterian. Olin, her executor, buried her in Hillcrest Cemetery between her friends Sarah Trent and Miriam Morgan.

Five years later came the move Ela had planned for. The Hoblitzelle Foundation, established by early Hockaday trustee Karl Hoblitzelle, donated 100 acres of land on Welch and Forest Roads for a new campus. In November 1961 the school moved to the site it still occupies. Today The Hockaday School is the largest independent girl's preparatory school in the United States.

In the new main administration building on Welch Road, the Alumnae Association built a memorial to the school's founder. From Olin Hockaday, the alums purchased a number of Ela's antique treasures; Olin and the other heirs donated additional pieces such as a replica of the original living room's paneled fireplace. Built to twice the scale of the old rooms in The Cottage, the three Memorial Rooms (bedroom, sitting room, and dining room) exhibit several hundred items from Ela's collection. Past alumnae president Harriet Olmstead Weber explained the reason for the rooms. "It has a meaning behind it: to let your children know what their past is and that they have a responsibility to their present and future when they go through school."

Just as Ela taught them.

One of four Memorial Rooms in the modern school
which highlight Ela's antique collection.

(Courtesy The Hockaday School, Dallas, Texas)

Notes—Chapter Six

1   A family history prepared by Ela's nephew Olin relates this story; another, written by an unknown person, says Thomas went with his parents to Tennessee. Thomas' father was probably John, who is the only Hockaday listed on the Lynchburg census in 1830, 1840, and 1850.

2   Giles County adjoins Maury on the south, so it is possible that some of the settlers knew Hockaday from Tennessee. A Texas Historical Marker was dedicated at the school site, now on the extreme eastern edge of Fannin County, in 1973. Giles Academy (later School) closed in 1936 after a tornado seriously damaged the building.

3   One source states that Thomas served under Brig. Gen. I. B. Ross, but there is no record of such a person. Possibly the author meant L. S. "Sul" Ross who took command late in 1863 of "Ross' Brigade,"composed of remnants of several Texas cavalry units, including the 6th. If so, Thomas Hockaday saw heavy fighting in Mississippi, Alabama, and Tennessee.

4   In 1921 new owners of the property dismantled Thomas Hockaday's house and built three rent houses from the materials on another part of the property. They then erected their own house just a few feet from the original site. The Hockaday cotton gin was converted to a barn. A Texas Historical Marker for the Hockaday homestead was placed nearby in 1982.

5   Albert appears to have been the only one of the boys to go to college; he attended Austin College in Sherman for a time. Because it was affiliated with the Presbyterian Church, Thomas Hockaday was a regular donor to Austin College.

6   Floy Crandall Hodge, *A History of Fannin County, featuring Pioneer Families*, 123.

7   Fred moved to Honey Grove and opened a hardware store. He married M. H. "Belle" Earley in 1880, and they

had two children; Fred died in 1909. Edgar worked at the Munger Gin Company in Dallas and later at Kelly Field in San Antonio. He married Nina Johnson in 1891, and they had three children; Edgar died in 1947. Brown farmed all his life (d. 1947) in Honey Grove. He and his wife Minnie had five children, including family historian Olin Scott Hockaday. Jimmie (d. 1947) eventually operated several electric plants; he and his wife had four children. Albert (d. 1958), father of four, owned the Itasca, Texas light plant. ("The Site of the Hockaday Homestead," no author, n.d., Dallas Public Library)

8   Olin Hockaday, "The Hockaday Family."
9   December 15, 1903, 1.
10 Camilla Starnes was the daughter of Marshall, Texas physician William Albert Starnes. After graduating from Mary Baldwin College in Virginia, she moved to Sherman in 1896 and became a lifelong supporter of North Texas Female College. Cammie Starnes Hall was named in her honor, and she was a close friend of Lucy and Joseph Kidd-Key. When Cammie married C. C. Mayhew in 1911, Bishop Key performed the ceremony. Mayhew had moved to Sherman shortly after Cammie did and founded the Texas Nursery, one of the largest plant nurseries in the Southwest. Cammie died in 1943.
11 Unfortunately, school records from this period are sketchy, and the author was unable to verify dates for Ela's attendance.
12 Durant is opposite Grayson County on the north side of the Red River, just 30 miles or so from Sherman.
13 Hodge, *op. cit.*, 123.
14 According to Dallas historian and author Vivian Anderson Castleberry, both Ripley Harwood and Juliette Harwood Collins, children of Alexander Harwood, claimed this meeting took place in their homes. It seems safe to say that Hockaday was founded in one of them. (*Daughters*

of Dallas: A History of Greater Dallas Through The Voices and Deeds of its Women, 226-227.)

15 Sarah B. Trent, "Miss Hockaday, the Founder," 6.

16 The building, which is now the YWCA's Proctor Hall, backed up to the Terrill School for Boys. Students remembered how the dividing fence was frequently lined with the heads of boys hoping for a glimpse of the Hockaday girls playing and taking physical education classes in the backyard.

17 Hockaday, *op. cit.*

18 Gerald D. Saxon, editor, *Reminiscences: A Glimpse of Old East Dallas,* 49.

19 Today the site is covered by Belmont Towers Nursing Home.

20 Saxon, *op. cit.,* 49.

21 An additional acre was later purchased to bring the campus to nine acres.

22 Located at what would become 5601 Bonita, The Cottage was razed after the school moved to the Welch Road campus.

23 Mary Frances Yancey, "Past History of Hockaday," 3.

24 Camille R. Kraeplin, editor, *Of Hearts and Minds: The Hockaday Experience, 1913-1988,* 38.

25 The Junior College closed in 1951 because most students wanted a full four years of higher education. Headmaster Hobart Mossman, who succeeded Ela, believed it did not have the facilities to achieve the excellence she had wrought in the rest in the school. The Music Institute continued until Ela's retirement in 1946; by then there were nearly 400 students and 46 faculty members. Among its directors was Ivan Dneprov, a Russian colonel until the Revolution of 1918 and one of the world's finest tenors. Students participating in Institute recitals were more nervous than normal, because Ela always sat in the center of the front row.

26 Kraeplin, *op. cit.,* 36.

27   Ted Dealey, *Diaper Days of Dallas*, 87.

28   Saxon, *op. cit.*, 51.

29   Eleanor Roosevelt spoke at the 1952 commencement ceremony, at which her granddaughter, Chandler Roosevelt Lindsley of Fort Worth, graduated. Ela, though a lifelong Democrat, was extremely conservative and not exactly pleased with the choice of a speaker, according to headmaster Hobart Mossman. But she graciously consented to introduce the former First Lady anyway.

30   Kraeplin, *op. cit.*, 49.

31   *Ibid.*, 61.

32   Sarah Trent had retired in 1935 after overseeing the first few years of the Junior College and died in 1950. Miriam Morgan retired in 1944 and died in 1951.

33   *Dallas Times Herald*, March 26, 1956; *Dallas Morning News*, March 27, 1956.

34   Kraeplin, *op. cit.*, 88.

35   *Ibid.*, 89, 91.

36   Obituary, *Dallas Times Herald*, March 26, 1956.

CHAPTER SEVEN

Edna Browning
Kahly Gladney

"There are no illegitimate children,
only illegitimate parents."

. . . Edna Gladney

To thousands of Americans—many of them Texans—Edna Gladney means one thing: the love and joy of having a baby. For this plump, ever-cheerful woman in the flowered hats, who had no children of her own, revolutionized the adoption industry in this country and made life brighter for many children and parents.

FAMILY HERITAGE

She was born Edna Browning Kahly in Milwaukee, Wisconsin on January 22, 1886, the daughter of watchmaker Maurice Kahly and Minnie Nell Jones Kahly (born 1869). Edna had a younger sister, Dorothy (born February 6, 1895), who later recalled that even as a child, Edna worried about

Edna, circa 1940.
(Courtesy Mrs. Earl Chester, Fort Worth, Texas)

others, bringing children in from the street to bathe and dress them. Their father died when Edna was just a child, and mother Minnie, concerned about her daughter's own recurring respiratory illness, decided to take Edna out of school and send her to Minnie's sister in the warmer climate of Fort Worth, Texas.

Edna was "very ill" when she traveled—shockingly, unchaperoned—by train to Texas in 1903 to live with her aunt and uncle, Arthur and Flora Goetz.[1] Goetz was a sales agent for two brick and coal companies located in Thurber, Texas and, at the time Edna came to stay with the family, resided at 120 St. Louis Avenue in south Fort Worth, not far from the modern site of the Gladney Center. Just seventeen when she arrived, Edna soon met and fell in love with a tall strapping Texan.

SAM GLADNEY

Samuel William Gladney was born in Comanche, Texas in 1877, the youngest of the six children of Thomas L. and Katharine Bowden Gladney, who had emigrated to Texas in 1848. A farmer and stock raiser in Harmony Hill, the elder Gladney had served in the Confederate army, then moved his family after the war to Comanche (between modern Killeen and Abilene). Sometime later they moved again to Gainesville on the Red River in North Texas.[2]

Sam eschewed his father's livestock business and at sixteen entered the business world as a collector and clerk for the First National Bank of Gainesville; his brother James also worked at the bank. About the time Edna Kahly moved to Fort Worth, so did Sam, and he went to work for the Medlin Milling Company.[3] He soon became assistant manager and then local manager of the flour mill. Edna said later that Sam and his brother-in-law, a Mr. Rogers, owned the mill.

TO CUBA

Just when and where Edna and Sam met is not known, but meet they did, and they married in Gainesville on September 22, 1906. According to Ruby Lee Piester, who knew Edna and wrote a history of the Gladney Center, Sam got in his buggy and drove all over town, inviting people to the wedding at his brother's home.[4] Afterwards, they sailed to Havana, Cuba, combining a honeymoon with business for the Medlin mill.

During their stay of at least six months, Edna suffered a tubal pregnancy that nearly killed her; the damage was such that she was unable to conceive another child.

It was a devastating loss, but Havana offered some recompense, for there Edna began to demonstrate her maturing interest in helping others. Sam was horrified when she announced she wished them to tour the city's leper colony, and he refused to go. But if he didn't already know his bride's determined nature, Sam learned it now. For Edna took him along on a visit to a close friend, a Catholic nun who, as it "happened," worked in the leper colony. She laughed about it afterwards: "I thought he'd never quit scrubbing himself after that visit."[5] Sam didn't balk again at anything she wanted to do and assisted her good works whenever he could, with money or time.

Sometime in 1907 the Gladneys returned to Fort Worth from Cuba. The evidence is sketchy and conflicting, but it appears they stayed until 1909, when Sam sold his interest in the Medlin mill. He then bought another mill in Wolfe City (Hunt County), and they moved there, living in a small, white frame farmhouse.

LIFE IN SHERMAN

Late in 1912 or early in 1913—even Edna was unsure of the date—they packed up once more, this time going north to Sherman, the Grayson County seat.[6] Sherman was one of Texas' major flour milling centers at the time, with four large mills. Sam bought the Sherman Mill and Grain Company on King Street in May 1913 and changed the name to Gladney Milling Company, with himself as president. The mill had been in operation since 1898, but Sam expanded it, building new concrete elevators and the first chemical laboratory in Texas for a flour mill. Gladney's primary product line was "Gladiola Flour," and all the bags were emblazoned with a stalk of those colorful flowers.

Sam and Edna lived in a new (1910), large white frame Victorian house which is still standing at 1318 South Crockett Street, and they entered quickly into the civic and social life of Sherman. Edna studied at North Texas Female College (the name was changed to Kidd-Key College in 1919), and in 1915 Sam won a seat as city councilman; he served at least three terms until 1920.[7] He was also on the board of the Grayson County Building & Loan Company.

The milling business was so good that Sam acquired more land for the plant and increased production capacity to 800 barrels of flour daily. He bought wheat from throughout Texas, Oklahoma, Kansas, and Missouri and found primary markets for his products in Texas, Louisiana, the West Indies, and Central America.[8]

Sam also ventured into Grayson County's then-new oil industry, purchasing leases for drilling rights from others. In his first transaction, in 1917, he acted in partnership with Sherman cotton buyer and exporter Maurice V. Johnson. But in his second lease in 1919, Sam acted alone. The records do not indicate whether he was successful.

Money from the mill enabled Sam to begin buying personal property in 1915, when he acquired the first of three adjoining plots in the Birge-Hopson Street area of Sherman. There he and Edna built a red brick, two-story Prairie-style house that today fronts on U.S. Highway 75 but which was then in a park-like section on the west side of town.[9]

About 1918 Edna's sister Dorothy came from Milwaukee to stay with the Gladneys while she, too, attended North Texas. In Sherman, she met "motor car" salesman Fred Dumas, a member of an old and prominent Grayson County family. Dorothy and Fred were married in the Birge Street home and their only child, Edna Jane, was born in Sherman.

TAKING ON THE COUNTY

Edna's foray into Sherman and Grayson County civic affairs began in 1916, when she was invited to visit the County Poor Farm not far from town. Such facilities were frequently little more than garbage dumps where the poor, indigent, mentally retarded, and physically handicapped were kept, willy-nilly, all together. Edna and the other ladies who visited with her were appalled at the conditions they found there: dirt everywhere, not enough beds, filthy linens, and, worst of all, orphaned children mixed in with the insane and sick.

They decided to do something about it.

With Edna as their leader and spokeswoman, the ladies started a publicity campaign with a scathing article in at least one Sherman newspaper which spelled out what they had found. They then requested and were granted a hearing before the county commissioners.

The *Sherman Courier* devoted a total of almost an entire page to coverage of that meeting with blaring headlines that read "Women Take Firm Stand to Better Conditions" and "Assertion Made That Not a Negro in Sherman is Sleeping on

Such Beds as Some of the Inmates of the County Farm."[10] Standing before the all-male Commissioners Court, the 5'1" Edna Gladney immediately went on the attack.

Dr. Swafford, the county physician under whose jurisdiction the Poor Farm fell, made the mistake of entering the fray. He declared the ladies' object a commendable one, but the publicity generated by it was "pinching" him and other county officials—though he hastened to add he was sure that was not the ladies' doing. He excused conditions at the Farm by saying it was too crowded to give everyone proper care. Edna then rose and informed him and the court politely that *she* had written the article in the newspaper and that "it correctly set forth the conditions."

The county auditor duplicated Swafford's mistake by asserting that, yes, the farm was bad, but there were a hundred private homes in Sherman just as bad. Edna took the floor again: ". . . that is just the point, we hope to get the county to take the lead in this matter and that this move will lead to a larger vision on the part of the whole people." She then silenced all further excuses by reminding the court that folks in Sherman were not a public charge, but "these children on the county farm are, these children are OUR children and it is OUR duty to properly care for them. . . ."

Not content with the county's reaction, Edna and her committee soon returned to the Farm armed with brooms, mops, new mattresses, and whitewash. They physically cleaned the facility, then turned their attention to the children and decided to send them to a refuge in Fort Worth.

THE REVEREND MR. MORRIS

The Texas Children's Home and Aid Society began unofficially in 1891 when the Reverend Isaac Zachary Taylor Morris arrived in Fort Worth. Born in Georgia in 1847, Morris graduated from Auburn and became an itinerant Methodist minister at age twenty. He served as a Confederate chaplain during the Civil War and was assigned to a Houston church in 1874. There he married Belle Waters.[11] In 1891 he was transferred to the Fort Worth mission.

"Cowtown" was then a booming railroad town, and it was the railroad—and what it brought to the city—that caught Morris' attention. For Fort Worth was the last major stop on the infamous "Orphan Train."

By the mid-nineteenth century, New York, Philadelphia, and other large East Coast cities were inundated with orphans and abandoned children, many of them offspring of newly arrived European immigrants who had not found the American pot of gold as they expected. At first there was no social agency to care for them. In 1854 the Children's Aid Society was established in New York, its major goal to place these children in good homes—wherever they might be. The first Orphan Train left for Michigan a few months later carrying forty-six boys. Until the trains stopped in 1929, 150,000 children were shipped west in "one of the largest social experiments in American history."[12]

At each stop, local committees would recommend couples to receive children, who had to be treated like family, clothed, churched, and educated until they were eighteen. Most of them went to farming families who needed the labor. By 1910 more than 2,000 orphans had been sent to Texas.

But at Fort Worth, the literal end of the line, rejected children were simply abandoned with their meager belongings and a nametag tied around their necks. Soon after the Reverend Morris arrived in 1891, he became aware of their plight and began taking the "leftovers" home until he could find families to adopt them. That was the beginning of the Texas Children's Home, formally chartered in 1896 and incorporated in 1904. Morris was the State Superintendent until his death in 1915, when he was succeeded by his wife, Belle.

By the time Edna learned of the Home as a possible answer to the Grayson Poor Farm children, the Morrises had "placed out" more than a thousand orphans and won awards at the Chicago and St. Louis World's Fairs for their work. While working with the Morrises to take the Grayson orphans there, Edna became interested in the Home's work. Belle Morris recognized a kindred spirit and asked Edna to serve on the Board, a position she would hold for nearly a decade. In that capacity, she "was mother confessor, legal counsel, nurse, and temporary guardian of every girl within forty miles of Sherman who needed confidential help."[13]

THE DAY NURSERY

"One thing about Edna," Sherman businessman Allan Birge would later recall, "when she had an idea, she had a way of getting everybody to help her put it over." And, added his wife, Pearl, "Edna's mind was an idea factory."[14]

Edna's latest idea was to help the many children she saw roaming around Sherman, children whose parents worked in the mills and shops and had no way of caring for them while on the job. Unattended, many also lacked proper medical care and nutrition.

What Sherman needed, she decided, was a day nursery.

According to many accounts, Edna convinced Sam that if they could have no children of their own, they could at least help others. Sam's response was immediate: he paid for Edna's trip to New York and Chicago where she studied other such facilities.[15] On her return, she rented the former S.W. Porter home on West Cherry Street, hired a matron and teacher, and, on May 20, 1918, opened the Sherman Nursery and Kindergarten for Working Women with thirty-five applicants.

Six days a week, the Nursery provided lunch, an early dinner, "entertainment," and qualified supervision for children one to seven years old. (Edna also brought the children to her home regularly for dinner and games on the lawn, while Sam took the boys fishing.) Initially admission was free, but later parents paid five cents per day. Many Sherman businesses gave funds, and Edna placed milk bottles for donations in stores and offices. She astutely pointed to the growing demand for female labor as the war in Europe dragged on: women would have to replace men, she said, and women needed day care.

Unfortunately, the Nursery was always underfunded. By 1920 Edna and the other women on the Nursery board were canvassing for money to eliminate more than $2,000 in debt. A presentation of "The Gypsy Rover" brought in some money while the students at Kidd-Key College staged dramatics to raise more.

LOSING EVERYTHING

In the meantime, the Gladneys' own financial picture was worsening. Early in 1919 Sam had bought more acreage on Natchez Street, possibly with an eye to development since it was not far from their home.[16] A year later, either unable to pay off the note or seeking a partner, he sold a half interest in the property to building materials entrepreneur Lewis T. Andrews.

Then disaster hit: wheat that Sam had bought on speculation for three dollars a bushel plummeted to one dollar. As Edna herself recalled, "We lost everything we had." By April of 1921 the Gladneys were forced to sell their land, home, and furnishings for $50,000 to Wichita Falls miller Frank Kell and J. P. Burrus of Collin County. Most of that went to pay off Sam's debts. He fought to save the Natchez Street property but finally lost it in 1923 when the sheriff seized it and sold it at auction. Fant Milling Company took over the mill and retained the "Gladiola" trademark.

As the prospect of having to leave Sherman grew, Edna persuaded the Tuesday Literary Club of Sherman to manage the Day Nursery.[17] On the day she went around town to gather up her "milk bottle money" for the last time, everyone she met cried. The *Sherman Daily Democrat* bemoaned the couple's leaving and paid tribute to their many activities.

The Gladneys then returned to Fort Worth.

At first they lived with relatives while Sam got work at a mill. An article in the Fort Worth *Star-Tribune* notes that Sam "discovered a way to utilize waste grain chaff and developed a process to turn it into a mill product."[18] By 1926 he had recovered enough financially to open a business again, the Gladney Grain Company, which was not a flour mill but traded in grains. In 1931 Sam gave up his company and went to work for Universal Mills in Fort Worth as export manager and, later, sales manager.

The Gladneys moved from one rented quarters to another, finally settling for several years (1928, 1930-1932) in the guest-house of the fifty-two-room Burton mansion on Crestline, which had been converted to apartments. When Dorothy, Fred, and Jane Dumas moved to Fort Worth in 1931 after Fred lost his automobile business in a fire, they lived in an apartment in the main house, so Edna had family close by.

While Sam struggled to regain their financial position, she continued her work on the board of the Texas Children's Home. Belle Morris died in 1924, but Edna was not named superintendent in her place until 1927. She later wrote that she accepted the position—unpaid—believing she would stay less than a year, just long enough to help raise money to eliminate the Home's indebtedness. But, she continued, "I have been here ever since [1941]; still in debt; accepting more children than we ought. This organization was organized in

1892 and has the distinction of never being out of debt."[19] The milk bottles that had worked so well in Sherman made their debut in Fort Worth, her response to the board's instructions that she not buy on credit.

The Children's Home that Edna managed was literally that—a large rambling frame house on Fort Worth's once exclusive El Paso Street. A. J. Duncan, president of Texas Electric Service Company, and his wife were persuaded by Edna's pleas to buy the house and donate it, despite the start of the Great Depression. To help furnish it, Edna brought some decorative items from home, and Sam borrowed on his insurance money for the rest.

In the upstairs sitting room were five rockers. One nursery was papered with blue morning glories and a second with red geraniums; chests in both rooms were filled with frilly layettes to dress the babies when they left for their new homes. A pink bassinet in the front room was the joyous site of first meetings between adoptive parents and their babies. In the backyard were a buggy walk and, in the very back, the laundry. The kitchen featured modern new juicing machines to provide fresh juices to even the smallest babies, Edna being a firm believer in the efficacy of carrot juice for skin problems.

And among the staff of the Home was a real resident mother: Minnie Kahly, who moved to Fort Worth in the 1920s to be near her daughters. Family photos show her surrounded by infants on whom she lavished a mother's care, overseeing that segment of the Home while Edna devoted herself to managing the entire operation and doing placements. (Minnie lived and worked in the Home for more than a decade until she died.)

Soon Edna had a house of her own again. After years of apartment living, she and Sam bought a Mediterranean-style house which still stands on elegant Medford Court West, in Fort Worth's Park Hill section. Niece Jane Dumas Chester recalls that the neighborhood was perched on top of a hill above Forest Park and that, at night, one could hear the animals in the zoo below. Jane was the Gladney's "surrogate" daughter; she traveled with Sam and Edna and helped out at the Home, taking care of the babies.

TAKING ON THE STATE

The Children's Home took in infants and children up to fourteen years of age only; birth mothers, doctors, and charitable organizations brought them in after the babies were born. But now Edna began turning her attention to the mothers and to legal considerations, the first steps in what would be a new direction for the Home.

She had soon learned that the infants' birth certificates marked them permanently as "illegitimate," if the birth parents were unmarried. In 1933 Edna began campaigning the Texas Legislature to have that changed. Fort Worth attorney Sproesser Wynn and Texas Senator T. R. Cotton helped her lobby for new legislation that faced a stiff uphill battle, for many thought it would condone immoral behavior. Not until 1936 did legislators finally surrender to the plump, pink-cheeked woman, who told them irately that "there are no illegitimate children, only illegitimate parents." The bill they passed made Texas the first state in the Southwest to legally remove the stigma of illegitimacy from birth records.

Today, because of Edna's lobbying, a baby to be placed for adoption in Texas is issued one certificate at birth listing his or her natural parents; after the adoption that document is sealed and a second issued with the names of the adoptive parents.

But Edna's triumph was marred by Sam's failing health as he succumbed to angina; and on Valentine's Day, 1935, he died in her arms. Probate records indicate that though he was receiving $300 per month plus a bonus from Universal Mills when he died, Sam Gladney's estate was relatively small because he was still doggedly paying off debts from Sherman.[20] [21]

After his death, a bereaved and lonely Edna considered leaving the Children's Home but was persuaded to remain. Her rector at Trinity Episcopal Church played an important support role for her and, with family and friends, encouraged her to enroll in sociology classes at Texas Christian University, which she did in the fall of 1939, though she never completed the requirements for graduation. To help Edna financially, the Home's board doubled her salary to $300 per month.

She moved out of the Medford Court house and lived in the Worth Hotel for several years before settling her residence permanently in the Children's Home on El Paso Street. (The Home's office, where Edna worked, was in the Medical Arts Building.)

BLOSSOMS IN THE DUST

Edna's first brush with national fame came in 1941. Ralph Wheelwright, a former journalist and then a publicist for Metro-Goldwyn-Mayer Studios, came to Fort Worth to adopt a daughter through the Children's Home. He quickly realized that Edna's story was a fascinating one and could be an excellent follow-up to the studio's successful *Boys Town*, which had starred Spencer Tracy. Giving the topic even more immediacy was the situation in Europe, where war had left thousands of children orphaned and homeless. (Edna added tartly that there were plenty of poor and homeless children in the United States.)

Louis B. Mayer, who liked the concept, had just signed a contract with a London stage actress named Greer Garson and decided to cast her as Edna. MGM bought Edna's story for $5,000, which she promptly signed over to the Home to ease its chronic debt.

Edna traveled to Hollywood—where a contingent of the Home's adoptive parents, including Ralph Wheelwright, met her train—to consult on the film. She stayed at the Ambassador Hotel, was feted at the Coconut Grove, and had lunch with Louis Mayer and tea with Greer Garson and her mother.

Edna and Greer became instant friends. The "big pink peach with an angelic face," as the actress described Edna, vowed that MGM "couldn't have flattered or pleased me more than choosing [*Miss Garson*]." Greer in turn declared it "a very great privilege . . . to be chosen to portray your image on the screen."[22] Their friendship endured for years; after Greer married Texas oilman Buddy Fogelson and moved to Dallas, she and Edna met regularly at Neiman-Marcus for lunch.

Originally intended to be a strict biography, *Blossoms in the Dust* was eventually fictionalized by screenwriter Anita Loos (*Gentlemen Prefer Blondes*), and very little of the storyline is actually true. There was no son who died young, no sister who proved to be illegitimate and adopted and who consequently committed suicide. Publicly, Edna praised the movie, and certainly she was happy with the publicity it brought the Home. But privately, she referred to the film as "Buds in the Dirt" and was annoyed that so many parts of her life were changed.

But she was pleased that MGM "glorified" Sam Gladney and his support of her work (Walter Pidgeon portrayed Sam). "Our love story, of course, is sacred ground to me," she wrote Mayer, "but not in any way have you encroached, or handled the story in a melodramatic or cheapened way."

Blossoms was to have been shot in black-and-white, but screen tests of Greer Garson convinced MGM to use the new Technicolor process, making it the first dramatic film to do so.

Greer Garson, star of *Blossoms in the Dust*, with Edna Gladney.
(Courtesy of Development Office, The Gladney Center)

Still from *Blossoms in the Dust* showing Greer Garson,
as Edna Gladney, addressing the Texas Legislature
in her fight to change Texas birth certificates.

(Courtesy of Development Office, The Gladney Center)

Sets and costumes were changed to enhance the actress' Irish coloring, and she would win her second Oscar nomination for the role.[23]

Edna first saw the finished product sitting alone with her memories in the projection room of Dallas' Majestic Theater. *Blossoms* had a successful prerelease in New York at Radio City Music Hall and its southwestern premiere in Fort Worth at the Worth Theater in July 1941. A dinner prior to the showing honored Edna, and MGM is said to have bought every pink and white gladiola in Texas to decorate the theater. Edna responded firmly to all the publicity: "It is all very wonderful. I am so happy and satisfied, but there still is work to be done." To another reporter, she stated her pleasure that *Blossoms* would bring attention to Texas' own needy children.

To her screen counterpart, she confided that she had seen the film three times.[24] In a letter to Greer Garson, she referred humorously to other movies that portrayed matrons in children's homes as always wearing "a black dress, low heel shoes, glasses" and an austere expression. "If any place on earth should be light, gay and [*have*] young people to have charge of them, surely a children['s] home should. . . . In summing up the whole picture and story idea, the only way I can express it best is—whenever I see a field of ripe wheat stacked for threshing I always feel it is a promise fulfilled and so is *Blossoms in the Dust*." An apt image for a miller's wife.

BUILDING AN INSTITUTION

Saved by the $5,000 from MGM, Edna moved to expand the Children's Home. While it had accepted only infants and children since its beginning, and ignored the birth mothers, Edna saw the need to include these young women, to bring them to the campus for the duration of their pregnancy where they could receive proper medical care and thus deliver healthier babies. She convinced the board to take the Home in a new direction, placing the emphasis on the birth mothers rather than solely on the disposition of their children. In 1949 the board purchased the thirty-five-bed West Texas Maternity Hospital, a necessity to fulfill Edna's new goal. In 1953 the facility was renamed the A. J. Duncan Memorial Hospital, in honor of the man who had served as board president for twenty years and donated the El Paso Street home. Five years later a new $100,000 hospital was built.[25]

Edna believed strongly in the privacy of both the birth and adoptive parents. In one suit brought against the Home, a judge threatened her with contempt of court unless she identified the birth mother of the baby in question. Edna refused.

The judge never knew that the baby's adoptive father was an attorney in his own courtroom.

Over the years, the Home's board of directors included some major Texas names: *Fort Worth Star-Telegram* publisher Amon G. Carter, whose namesake museum is today a major repository of Western art; candy manufacturer John P. King; former Fort Worth mayor William Bryce; Kay Kimbell, who built a massive flour milling and cottonseed oil empire and left his collection for the Kimbell Museum of Art; oilman A. M. "Aggie" Pate Jr; Perry R. Bass; Charles E. Green, editor of the *Austin American Statesman*; Sproesser Wynn; John S. Justin, Jr. of the Justin Boot Company; and Edna's first donor, A. J. Duncan. Even Louis B. Mayer was pressed into service as an honorary vice president.

The forty-one directors were mostly businessmen since Edna believed chauvinistically that men were "much kinder in their attitude toward unmarried mothers than women. Also, we keep completely secret the names and identities of our unwed girls. You can imagine how long they would be secret if we had women on our board."[26]

Of course, she was also quite capable of tongue-lashing the men if they needed it. Refused the money for a new recreation building and laundry, Edna faced down her board as she had once faced down the Grayson County Commissioners Court. "I just wish that all of you men were pregnant! I wish that you had to wear barrel-like clothes over your misshapen figures. I wish that you had to live like this for nine long months—among strangers. Then I wish that you had your babies and had to give them up for adoption. You'd give me that recreation building soon enough!"[27]

They did.

And they learned soon enough, too, that Edna would ask for anything. And expected to get it.

One board member recalled the day Edna called to ask him for money for new filing cabinets. Promised the money, she added "you'd better get it up here fast—the cabinets came yesterday and we're already using them!"[28]

Their respect and love for—and possibly their fear of—the diminutive woman in the flowered hats led them to give her her greatest honor. In 1950 they renamed the Texas Children's Home & Aid Society the Edna Gladney Home. Today it is known simply as The Gladney Center.

Edna took up another legislative battle with the state in the late 1940s, lobbying to give adopted children the same inheritance rights as natural ones and allowing them to be legally adopted rather than placed in a guardianship. That bill passed in 1951.

EASING MONEY WOES

The Home's everpresent need for financial stability was eased with the formation of the Edna Gladney Foundation, Inc. (1948) and the first auxiliaries in Houston (1952) and Dallas (1953), which set as their goals raising $600,000 for an endowment fund.

The Emerald Room of Houston's famous Shamrock Hotel was the setting for the first major event, a Charity Ball in 1952 to benefit the Home: 800 people attended and hundreds more were turned away. Adoptive parents crowded about Edna that night to show her snapshots of their Gladney babies, and Houston proclaimed Edna Gladney Day. Since 1952 also marked Edna's twenty-fifth anniversary as State Superintendent, guests presented her with a platinum ring set with five diamonds. Overcome by this tribute, Edna tried to speak but could only cry.

With the Charity Ball and Dallas' Little Theater Night and other fundraisers, the Auxiliaries reached their goal in 1954, to

Edna's delight. Today there are Gladney auxiliaries across the country which carry on this important work.

MEDIA ATTENTION AND HONORS

Blossoms in the Dust was one of the top ten films of 1941 but only the first of several major media events featuring Edna and her work. In December of 1953 she was the star of television's "This Is Your Life," where a former suitor (Garland Jones of Raleigh, North Carolina) and a Gladney baby with two children of his own adopted from the Home were among those paying tribute. Greer Garson also appeared. The show's staff presented Edna with a gold charm bracelet representing the important events of her life: a baby cradle, castañets for the trip to Cuba, Sam's oil wells, a flour sifter for his milling business, etc. "Surprises like this aren't good for an old lady!" exclaimed Edna, who had been lured to the studio by promises of magazine publicity for the Home.

The nationally broadcast show turned a major spotlight on the Home and brought such a spate of birth mothers that the staff was forced to use dresser drawers for the babies to sleep in until more cradles could be located.

The *Christian Science Monitor* published a long article about Edna's work, and in January 1954 came the *Woman's Home Companion* article "I Gave Away 10,000 Babies." (*Reader's Digest* excerpted the story.) Author Eleanor Harris described the sixty-six-year-old Edna, who by then weighed 190 pounds as the result of diabetes and a knee injury that left her walking with a cane: "Above all this poundage is a charmingly pretty face—to which she gives a lot of attention . . . she still wears carefully applied eye shadow and mascara day and night; her eyebrows are plucked and penciled. She races through life wearing blue, purple or white dresses under a series of gay little flowered hats and leaving behind her the scent of perfume."

AUNT EDNA

Edna, reported Harris, tootled around Fort Worth and the Home's campus in a grey sedan given her by some of the adoptive parents. Later, appalled at finding she drove by punching the gas pedal with her cane, they modified the car with hand operated pedals. Niece Jane Chester recalls that Edna's driving scared her to death. On one trip downtown together, Jane watched helplessly as her aunt backed up the wrong way on a one-way street. A Fort Worth policeman pulled Edna over but was so stunned at what she'd done that he let her go with only a warning. As soon as Jane got her learner's permit, she drove.

Despite her diabetes, Edna loved to eat and kept candy in every drawer. She would make up for apple pie a la mode and other forbidden foods with an extra insulin shot. She also became quite hard of hearing. Ruby Lee Piester, who joined the Home' staff in 1961, recalled the great booming voice that would answer her over the telephone when she called to ask a question.

Among the numerous newspaper articles published about the Home during this period was one which gave this description of Edna: "Aunt Edna Gladney, who goes about her works with the fervor of a Billy Graham and a smile and touch that makes even newborn babies giggle."[29]

Several important Fort Worth organizations honored Edna for her work: B'nai B'rith with the Americanism Citation for Meritorious Service (1955) and Texas Christian University with an Honorary Doctor of Law degree (1957). The Carnation Company and Cal Farley's Boys Ranch also presented her with awards for her work. Even the *Congressional Record* paid tribute to "the commendable work of Edna Gladney. It took much love, much courage, much hard work and much of every form of human devotion to accomplish the truly great work that has been the achievement of this gracious Texas lady. . . ."

TRIBUTE TO A CAREER

Plagued by her diabetes, Edna decided to retire in April 1960, at the age of seventy-four, after more than three decades as Superintendent of the Gladney Home, but continued to work "ex-officio" as an adviser and fundraiser. (Members of her family believe the board forced her to retire not only because of her health and age, but also because she had never completed her sociology degree.) By the time she left, Edna had built the Home's budget to $250,000—a far cry from the days when she worked unsalaried because there was no money.

After her retirement, Edna moved from the El Paso Street facility to her final home in the Chateau De Ville apartments. Her seventy-fifth birthday in January 1961 was to have been marked by a testimonial dinner, but Edna was too ill to attend, and it was cancelled.

Her devotion to her life's work was such that she was still going over plans for a new nursery and dormitory two days before she died of complications from diabetes on October 2, 1961. Her successor, Walter Delamarter, later recalled that just a week before, he had visited with her to show her the latest blueprints. Ill and long past an age when most people retire, Edna only wanted to know "When do we get started?" To the last, her thoughts were there, as she requested that memorial donations be made to the Home.

Newspapers across Texas eulogized her. "Mrs. Gladney dealt in one of the emotional areas of human relations, and she did so with compassion and devotion. Psychologists might have called it a sublimation of her own frustrated mother instinct, but whatever it was it made her an almost irresistible crusader for the rights of children born out of wedlock. . . . 'What on earth,' she once asked, 'could anyone find to write about me?' The fact is that a great deal was found to write and say about her. . . . These things answered her question and brought wide public attention to her and the work for unfortunate mothers and children that she spent most of her life in furthering."[30]

She had written her will nearly a decade earlier, leaving all her goods to her sister Dorothy Kahly Dumas (Mrs. Fred Dumas), who had also lived in Fort Worth for some years.[31] It was a modest estate, just under $27,000 in stocks, bank deposits, and furnishings: Edna had given so much of herself, in every way, over the years to the Home.

Today the Gladney Center is a multimillion-dollar facility, the oldest adoption agency in Texas. Many more thousands of babies have left it for new and loving homes since the days when Edna Gladney herself placed each infant in a pink bassinet to meet parents who had waited anxiously by the phone for "the call" for months and even years. This compassionate woman with a generous, loving heart believed sincerely that "God intended these girls [*the birth mothers*] to become pregnant" so their babies could bring joy and life to otherwise childless couples.

Today, in the small, cheerful mural-painted room of the Gladney Center, where new parents wait to see their son or daughter, hangs a poem from an adoptive mother to her child. It concludes with these lines: "You were not born under my heart/You were born in it."

Every single baby that leaves that room was born in Edna Gladney's heart.

Notes—Chapter Seven

1   Letter from Edna to Mrs. Arthur G. Hopkins Jr. of Sherman, Texas, September 8, 1958. Edna wrote she came to Texas in 1903, but the Fort Worth City Directory does not list her until the 1905-1906 volume.

    Texas and Texans, 1914, says Maurice Kahly was "a well known businessman . . . who retired some years ago and died in June, 1913." But Edna's niece, Jane Dumas Chester of Fort Worth, says Edna was 17 when Maurice died, which would have been in 1903.

2   Thomas moved his cattle to the Indian Territory to graze and later to New Mexico; he retired in 1912. Katharine Gladney died in 1908.

3   By 1913 Medlin had been bought by Bewley Milling, established in 1882. In the letter cited in #1, Edna erroneously referred to it as the "Beauty" Mill.

4   Ruby Lee Piester, *For the Love of a Child: The Gladney Story, 100 Years of Adoption in America*, 11. Unfortunately all September 1906 issues of the Gainesville newspaper, which would have given an account of the wedding, are missing. But Edna's niece Jane Chester confirms that such an action sounded very much in character for Sam.

5   *Ours: A Quarterly Publication of the Edna Gladney Home*, Vol. 1, No. 3, Special Memorial Issue, October 1961, 1.

6   Grayson County adjoins on the east Cooke County (county seat, Gainesville), where Sam grew up.

7   Sam served on the city council 1915-1916, 1917-1918, and 1919-1920. The records for 1916-1917 are missing.

8   *Texas and Texans*, Vol. LLL, 1914.

9   Shermanites were astonished that they built on mosquito-ridden Post Oak Creek (517 W. Birge). The 1920 census also listed a Negro gardener, Doc Britton, who lived on the premises.

    According to Jane Chester, the Gladneys had engaged famed architect Frank Lloyd Wright to design yet another house for them, but Sam's financial misfortunes cancelled the plans to build it.

10   *Sherman Courier*, January 9, 1917, 1.

11   One of Morris' seven children, born in 1898, was *Lucy Key* Morris, undoubtedly named for Lucy Kidd-Key, wife of a Methodist bishop. See her chapter.

12   "Lost Ties" by Elaine Schad, *Fort Worth Star-Telegram*, September 29, 1991. Information on Orphan Trains from this article and "Waifs of 1880's Given Home by Minister" by Ted Stafford, unidentified clipping. The Orphan Train Heritage Society of America is in Springdale, Arkansas; an estimated 500 to 600 riders are still alive today.

13   Undated (circa 1940) clipping, "Edna Gladney Is Heroine to Sherman," by Bess Stephenson, *Fort Worth Star Telegram*.

14   *Ibid.*

15   Edna's sister Dorothy could not verify these trips and stated that she did not believe Edna made them.

16   Natchez Street no longer exists, demolished when Highway 75 was built. Roughly it was in the modern Kam Korners Shopping Center-Burger King area. There were only a few houses on it, all belonging to "coloreds."

17   The Club ran the Nursery for six years, raising money through rummage sales, theatrical performances, and teas. The City of Sherman took it over in 1927 (Edna complained that "the young matrons . . . soon tired of it and in turn the City took it over") and still operates it today. With funds donated by a friend of Edna's, they built a new facility on Lamar Street in 1932—"bigger and better than I ever hoped for the little institution I had started"—which now houses the Boy Scouts. Today the Nursery is in a wing of a Sherman school.

18   Unattributed article, "Greer Garson Movie Made Edna Gladney Famous" by Ted Stafford, October 24, 1980.

19   Letter from Edna Gladney to Guy Yowell of the *Sherman Democrat*, April 17, 1941. Copy in Flemming Collection of Sherman Public Library.

20 Sam had a suit against Smith Brothers Grain Company that dated to 1929 and had to do with an earlier agreement between them setting the price of grain: he lost a great deal of money as a result of changed market conditions. The grievance was first heard by the Board of Arbitration of the Fort Worth Grain and Cotton Exchange and eventually went all the way to the Texas Supreme Court in 1934. The case was heard late in 1936, after Sam's death, and the court reversed earlier decisions and ruled against Sam.

His will, handwritten in 1920 on Gladney Milling Company stationery, was one paragraph long and left Edna everything.

21 Several sources report that Edna met attorney Sproesser Wynn, who helped her fight for new adoption laws, when he probated Sam's will. But the probate records list Charles Kassel as the attorney.

22 Private correspondence between Edna Gladney and Greer Garson in Garson's *Blossoms in the Dust* scrapbook, in the collection of The Gladney Center.

23 Critics raved about Greer Garson's Technicolor beauty. "You've seen dawn on the Grand Canyon, maybe, and moon over Miami, the sunset in *A Star Is Born* and opening night at the Metropolitan Opera, but you haven't seen anything gorgeous until your mortal eyes have beheld Miss Garson in a blue party dress." (*New Orleans Times Picayune*)

24 Letter from Edna to Greer Garson, July 9, 1941.

25 The original West Texas Maternity Hospital was razed to build a driveway and the site of the El Paso Street facility is now a parking lot. The later Duncan Memorial is still standing, though it is no longer used as a hospital. Today's birth mothers deliver in a Fort Worth hospital.

26 Eleanor Harris, "I Gave Away 10,000 Babies," *Woman's Home Companion*, January, 1954, 92.

27 *Ibid.*

28 Piester, *op. cit.*, 16. She also reported that the milk bottles that had proved so successful in Sherman made their appearance in Fort Worth stores and offices, raising money to buy window air conditioners for the dormitories.

29 *Dallas Morning News*, August 15, 1954.

30 *Fort Worth Star*, October 2, 1961.

31 After living in Sherman until 1930, Dorothy and Fred Dumas followed the Gladneys to Fort Worth. Fred's father Louis was the namesake of Dumas, Texas; his wife Dorothy, Edna's sister, died in 1981. Their daughter Edna Jane Dumas Chester (Mrs. Earl Chester), who was born during their residence in Sherman, still lives in Fort Worth and was kind enough to share her family memorabilia with the author.

CHAPTER EIGHT

Enid Mae Justin

"Listen, things are either right or
they are wrong. There is no in-between."

. . . Enid Justin

To folks in Nocona and to those who knew her, she is and
always will be simply "Miss Enid." They tell stories of her with
laughter and respect in their voices and make it clear that they
miss her. She defied just about everybody along the way but
would not stop until she became the world's only lady bootmaker.

BORN ON THE RED RIVER

Enid Justin was born in Nocona, Texas on April 8, 1894, the
fourth child of H. J. (Herman Joseph) and Annie (Lovanna)
Allen Justin. Her father's parents were German immigrants
who eventually had settled in Lafayette, Indiana where H. J.
was born in 1859.[1] Joe, as most people called him, was not
interested in his father's cigarmaking business and decided to

head out to Texas at age eighteen. In Gainesville (Cooke County), he worked for the Norton Shoe Shop from 1877 to 1879 before moving north to Burlington (today Spanish Fort) on the Red River. Burlington wasn't much of a town, but it was right on the Chisholm Trail, and Joe Justin had arrived there at the peak of the cattle drive era.

With twenty-five cents, some tools, and enough leather to make one pair of boots, Joe opened a one-room shoe repair shop. When the town barber rewarded his hard work with a loan of thirty-five dollars to buy more leather, Joe was on his way. He knew that a properly fitting boot was an essential tool for the thousands of cowhands riding the Chisholm Trail. Joe would take their measurements as they headed north and have their boots ready on their return. Word of mouth about the quality of his work soon brought him more business than he could handle, and his brother Willie moved from Indiana to help him.

In Burlington Joe met a young woman named Annie.

Annie Allen was a native Texan, born in Lipan (near Granbury) in 1863 to Dr. S.A. and Elizabeth Jane Allen. When she was thirteen, the family moved to Burlington where her father had a busy practice patching up cowhands. Annie grew up helping him in his surgery and building a reputation for a feisty temper: once she tried to beat up the town whore because the woman was wearing a hat almost identical to Annie's new one. Both women wound up in court.

Annie and Joe married January 12, 1886 in Burlington, where their first son, John S., was born two years later. But by then the cattle drives were beginning to dry up and the Gainesville, Henrietta & Western Railroad (a branch of the Missouri Pacific) was building into nearby Nocona, draining the life from Burlington. So in 1889 the Justins packed up their home, shop, and Joe's reputation as a perfectionist bootmaker and moved to Nocona.[2]

NOCONA

Named for Comanche war chief Peta Nocona, father of Quanah Parker, the town was just two years old in 1889, the seat of a county already boasting more than 10,000 people. It was raw and bustling with ranchers and their hands who worked large cattle spreads both in North Texas and across the Red River in the Chickasaw Nation of the Indian Territory (now Oklahoma). This ready-made market, along with the shipping facilities provided by the new railroad, was what Joe needed to expand. He and Willie found a shop and immediately hired workers to meet the expected demand.

About the same time, Joe and Annie developed Justin's original "self-measuring system" which let customers order by mail, an innovation now used by most bootmakers. About 1902 Joe would try branching out with a store on Fort Worth's Main Street, but it only lasted a year or so; he advertised himself there as "H. Joseph Justin, the celebrated cowboy bootmaker."[3]

As the business grew, so did the family. Earl was born in 1890, Fern in 1892, Enid in 1894, Samuel Avis in 1896, and Anis in 1898. Myrl D., the last, was born in 1909. They were an extremely close family and grew up in a simple, two-story frame house that Joe had built. The backyard was filled with swings and gym-type equipment, but the children's favorite place was the "clubhouse," originally built to be Joe's shop but quickly outgrown. In it, they danced to music from the Victrola, played billiards, and sought the shade of its enveloping veranda on hot days. In later years the clubhouse served as a honeymoon cottage for newly married Justins.

From the time they were ten years old or so, the children all helped out in the shop.[4] "Daddy Joe," as Enid called her father, "was a stern boss, but he was a wonderful boss. He demanded quality in everything he did. . . ."[5] Enid's first job after school and on Saturdays was folding catalogs and

Enid, circa 1985.

(Courtesy Nocona Boot Company, Nocona, Texas)

stuffing them into envelopes along with a tape measure and price list, ready for mailing. When she was twelve, she began stitching boot tops on a foot-pedal Singer sewing machine.

At school, the blue-eyed Enid enjoyed writing compositions and put her six feet of height to good use in basketball games. But in 1906, when she was twelve and just out of seventh grade, Enid had her first brush with authority.

Brother John's eighteenth birthday party featured dancing in the long, wide hallway of the Justins' home. Enid joined in with pleasure, for she loved dancing. But the next day, she learned the price of her night's fun: suspension from school for three weeks. Enid gathered her books and left her teacher with this parting shot: "Anybody that thinks there's a party going on in my own home and I'm going upstairs to bed has something else to think about!"[6]

She never went back to school and later explained why: "... it's not what you know that counts. It's what you do with what you do know that makes a difference."

Enid went to work for her father full time. By this time, the H. J. Justin Boot Company had several dozen employees who produced a pair of boots each day by hand.

Office of H. J. Justin & Sons Boot Company, circa 1919.

(Courtesy of Marsha Taylor, Nocona, Texas)

At fourteen, Enid designed her first pair of boots, her inspiration for the pattern found in a velvet brocade couch. But she functioned primarily as Joe's assistant and ran the office, overseeing orders and shipments. As she grew older, she spent her Saturdays at home helping with the laundry and baking eighteen or twenty pies which were mostly consumed by the next day.

JULIUS

Enid's life was full enough for years without boys. When she was nineteen, her sister-in-law dared her to put a message into a pair of boots bound for Montana. She corresponded with the cowboy who received them a few times—until he sent his picture. The six foot tall Enid decided she wasn't interested in a short, bowlegged cowboy.

Then she met Julius Stelzer, a railroad telegrapher recently arrived in Nocona. He was handsome and "a wonderful dancer," and their courtship survived a short stint while he worked in Illinois. Enid was so in love that she forsook Annie's Christian Church and took instruction as a Catholic, the religion of both her fiancee and Daddy Joe. She and Julius were married in nearby Muenster on August 10, 1915 and left by train for their honeymoon in Galveston; Daddy Joe cried as the train pulled out.

But they stayed in Galveston only two days before Enid declared she wanted to go back to their rented house in Muenster. Julius complied to please her and was no doubt happy he'd done so when they learned that a major hurricane hit Galveston the following day and destroyed the Beach Hotel where they had stayed.

Two weeks later, Julius went to work for Daddy Joe as a bootmaker, Enid went back to her old job there, and the couple moved to Nocona.

ANNA JO

Enid and Julius lived in the clubhouse for some time after their return; and on December 26, 1916, she gave birth there to a daughter, Anna Jo, after working full time until Christmas Eve. They named the child for Annie and Joe. Enid left H. J. Justin & Sons Boot Company to stay home and care for her daughter, of whom she said, "everything we did centered around her."[7] With $600 in Liberty Bonds given her by Daddy Joe, she bought a four-room house nearby and moved there not long after the baby's birth.

But when Anna Jo was just over a year old, she contracted whooping cough in an epidemic that hit Nocona. The illness worsened into pneumonia and Enid took the baby to her parents' home, which was warmer. What followed was a hard dying for a baby, her tiny body wracked with convulsions and nothing that medicine could do to help her. Anna Jo died on January 27, 1918. At the funeral, a grieving Enid demanded that the coffin be raised from the grave so she could see her child once more.

She desperately wanted more children but that wish would remain unfulfilled. No doctor could find the problem that kept her from conceiving again and, at an older and more philosophic age, she decided it had worked out for the best. "I've always believed after Julius did what he did in later years, that God had more to do with it than I did. I think God knew what was going to happen. . . ."

She and Julius moved to Hollister, Oklahoma, hoping that a change of scenery would help Enid recover. But they stayed only a few weeks before hurrying back home. Daddy Joe had suffered a stroke the previous year, and now he was declining rapidly. He died not long after Anna Jo, leaving his favorite child reeling from this second blow.

CHANGING TIMES

Joe had bought land for a new factory, but his stroke prevented him from building it. After his death, the boys took over H. J. Justin & Sons, and Earl even went out on his own to open Justin Leathergoods Company in 1919, using scrap leather from the big plant to make small items such as key cases. But Enid could not bring herself to return, and to her dismay, her brothers began seriously considering leaving Nocona.

The Fort Worth Chamber of Commerce had been courting the Justins for some time to move their operation to "Cowtown." Enid strongly opposed it, for she felt that Joe would never have left Nocona. But in 1924 the boys decided to go ahead. A caravan of moving trucks carried the business—and more importantly, the Justin name—south to Fort Worth, where the plant opened in July 1925. The move was probably a wise one: business increased rapidly, and by 1926 Justin was the largest manufacturer of cowboy boots in the United States.[8]

Even Annie would eventually follow her sons, but Enid dug in her heels. Not only did she refuse to move but she decided to keep her father's memory alive in Nocona by starting her own bootmaking company.

Her brothers scoffed at her, told her she'd "lose every damned cent. . . [*she had*] in six months," and even predicted that soon there would be no cowboys to need boots. Enid's response was pointed: if she went broke, she'd do something else. And in her opinion, people would always eat meat, and there would always be cowboys. The boys shrugged and went to Fort Worth.

THE LADY BOOTMAKER

In September 1925, three months after H. J. Justin & Sons left with most of the equipment, employees, and customers, Enid and Julius opened Nocona Boot Company in the 1,000 square foot plant just vacated by her brothers, and with six employees who also chose not to leave. She tried to sell her Justin stock to finance the startup but couldn't find a buyer. Finally she went to Cadmus McCall, president of Nocona's Farmers & Merchants National Bank and a friend of Daddy Joe's, and borrowed $5,000 on her own; Julius' name did not appear on the loan form. She also found ten people willing to bet on her by buying stock in the new company.

Enid leased machines and set to work. Now she was competing with her brothers but "I didn't feel bad about it at all . . . I never have felt bad about it to this day."[9] Julius was nominally the president but Enid ran the business.

And that caused her her first problem.

It seemed that cowboys and ranchers didn't want to do business directly with a woman. Buying boots from Daddy Joe was one thing; buying them from his daughter was another entirely. Business at the factory was slow, and, to keep the family afloat, Enid took in boarders, cooked lunches, sewed and ironed, and sold coal and washing machines—in fact, the first electric washing machine in Nocona. To make a sale, she would run a load of wash and even hang it out to dry. She would even walk across town to collect twenty-five cents owed to her. "I developed a trait that has stood me in good stead all my life: just plain, mule-headed persistence."[10]

Enid also took to the road as Nocona Boot Company's first sales"man." She loaded up her Model T with samples and, with sister Myrl, traveled "highways" that were little more than cow trails. It was an adventure that might have left most men reeling. Enid made her first big sale in Jacksboro, their car caught on fire from an oil leak, and Myrl was nearly run down by another car while changing a flat tire near Mineral Wells. In a Gatesville hotel, the sisters stayed on the second floor; when they asked what they should do in case of fire, the bellman told them to jump.

Enid prided herself that she made a sale at nearly every stop. "Thank goodness, we didn't have women's lib back then," she recalled. "I usually was lucky enough to have a gentleman offer to help me get my samples out of the car and into the store when they'd see me struggling with that old sample case . . . I found out that a woman selling boots was pretty much like a man selling boots. The store owners were interested in quality and price. I had both to offer in my boots. . . ."[11] Someone finally called from the factory and told her to come home because they couldn't keep up with the orders pouring in from across West Texas.

Still, it was oil, not cowboys, that saved her the first few years. Nocona made a tall lace-up boot that became very popular with the workers in the new oil fields around the area. Enid got into her first legal flap with her brothers over a tongue designed specifically for that boot when Justin was still located in Nocona. When told the tongue was patented by Justin, and threatened with a lawsuit, Enid contacted the Patent Office, only to discover that her own name was on the form, along with those of all Daddy Joe's children. She continued using it.

The oil workers spread the word about the quality of Nocona boots, and soon the cowboys came back, too.

Even so, she ended her first year of business with a checking account overdrawn by $267.61. Almost fifty years later, that statement still hung, framed, on her office wall to remind her of the lean times. But Enid didn't worry too much. She knew she had the assets and a marketable product, so she simply issued more stock and expanded. For years, she drew a salary of only three dollars per week in order to plow everything else back into the business.

Enid also continued to design boots, drawing more inspiration from that old brocade sofa and from some distinctly different sources. One of her favorite patterns was "The Neck," designed while she attended a funeral one day. It seemed there was an elderly man seated in front of her with a heavily wrinkled neck. Enid started sketching and finished it despite the multitude of prayers the preacher insisted on.

A BROKEN MARRIAGE

But just as the business was prospering, Enid's personal life began falling apart again. Annie Justin had moved to Fort Worth and rented out the old family home; a boarder smoking in bed burned it to the ground. Now Enid was bereft of family and home.

The one sure thing she thought she had was her marriage. Julius "was like a little boy who never grew up," she said. "But I liked his dependence on me . . . [*he*] was everything I could have hoped for. We didn't have a lot of problems many married couples have . . . But Julius was changing and I didn't notice the changes."[12]

Her husband started drinking and cheating on her with "one of the devil's imps in women's clothing."[13] Enid didn't know what was wrong, only recognized that something was, and began losing weight and sleep. A friend called Annie Justin back to Nocona and it was she, with bank president Cadmus McCall, who broke the news to Enid. To add insult to injury, as far as she was concerned, the woman was an employee of Nocona Boot Company. "I finally lost my temper. I fired her! She said I couldn't do it, but I did. I'd just come from the beauty shop and my hair was up in curlers. She grabbed me by the hair and pulled all the pins out.

We were by a cutting table and I grabbed a weight used by the cutters. Luckily it fell to the floor or I would've hit her with it and killed her." Annie's own feisty daughter concluded with some satisfaction. "I still have that weight around here somewhere."[14]

Cadmus McCall had already called an attorney, but Enid, as usual, took matters into her own hands. She hired a detective to follow Julius and his girlfriend; when that didn't work, she trailed him herself with close friend Ruby Anderson. They followed the illicit couple over the state line into Oklahoma, and there Enid had him: it was illegal for a married person to carry another out of Texas for immoral purposes. Enid called the sheriff and had the two arrested. She visited the woman in the Waurika jail but did not talk to Julius because she couldn't bear to see him behind bars.

They eventually reconciled, but it only lasted about a year. He really tried to make the marriage work, Enid acknowledged, but his girlfriend stalked them. In 1934 Julius resigned as president of Nocona Boot Company and "he just walked away and left everything behind."[15] "He gave me my stock, his stock and a home, everything and only asked for $3,000. He wasn't all bad. He was just weak and got off on the wrong foot, and he didn't feel my equal."[16]

Sadly, Julius continued to drink and to hope for another chance with Enid, but the alcohol finally killed him. To reporters who asked her about the marriage, she would give almost flippant answers: "He was like a lot of men. He just up and went away after 20 years."[17] Or "He began associating with persons of whom I didn't approve. We broke up."[18] But the hurt was real and decades later, Enid could still admit, "You see, I really loved Julius . . . and I always will."

DEPRESSION

Enid pushed the company to stay even with the competition, selling her boots for little more than the $18.50 she'd charged back in 1925 and developing ever fancier ones. She hired salesmen to travel Texas and the Southwest until she had a national market. (She resisted world distribution, knowing she couldn't keep the quality and meet the demand, too.)

The Great Depression that flattened many other businesses didn't faze Enid. "I just made up my mind I was going to keep on working." Leather was sometimes hard to obtain, but she never laid any of her workers off. Her goal to keep the company a workable size paid off.

But federal austerity regulations that came out of the Depression and lasted through World War II irked her enormously: only black and brown boots, no fancy boots, just one row of stitching, and no stitching across the toes. That last rule really riled her because toe stitching was fundamental in a boot for a working cowboy, who stands in the stirrups frequently and puts pressure on the toes. Enid Justin picked up the telephone and called Washington to demand a hearing. (Her brothers had already tried that and been turned down.) Told that the official she needed to talk to was busy, she replied tartly that she was busy, too, trying to make money to pay her taxes. She finally coerced the proper official into a meeting in St. Louis: "I got the boot people together and we went up there and convinced him the stitching was functional, not just decoration as he believed it to be. So, we got that changed."[19]

The Texas Centennial in 1936 spurred growth because of the craze it created for Western attire, and Enid even bought a company in Paul's Valley, Oklahoma that made bits and spurs. But World War II brought a critical shortage in leather, sheepskin, and wooden lasts, and frequently the workers were idled. Enid couldn't bring herself to lay them off so she installed a piano on the factory floor and encouraged them to sing while she paid them. When supplies were available, Nocona shipped military boots all over the world.

Enid fought hard to keep the business going, feeling a responsibility "to my employees and to my town," where she was the major employer.

HARRY

Her devotion to her work after Julius left wasn't enough to fulfill her. When Harry Whitman walked into her office one day on business, she agreed to go out with him. The son of an itinerant Baptist preacher, raised in Waco and educated at Baylor College, Harry was personable, funny, played bridge well, and, most importantly, was a good dancer. Several friends and relatives, however, sensed that he was a fortune hunter and tried to warn Enid. She married him anyway on November 9, 1940 at her brother John's house in Fort Worth.

Harry "went to work" at the company but even Enid admitted he did little beyond wander around and be friendly with the workers. The couple built a $100,000 frame and stucco house a few blocks from the site of today's plant. Enid paid for it as she did everything else, and Harry painted every surface in and on it yellow, his favorite color.

She indulged his wants but retained enough sense to refuse to give him control of anything financial. When Justin Boots dividend checks arrived, Harry would ask they be put in his name, but Enid just smiled and replied, "I would rather keep my stuff together. We will enjoy the fruits of it."[20] His teenaged daughter from a previous marriage was always asking about Enid's possessions, as if anticipating the day they would be hers.

The marriage lasted five years. Then on October 17, 1945, his birthday, Harry walked into Enid's dressing room and informed her she'd better call her lawyer. Her immediate response was to think that someone had been injured at the plant. "Did someone get hurt?" she asked. "You're going to get hurt," was the cold reply.

"I'm leaving," Harry continued. "I came here broke but I'm not leaving that way. You get your chips out on the table and I mean get them all out." Harry asked for half of everything she owned and Enid replied that he didn't deserve any because he hadn't helped her make any of it. Her attorney agreed and so did the court.

After the divorce, Harry returned to Wichita Falls, Texas, where he had been working when he met her, and opened Whitburn Boot Company.[21] Harry claimed that his boots were made by part of the Justin family; Enid laughed, said he should have called it "Will-Burn Boots," but never challenged him. She didn't have to. The business lasted only a year or so and closed. She gleefully sent several men to buy up equipment and supplies for ten cents on the dollar.

The passage of time didn't change her feelings about Harry, either. Forty years later, in 1985, when she told her story to writer Dale Terry, she included several photographs of Julius Stelzer in the book but not one of Harry Whitman. (*"Miss Enid:" The Texas Lady Bootmaker*)

Harry eventually died in New York State, where his daughter lived, of a skin cancer that "ate his face up." But the experience with him caused several fundamental changes in Enid. She who had loved dancing forbade her employees that pleasure, even on their own private time, to protect Nocona's reputation. She expected everyone in the plant to have and practice a high tone of moral conduct. In hiring women, she selected only widows, until she finally relaxed that rule in the mid-1950s.

As she later told employee Ann Lawyer, "Just the minute that bastard went out the door, I grabbed a paintbrush and started painting everything pink." The house remained pink as long as Enid Justin lived in it.

BUILDING NEW

After the war, Enid knew she had to expand again to keep up with demand for her boots. Heeding Cadmus McCall's advice, she decided to buy land to build a new facility rather than renting an already existing structure. The property she wanted was on the highway and backed onto a rail line—ideal for her purposes. Symbolically, it was also only a few hundred yards west of the old Chisholm Trail, the route that had given Daddy Joe his start nearly seventy years earlier. But the land belonged to an estate she felt would not sell. To her surprise and gratification, the estate manager declared he would sell it only to her for "I know you'll build something the town will be proud of."[22]

Enid broke ground on July 29, 1947, with Associate Justice Earl P. Hall of Fort Worth's Second Court of Civil Appeals helping her and with two radio stations broadcasting the ceremonies. A Lubbock architect designed the 33,000-square-foot facility and a Dallas contractor completed it in time to move in on June 9, 1948. Nocona's mayor declared that day a town holiday, and most businesses closed to be there at the festivities. Enid was astounded when 7,000 people turned up to tour the plant.

Now she developed the routine of work she would maintain for years: rising at 5 A.M. to bathe and breakfast, picking up mail before arriving at the plant at 7 A.M., opening and sorting the mail, and having the office ready when the employees arrived at 8:00. She supervised all the orders that came in and personally knew many of the dealers from her travels around the country to buy leather and promote Nocona.

SELLING BOOTS

Promotion was all important in the increasingly competitive boot business, and Enid took to it with a passion. Her first exposure came in 1935 when Paramount Pictures did a film entitled *Unusual Occupations* and included her.

But it was the Pony Express stunt she dreamed up in 1939 that really put her on the world media map.

Seventeen riders signed up to race "2,000" miles from Nocona to the Golden Gate International Eposition Park in San Francisco, Pony Express style: no relief riders and only two horses per contestant. Along the route they picked up letters at Nocona Boot outlets to deliver in San Francisco. Enid served as Chamber of Commerce Publicity Chair for the event and furnished the prize—a wheelbarrow containing 750 silver dollars.

Newspaperman and art collector Amon G. Carter, who had grown up in Nocona, came from Fort Worth to open the race on March 1, 1939. The winner, Shannon Davidson of Matador, Texas, finished 100 miles ahead of his closest competitor on March 24, with his mother, Miss Enid, and the great-great-grandson of the Pony Express founder waiting to greet him.

Of course, there were repercussions. The California Humane Society complained the horses were ill-treated, and one member even called Enid's hotel room at 3 A.M. to fuss. "I told her she didn't know what she was talking about, that those boys thought more of their horses than they did of their wives. I hung up on her."[23] But she had no regrets about staging the event: "I guess the Pony Express Race was about the craziest thing I ever got involved in, but believe me, if I had the chance I believe I'd do it all over again."

To put Nocona Boot Company in everybody's mind, Enid traveled the world. She exhibited at Fort Worth's prestigious

Fat Stock Show and at apparel marts around the country. She went to Houston for the 1952 Annual Governors' Conference and presented each governor with boots. (Adlai Stevenson refused to wear his, and an indignant Enid gave them to his son.) Texas Week found her on the French Riviera. Any celebrity or world figure who crossed her path received or was flattered into buying Nocona boots: King Gustaf VI of Sweden, George Burns, Lawrence Welk, Carol Burnett, Lyndon B. Johnson, Reba McEntire, Glen Campbell, Henry Ford II, Harry Truman, Roger Staubach, and Lorne Green, among them. She even wanted to present a pair to Pope Pius XIII during a 1949 audience granted her but was dissuaded by the U.S. Ambassador.

Publicity would always be her forte. When she was eighty-four, Nocona Boots inaugurated its most famous ad campaign to target the youth market. The award-winning "Let's Rodeo" series featured a cowboy in Nocona Boots fending off or ignoring a variety of western wildlife, such as a rattlesnake, Gila monster, and tarantula. However, Enid wasn't too thrilled when the ads turned up in *Playboy*.

Nocona stayed on the cutting edge of the footwear industry by introducing such improvements as the patented Thin-Line Cushion Shank (1960), the Seamless Saddle-Side boot, which eliminated the unconfortable vertical seam on the inner, saddle side (1962), and the Flex Line Sole (1963). Today the company is one of the few to still use wooden pegs to hold the steel shank in place, an expensive mark of quality that most bootmakers have forsaken.

Even in her personal life, Enid was a Nocona promoter. Her Cadillac—pink, of course—carried vanity plates that read "E J Boot" and flaunted boot hood ornaments.[24] Until they became too expensive, her business card was a leather boot, and she collected miniature boots from countries around the world. There were several hundred pairs by the time she died, some of which are still on display in the plant's employee break room and exhibit area.

THE PERSONAL WOMAN

Enid developed a real love of travel from doing Nocona promotions. She went abroad many times, took cruises, and fell for the dollar slots in Las Vegas, her favorite destination. At home, she played relentless bingo at the Nocona Hills Country Club.

In addition to the miniature boots she collected "for work," Enid had a passion for Royal Doulton figurines and filled her house with them. She enjoyed cooking and didn't smoke or drink—although she did "almost" drink a beer once—but confessed that, when angry, she would "cuss a little." Friends always came to the back door, not the front, and her den was filled with trophies won by the baseball teams she sponsored.

"Old women clubs" were not much in her line; her hobbies were people and boots, and jewelry, especially diamonds. Pat Keck, who grew up across the street and has worked for Nocona Boot Company since 1975, well remembers the wild Texas storms that drove everyone into storm cellars. Enid always took with her a pouch containing her precious jewels—and her driver's license. "For she knew," laughs Pat, "that she couldn't pass her driver's test again."

Enid lived by what she called her Creed for Success. "I believe what I'm doing helps other people be happy. I believe in earning a promotion every day. I give twice as much and as a result, receive twice as much . . . I believe if I add to prosperity, I will prosper in return . . . I believe it's easier to win than to lose . . . I believe opportunities are everywhere . . . I have the seed for achievement and it's called brains. I am president of my own life."[25] She never failed to credit Daddy Joe for what she became in life and maintained a musem of his career in the plant.

And Annie's feisty daughter admitted that she'd had "to be sort of tough" along the way "to keep from being stepped on." She proudly proclaimed that she'd been a women's libber "before the word and the definition were even invented," the result of "a bad case of German independence" she'd inherited from Daddy Joe.

Her vulnerability would surface, however, when she was shown photos of other people's children. Enid responded by pulling out snapshots of her factory and boots, saying "These are my children."

EMPLOYEE RELATIONS

Enid treated her employees as family but expected them to work or go home. "It was always a pleasure to see a person who had no skills when hired, grow into a skilled worker . . . and to see them raise their families, to share their happiness as well as their sad times." She established a profit sharing plan for them about 1971, long before others followed suit, provided insurance, and threw elaborate Christmas parties with gifts for both employees and their spouses. Trips to the rodeo in Oklahoma City and the Ice Capades in Fort Worth were also employee benefits. At breaktime, she visited with the workers, laughing, talking, telling jokes and stories about her youth or her travels. And the plant shut down every year for two weeks to give all the staff a paid vacation.

Even in the cowboy craze of the 1970s, when the company labor force grew rapidly to keep up with the demand for 1,200 pairs of boots a day, Enid vowed to keep the family atmosphere. "We're adding employees so fast I don't even know them," she complained to a reporter. "But I will." She added that she didn't have factory workers, she had friends.

Enid hired only the best, recalls stitching supervisor Darla Linn: being a Nocona Boot employee was a mark of pride. Turnover was low, and some families could boast three and even four generations of workers.

But Miss Enid on the factory floor could be a terror. Linn well remembers the day she dropped empty wooden thread bobbins on the floor by her sewing machine. "Young lady," Enid informed her, "these bobbins are a nickel apiece. We don't waste them." The owner who had started out stitching boot tops herself was not above sitting down and showing a new employee exactly how to do the job.

For years Enid imposed a strict dress code: no jeans—high heel shoes and dresses for the women. Those who didn't comply were sent home to change. Long-haired young men of the '60s and '70s who applied were turned away until the plant manager finally convinced Enid he needed workers, regardless of their hairstyle.

But when the employees voted in a union in the mid-1970s, Enid had a fit. "Oh, that just burned me down. That just killed me. I felt like almost that we were a family, you know."[26] Employee Ann Lawyer remembers Enid tongue-lashing the president of the union on the floor, something she rarely did. A year later, the workers voted to go back to the old ways and killed the union: "It just went out like Lotty's eye," Enid said with satisfaction. "You know, it just makes you mad when you're doing everything for your employees you can and someone from the outside sticks their nose into your business."

IN THE COMMUNITY

Enid had demonstrated her love for the town of Nocona back in 1925, when she refused to move to Fort Worth with her brothers. She never lost that love, giving back to Nocona in many ways.

Besides being the largest employer, Enid donated additional land, a band shell, tennis courts, and playground equipment for the City Park[27] and built the public library. She presented specially designed boots every year to the winners of the Future Farmers of America projects and to Montague County 4-H Gold Star winners; and she built the Youth Center, since she thought teenagers were "the future of the nation and smarter than we give them credit for." On her frequent travels, she took every opportunity to speak to young people and urge them not to drop out of school as she did. She later explained her deep interest in youth: "Every time I do anything for children, I think I am doing it in honor of my little girl that I lost."[28]

Through the company, she sponsored Little League baseball teams and a riding club. She served on the boards of the Nocona Rodeo Association[29] and of the Cowboy Hall of Fame in Oklahoma City.

Nocona children referred to her fondly as the Crackerjack Lady, for Enid ordered cases of that treat to dispense at Halloween. Before the property behind her house was developed, she kept it as a playground for the neighborhood children, who helped themselves to archery and croquet equipment in her garage.

In return, Nocona, Texas, and even the country honored her.

Over her lifetime, Enid received many awards, among them the Lone Star Farmer Award from the Future Farmers of America, the Lions Club International Honor Award, and a government citation for Significant Contribution to Industrial Expansion. She was Honorary Chief of the Nocona Fire Department as well as an Honorary Okie and Tarheel, and an Aide-de-camp to New Mexico's governor. The Texas Angus Association recognized her "devoted and unselfish service to your fellowman and country," and the Western Image Awards

Hall of Fame singled her out for Lifetime Achievement in the Western Industry. She was inducted into the National Cowgirl Hall of Fame and was listed in *Who's Who in American Women*.

RETIREMENT?

Long past a "normal" retirement age, Enid continued to oversee all operations of Nocona Boot Company. Several expansions took the plant to 125,000 square feet with 500 employees, and the 1970s saw production increase 180 percent to a record 400,000 pairs of boots made in one year. Nearly two dozen salesmen fanned out across the country to sell more. By 1980 Nocona had garnered 25 percent of the handcrafted boot market, and net sales were $19 million.

In 1973, when she was seventy-nine, Enid bought the Tex Tan Boot Company from Fort Worth's Tandy Corporation. She and Charles Tandy were good friends, even though he had tried for years to buy her company. Nor was he the only entrepreneur interested in Nocona. But Enid turned them all down. "In polite words I told them to get lost. This company is my life and I aim to keep on running it."[30]

She couldn't hire enough workers in Nocona to meet the demand, so she built a second plant in Vernon, Texas (1977) which she personally financed and then a third in Gainesville (1981). That year net sales rose to $27 million. When she was eighty, rumors began to fly that Miss Enid would at last retire. But she scoffed at them. "Why would I do that? I'll not let the rockin' chair get me! Besides, I've got too much to do to be worryin' about myelf."[31]

Her one concession to her age was to hire nephew Joe Justin in 1974 as vice president, general manager, and heir apparent. Joe had worked for her once before, from 1954 to 1957, then moved to Wichita Falls with Amsco Steel Products.

He had cut his teeth in the leather business, working for his father and uncles' company, Justin Boots, in Fort Worth for more than a decade.

Enid continued to be principal stockholder, president, and chairman of the board despite the stroke that paralyzed her left side a few years after Joe's return. In a wheelchair pushed by her nurse, she still visited the plant as frequently as possible.

MERGER

In 1981, at the age of eighty-seven, Enid gave in to age, health, and changing times. She agreed to merge with Justin Industries (the parent company of Justin Boots) in a stock exchange so that her company would at least stay in the family. She had been fighting a takeover by her nephew John Jr. for a year, after Justin claimed it held an option to buy Nocona for $5 million. Enid believed that John was "obsessed" with owning Nocona, and she was offended by the party he threw at the Fort Worth Club to celebrate their deal: "I have never seen so many people in my life and so much whiskey flowing. I don't do that."[32] She was pleased, however, that Nocona remained an independent subsidiary in competition with Justin, and she retained her title as president and chairman.

But that was one of the few things she was happy about. Joe Justin had turned on her for agreeing to the merger in the first place, causing her much grief. And John, she believed, was trying to steal funds from Nocona behind her comptroller's back. Justin balked at continuing her employee profit sharing plan, and she complained that their sales manager gave away boots to friends. She summed up her irritation in an interview with North Texas State University business professor Dr. Floyd Jenkins: "I have two nephews by the name of Justin, much to my amazement and regret. They don't live right . . . [*the Fort Worth office has*] antagonized and harassed me, you know, because I haven't died, that's all."

A year after the merger, in September of 1982, Enid retired, though she continued to hold the titles of Honorary Chairman of the Board and consultant. A few days later, she returned to her office to find the picture window blocked with a new wall. Infuriated, she called Fort Worth and complained; the wall was promptly removed.

LAST YEARS

Now Enid stayed closer to home, bound by her stroke to a wheelchair and round-the-clock nursing care. The telephone and police scanner became her main links to the world although she went out as often as possible. Finally, she had to be hospitalized.

Enid Justin died October 16, 1990 at the age of ninety-six and was buried in the cemetery in Nocona, where she had lived all but a few weeks of those years. The bulk of her estate went to her nieces and nephews, including such items as a black Russian sable stole, her coveted diamond earrings, watch, ring, and pendant, real estate in Nocona and Wise County, and her Cadillac. To the Nocona Library she bequeathed her china cabinet and the Royal Doulton figures within it.

To the end she lived by the teachings of Daddy Joe. "There are a lot of people who will compromise when it's to their advantage, but I won't compromise."

Notes—Chapter Eight

1   H.J.'s siblings were Matthew and Elizabeth, both of whom lived, unmarried, in Lafayette, Indiana all their lives; Albert, who moved to California; and Willie, who worked for brother H.J.

2   Another Nocona newcomer at this time was a blacksmith whose son would become one of Texas' most prominent men: Amon G. Carter, publisher of the *Fort Worth Star-Telegram* and Western art collector, whose namesake museum in Fort Worth is today one of the Southwest's most prestigious.

3   Fort Worth City Directory, 1902-1903.

4   Annie Justin didn't work in the shop but was an excellent seamstress who sewed for others, including making costumes for the Mollie Bailey Circus. Enid often declared that her own sewing skills were inherited from her mother.

5   Enid Justin as told to Dale Terry, *"Miss Enid:" The Texas Lady Bootmaker*, 11.

6   *Ibid.*, 12.

7   *Ibid.*, 21.

8   Today Justin Industries is still "the preeminent producer of western boots, and quality work and sport footwear." The conglomerate also owns several building supply firms, including Acme Brick, the oldest in Texas; and Northland Publishing. When the firm opened in Fort Worth in 1926, Annie Justin was president, Earl vice president, John secretary/treasurer, and Samuel a worker.

9   Justin, *op. cit.*, 28.

10   Henry R. Ferguson, "Enid Justin: Woman Bootmaker," *Texas Woman*, February 1979, 34.

11   Justin, *op. cit.*, 35.

12   *Ibid.*, 40-41.

13   North Texas State University Oral History Collection (Business Archives Project): Number 63: Interview with Enid Justin, November 13, 1981, 13.

14   Justin, *op. cit.*, 43.

15   *Ibid.*, 45.

16   North Texas State University, *op. cit.*, 16.

17   Ferguson, *op. cit.*, 35. Enid's tolerance for affairs within the ranks of her employees dwindled to nothing after Julius. She was known to fire those who "fooled around."

18   Kent Biffle, "These boots were made for kicking," *Dallas Morning News*, September 21, 1980.

19   Justin, *op. cit.*, 52-53.

20   North Texas State University, *op. cit.*, 65.

21   Enid declared contemptuously that Harry got "a bunch of Jews" to back him: Bernbaum, Novin, Finklestein, and Whitman was the official name of the entity. Later she suspected that his rambles around the Nocona plant had been to gather information for this venture.

22   Justin *op. cit.*, 55.

23   *Ibid.*, 78.

24   Longtime employees recall that no one parked within two car lengths of Miss Enid's prized Cadillac so as not to risk scratching it.

25   Justin, *op. cit.*, 80.

26   North Texas State University, *op. cit.*, 78-79.

27   Grateful Noconans renamed it the Enid Justin City Park.

28   North Texas State University, *op. cit.*, 62.

29   The president of one of the largest boot manufactories in the world didn't ride horses herself, the result of being felled from horseback by a clothesline when she was young. In an early Nocona rodeo parade, the horse pulling Enid's buggy spooked and ran and had to be caught by a cowboy on a speedy horse. (In another interview, Enid said her fear resulted from a Colorado parade in which actor Rory Calhoun, riding behind her, was injured when his

horses bolted.) "Now whenever they want me in a parade, they get me a Cadillac." Nonetheless, she donated or helped raise most of the $100,000 cost of a new arena.

Nor did she wear boots, except on special occasions. "Does a doctor ever take his own medicine?"

30 Ferguson, *op. cit.*, 35.
31 "There's a Difference Between Talkin' and Livin'," unindentified Clay County newspaper in collection of Nocona Boot Company.
32 North Texas State University, *op. cit.*, 35.

Bibliography

CHAPTER ONE—SOPHIA PORTER

PRINTED SOURCES

Allen, Winnie and Allen, Corrie Walker. *Pioneering in Texas: True Stories of the Early Days.* (Dallas, Texas: The Southern Publishing Company, 1935).

Brownlee, Richard S. *Gray Ghosts of the Confederacy: Guerrilla Warfare in the West,1861-1865.* (Baton Rouge: Louisiana State University Press, 1958).

Connelly, William Elsey. *Quantrill and the Border Wars.* (Cedar Rapids, Iowa: The Torch Press, 1910).

Cramton, Willa G. *Women Beyond the Frontier: A Distaff View of Life at Fort Wayne.* (Historic Fort Wayne, Inc., 1977).

Drago, Harry Sinclair. *Red River Valley.* (New York: Clarkson N. Potter, 1962).

Foreman, Carolyn Thomas. "Pierce Mason Butler." *Chronicles of Oklahoma* (Volume 30,1952).

Foreman, Grant. "Sources of Oklahoma History." *Chronicles of Oklahoma* (June 1925).

_____"The Texas Comanche Treaty of 1846." *Southwestern Historical Quarterly* 51 (April 1948): 313-332.

_____*Pioneer Days in the Early Southwest.* (Cleveland: Arthur H. Clark Company, 1926).

_____(editor). "The Journal of Elijah Hicks." *Chronicles of Oklahoma.* (March 1935).

_____(editor). "Journal of the Proceedings at our First Treaty with the Wild Indians, 1835." *Chronicles of Oklahoma* (December 1936).

Genealogical Biographies of Landowners of Grayson County, Texas, 1836-1869. (Sherman: Oak Room Emporium Press, 1967).

Greene, A. C. "Texas Sketches." *Dallas Morning News*.

Jenkins, John H. *The Papers of the Texas Revolution, 1835-1836*. (Austin: Presidial Press, 1973).

Landrum, Graham. *An Illustrated History of Grayson County, Texas*. 1st edition. (University Supply & Equipment Co., 1960).

Lucas, Mattie Davis, and Hall, Mita Holsapple. *A History of Grayson County, Texas*. (Sherman: Scruggs Printing Company, 1936).

McComb, David G. *Houston: The Bayou City*. (Austin: University of Texas Press, 1969).

McLeRoy, Sherrie S. "A Love Feast of the Olden Time." *World's Fair*. (October, November, December 1989).

_____ "The Short Life and Hard Death of Holland Coffee." *True West*. (December 1989).

_____ "The Adventures of Sophia." *Texas Highways*. (February 1991).

_____ *Mistress of Glen Eden: The Life and Times of Texas Pioneer Sophia Porter*. (Sherman, Texas: White Stone Publishing Group, 1991).

Maguire, Jack. "Sophia Porter: Texas' Own Scarlett O'Hara." In *Legendary Ladies of Texas*, edited by Francis Edward Abernethey. (Dallas: E-Heart Press, 1981).

Middlebrooks, Audy J. and Glenna. "Holland Coffee of Red River." *Southwestern Historical Quarterly* (October 1965).

Pierce, Gerald S. *Texas Under Arms: The camps, posts, forts, and military towns of the Republic of Texas, 1836-1846*. (Austin: Encino Press, 1969).

Ray, Bright. *Legends of the Red River Valley*. (San Antonio: The Naylor Company, 1941).

Ray, Worth Stickley. *Austin Colony Pioneers, including history of Bastrop, Fayette, Grimes, Montgomery, and Washington Counties, Texas.* (Austin: Pemberton Press, 1970).

_____*Tennessee Cousins: A History of Tennessee People.* (Baltimore, Maryland: Genealogical Publishing Company, Inc.,1966).

Rister, Carl Coke. "A Federal Experiment in Southern Plains Indian Relations, 1835- 1845." *Chronicles of Oklahoma* (December 1836).

_____*Robert E. Lee in Texas.* (Norman: University of Oklahoma Press, 1946).

Scott, Lt. Col. Robert N., preparer. *The War of the Rebellion: A Compilation of the Official Records of the Union and Confederate Armies.* (Washington, DC: Government Printing Office, 1891).

Strickland, Rex Wallace. "History of Fannin County, 1836-1843." *Southwestern Historical Quarterly* Volumes 33 and 34.

Swisher, Mrs. Bella French, editor. *American Sketch Book: An Historical and Home Monthly* Volume 5, no. 5 (Austin, 1880).

Texas State Library, Archives Division. *The Indian Papers of Texas and the Southwest, 1825-1916.* (Austin: Pemberton Press, 1966).

"The Reminiscences of Mrs. Dilue Harris." *Southwestern Historical Quarterly* 4 (October 1900): 85-127.

Tolbert, Frank X. *The Day of San Jacinto.* (New York: McGraw-Hill Book Company, Inc., 1959).

Webb, Walter Prescott, editor in chief. *The Handbook of Texas.* Volumes 1-2. (Austin: Texas State Historical Association, 1952).

White, Dabney, editor. *East Texas: Its History and Its Makers.* Volume 2. (New York: Lewis Historical Publishing Company, 1940).

Wilbarger, Josiah. *Indian Depredations in Texas.* (Austin: Hutchings Printing House, 1889).

Wingo, Elizabeth B., compiler. *Marriages of Princess Anne County, Virginia, 1749-1821.* (Privately printed, 1961).

MANUSCRIPT AND GOVERNMENT SOURCES

Allen County (Fort Wayne, Indiana): Deeds, Wills, Marriages.

Amherst County (Amherst, Virginia): Deeds, Wills, Marriages.

Britton, Dr. Morris L. "The Red River Frontier: Posts and Trails of the Middle River, 1542-1861." Unpublished manuscript, volumes 1-2.

Census of the United States:
Allen County, Indiana: Population Schedules for 1830, 1840.
Fannin County, Texas: Population Schedule for 1840.
Grayson County, Texas: Population Schedule for 1850, 1860, 1870, 1880. Slave and Agricultural Schedules for 1850 and 1860.
Princess Anne County, Virginia: Population Schedule for 1840. Slave Schedule for 1850.

Coffee, Holland. Letter to Sam Houston. March 21, 1838. A. J. Houston Collection, Texas State Library, Austin, Texas.

Collin County (McKinney, Texas): District Court Records.

Edwards, Chris (President, W. C. Quantrill Society). Phone interview with author, July 1991.

Fannin County (Bonham, Texas): Minutes of Board of Land Commissioners, Deeds, Wills.

Foreman, Grant, compiler. "Copies of Manuscripts in the Office of the Commissioner of Indian Affairs, Washington, DC." Unpublished, 1930. Copy in Oklahoma Historical Society.

Grayson County (Sherman, Texas): Deed Books, Will Books, Marriage Registers, Probate Records, Tax Rolls, District Court Records.

Harris County (Houston, Texas): District Court Minutes, Tax Rolls.

Holland Coffee Collection in Sherman Public Library, Sherman, Texas: deeds; bills of sale; newspaper clippings; correspondence; land grants; powers of attorney.

"Journal of the House of Representatives of the Republic of Texas, (1) Regular Session of 3rd Congress, November 5, 1838 (2) Called Session of September 25, 1837." Texas State Archives.

"Journal of the Senate of the Republic of Texas; First Session of the Third Congress, 1838." Texas State Archives.

Lucas, Elizabeth and Wall, Christine. "Glen Eden and Preston Bend: Sophia Coffee Biography." Unpublished manuscript, 1929.

Lusk/Coffee Family Folders, McMinnville (Tennessee) Public Library.

McLennan County (Waco, Texas): Marriage Records.

Mosley, Joe, compiler. "Genealogy of George Washington Jewell and Elizabeth Coffee Jewell" in McMinnville (Tennessee) Public Library.

Old Settlers Association of Grayson County: Minutes of.

Princess Anne County (Norfolk, Virginia): Deeds, Wills, Marriages.

Sophia Porter/Glen Eden Collection in Red River Historical Museum, Sherman, Texas: correspondence; furniture; clothing; decorative arts; maps; photographs.

Treybig, Arliss. Letters to author recaptivity of Theresa Juergens. November 26, 1990; May 23, 1991.

Washington County (Brenham, Texas): Deeds, Wills, Marriages, Probate Records.

NEWSPAPERS

Arkansas Gazette (Fort Smith, Arkansas)
Arkansas Intelligencer (Fort Smith, Arkansas)
Baltimore Patriot (Baltimore, Maryland)
Dallas Morning News (Dallas, Texas)
Denison Herald (Denison, Texas)
Northern Standard (Clarksville, Texas)
Sherman Courier (Sherman, Texas)
Sherman (Daily) *Democrat* (Sherman, Texas)
Sherman (Daily) *Register* (Sherman, Texas)
Sunday Gazetter (Denison, Texas)
Telegraph & Texas Register (Houston, Texas)

CHAPTER TWO—LYDIA MCPHERSON

PRINTED SOURCES

Baillio, F. B. *A History of the Texas Press Association*. Dallas, Texas: Southwestern Printing Company, 1916.

Bryan County Heritage Association, Inc. *The History of Bryan County, Oklahoma*. 1983.

Carter, L. Edward. *The Story of Oklahoma Newspapers, 1844 to 1984*. Muskogee: Western Heritage Books, Inc., 1984.

Chronicles of Oklahoma. Article on Masonry, Volume 22, Spring 1944.

_____"Chief Wilson Nathaniel Jones" by John Bartlett Meserve, Volume 14, December 1936.

Ferguson, Mrs. Tom B. *They Carried the Torch: The Story of Oklahoma's Pioneer Newspapers*. Norman: Levite, 1989. Originally published 1937.

Foreman, Carolyn Thomas. *Oklahoma Imprints, 1835-1907: A History of Printing in Oklahoma Before Statehood.* Norman: University of Oklahoma Press, 1936.

History of Free Masonry in Oklahoma. Prepared for the M.E. Grand Chapter, Royal Arch Masons of Oklahoma.

Hunter, E.C. Series of articles on Indian Territory for *Dallas Morning News Magazine Section,* January 30-March 20, 1921.

Jenkins, Janet and Taylor, Erma L. *Kadohadacho: Real Chief, History of Caddo.* Durant, Oklahoma: Plyler Publishing Co., 1976.

Liahona Research, Inc., compiler. *Iowa Marriages: Early to 1850.* Orem, Utah, 1990.

McPherson, Lydia Starr. *Reullura: A Book of Poems.* Buffalo: Charles Wells Moulton, 1892.

Moursund, John Stribling. *Blanco County Familes for One Hundred Years.* Austin, Texas: privately printed, 1958.

_____*Blanco County History.* Burnet, Texas: Nortex Press, 1979.

Ray, Grace Ernestine. "Early Oklahoma Newspapers: History and Description of Publications from Earliest Beginnings to 1889." In *University of Oklahoma Bulletin,* 1928.

Ross, Ishbel. *Ladies of the Press.* New York: Harper & Brothers, 1936.

Sherman City Directory, 1887-1909.

Swisher, Mrs. Bella French. *The American Sketch Book: An Historical and Home Magazine.* Austin, Texas: Sketch Book Publishing House, 1881.

Willard, Frances E. and Livermore, Mary A., editors. *A Woman of the Century.* Buffalo: Charles Wells Moulton, 1893.

Womack, Lillian. "Civic-Minded Widow, Printer Sons Founded Democratas 'People's Paper' 75 Years Ago." *Sherman Democrat*, August 29, 1954.

MANUSCRIPT AND GOVERNMENT SOURCES

Bryan County Historical Society: Caddo, Oklahoma: Files.

Census of the United States:
> Belmont County, Ohio: Population Schedule for 1820.
> Blanco County, Texas: Population Schedule for 1880.
> Grayson County, Texas: Population Schedule for 1880, 1900.
> Pulaski County, Arkansas: Population Schedule for 1860.
> Saline County, Arkansas: Population Schedule for 1850.
> Van Buren County, Iowa: Population Schedule for 1840, 1850, 1860.

Center for American History, University of Texas at Austin: Vertical file on Granville McPherson.

Foreman, Grant, editor. "Indian-Pioneer History Collection." Oklahoma City, 1978.

George, Gregory A. Private letter to author re David Hunter family history. August 25, 1995.

Grayson County (Sherman,Texas): Deed and Probate Records.

McPherson, Granville. "Address of Grand Master Granville McPherson Delivered at Vinita, Indian Territory, September 4, 1877." Type-written copy given author by family member.

NEWSPAPERS

Caddo International News (Caddo, Indian Territory)
The Daily Oklahoman (Oklahoma City, Oklahoma)
Dallas Morning News (Dallas, Texas)
Dallas Weekly Herald (Dallas, Texas)
Galveston Daily News (Galveston, Texas)
Oklahoma Star (Caddo, Indian Territory)
Sherman Daily Democrat (Sherman, Texas)
Sherman Daily Register (Sherman, Texas)
Sherman Democrat (Sherman, Texas)
Whitesboro News Record (Whitesboro, Texas)

CHAPTER THREE—LUCY HOLCOMBE PICKENS

PRINTED SOURCES

Able, Gene. " 'Fleur de Luce' Legends, Lure, Linger Long." *The Edgefield Advertiser* (S.C.), May 29, 1985. Also Parker, David. "Lucy Holcombe Pickens 'Cult' Continues."

Barnwell, John. *Love of Order: South Carolina's First Secession Crisis.* Chapel Hill: University of North Carolina Press, 1982.

Brooks, Elizabeth. *Prominent Women of Texas.* Akron, Ohio: The Werner Company, 1896.

Channing, Steven A. *Crisis of Fear: Secession in South Carolina.* New York: W. W. Norton & Company, 1974.

Chapman, John A. *History of Edgefield County from the Earliest Settlements to 1897.* Spartanburg, S.C.: Reprint Company, 1980. Originally published 1897.

"Charleston, S.C. and Mount Vernon: 22d-23d February, 1884." Charleston, S.C: Walker, Evans & Cogswell, 1884.

Chesnut, Mary Boykin. Martin, Isabella D. and Avary, Myrta Lockett, editors. *A Diary from Dixie.* New York: D. Appleton & Company, 1914.

Bibliography

Civic League of Edgefield, S.C. *Welcome in Edgefield, South Carolina*. Edgefield, S.C.: Advertiser Print, 1963.

Coit, Margaret L. *John C. Calhoun: American Portrait*. Boston: Houghton Mifflin Company, 1950.

Coulter, E. Merton. *A History of the South: Volume VII: The Confederate States of America, 1861-1865*. Baton Rouge: Louisiana State University Press, 1950.

Current, Richard N., editor-in-chief. *Encyclopedia of the Confederacy*. New York: Simon & Schuster, 1993.

Faust, Drew Gilpin. *James Henry Hammond and the Old South: A Design for Mastery*. Baton Rouge: Louisiana State University Press, 1982.

Greer, Jack Thorndyke. (Greer, Jane Judge, editor) *Leaves from a Family Album*. Texian Press, 1975.

Hardiman, H. M. (pseudonym) *The Free Flag of Cuba: Or, the Martyrdom of Lopez: A Tale of the Liberating Expedition of 1851*. New York: De Witt & Davenport, nd. (University of Texas, Austin collection).

Hennig, Helen Kohn. *Great South Carolinians from Colonial Days to the Confederate War*. Chapel Hill: University of North Carolina Press, 1940.

Horton, Mrs. Thaddeus. "Romances of Some Southern Homes." *Ladies Home Journal*, January 1900.

James, Edward T., editor. *Notable American Women, 1607-1950: A Biographical Dictionary*. Cambridge, Mass: Belknap Press of Hardvard University Press, 1971.

"Lady Lucy, Queen of the Confederacy." *The Medallion*, Texas Historical Commission, December 1990.

Lake, Mary Daggett. "Russians Liked the Beauty from Texas." *Fort Worth Star-Telegram*, July 30, 1944.

Lander, Ernest McPherson Jr. *The Calhoun Family and Thomas Green Clemson: The Decline of a Southern Patriarchy*. Columbia: University of South Carolina Press, 1983.

254

Lewis, Kathleen. "The Woman Called Lucy." *The State Magazine*, November 2, 1952.

McClendon, Carlee T., compiler. *Edgefield Death Notices and Cemetery Records*. Columbia, South Carolina: Hive Press, 1977.

McPherson, Hannah Elizabeth (Mrs. Lewin D.). *The Holcombes, Nation Builders: Their Biographies, Genealogies, and Pedigrees*. Privately printed, 1947.

"Marshall C.S.A. . . 1861." *Marshall News Messenger*, February 26, 1961.

Meredith, Roy. *Storm Over Sumter*. New York: Simon & Schuster, 1957.

Mims, Nancy Crockett. Articles on Francis and Lucy Pickens and "Edgewood" in *Annals of Edgefield District: Heritage Series*, #11, July 1990.

Minutes of the Council of the Mount Vernon Ladies' Association of the Union. Held at Mount Vernon, Va. May, 1900. Kansas City, Mo: Hudson-Kimberly Publishing Company, 1900.

Moore, Ellis. "La Grange Lives In Aura of Glorious Past." *Commercial Appeal*, Memphis, Tennessee: June 8, 1952.

Moore, Valvera and Burba, Alma. "Only Texas Girl Ever Pictured on Money." *Dallas News*, May 19, 1929.

Muhlenfield, Elisabeth. *Mary Boykin Chesnut: A Biography*. Baton Rouge: Louisiana State University Press, 1981.

Revill, Janie, compiler. *Edgefield County, S.C. Records*. Easley, S.C: Southern Historical Press, Inc., 1984.

Simkins, Francis B. "Francis Wilkinson Pickens." In *Dictionary of American Biography*.

Wallace, David Duncan. *South Carolina: A Short History, 1520-1948*. Columbia: University of South Carolina Press, 1961.

Woodward, C. Vann, editor. *Mary Chesnut's Civil War*. New Haven: Yale University Press, 1981.

Yearns, W. Buck, editor. *The Confederate Governors*. Athens: University of Georgia Press, 1985.

Youmans, Leroy F. *A Sketch of the Life and Services of Francis W. Pickens of South Carolina*. Charleston, South Carolina: The New Job Presses, nd.

Young, Marjorie W. "Lucy Pickens To Be Recalled When Homes Tour Begins." *Independent*, Anderson, S.C., March 27, 1966.

MANUSCRIPT AND GOVERNMENT SOURCES

Census of the United States:
Edgefield County, South Carolina: Population and Slave Schedule for 1860, Population Schedule for 1870. Harrison County, Texas: Population Schedule for 1850.

Edgefield County (Edgefield, South Carolina): Marriage and Probate Records.

Harrison County Historical Museum, Marshall, Texas - Vertical files on Lucy Holcombe Pickens and Holcombe Family: including newspaper and magazine clippings, letters, speeches, copy of Eugenia Holcombe diary, revised entry for *Handbook of Texas* (1984).

NEWSPAPERS

Texas Republican (Marshall, Texas)

CHAPTER FOUR—OLIVE ANN OATMAN FAIRCHILD

PRINTED SOURCES

Biffle, Kent. "Old West tale, secrets hidden behind a veil." Kent Biffle's Texana, *Dallas Morning News*, August 7, 1994.

Centennial Celebration, 1872-1972: St. Stephen's Episcopal Church, Sherman, Texas. np. 1972.

"Death's Call Was Sudden." *Denison* (Texas) *Daily Herald*, April 25, 1907.

Gilmore, Jean Fairchild. *Early Fairchilds in America and Their Descendants*. Baltimore: Gateway Press, Inc., 1991.

"Grayson Link to Arizona Indian Saga Published." *Denison* (Texas) *Herald*, November 10, 1968.

"Historical Marker Okayed for Olive Oatman's Grave." *Denison* (Texas) *Herald*, September 21, 1969.

Maloney, Alice Bay. "Some Oatman Documents." *California Historical Society Quarterly*, Volume 21, 1942.

Peckham, Howard H. *Captured by Indians: True Tales of Pioneer Survivors*. New Brunswick, New Jersey: Rutgers University Press, 1954.

Pettid, Father Edward J. "The Oatman Story." *Arizona Highways*, November 1968.

Rice, William B. "The Captivity of Olive Oatman: A Newspaper Account." *California Historical Society Quarterly*, Volume 21, 1942.

Sanderlin, Walter S., editor. "A Cattle Drive from Texas to California: The Diary of M. H. Erskine, 1854." *Southwestern Historical Quarterly*, January 1964.

Sherman City Directory.

Smith, Robert Benjamin. "Apache Captives' Ordeal." *Wild West*, June 1993.

Stratton, R. B. *Captivity of the Oatman Girls*. Originally published 1859. Reprinted: Upper Saddle River, N.J.: Literature House/Gregg Press, 1970.

"What Happened to Olive Oatman?" *Denison* (Texas) *Herald*, July 2, 1967.

MANUSCRIPT AND GOVERNMENT SOURCES

Census of the United States:
Albany, New York: Population Schedule for 1860.

El Dorado County, California: Population Schedule for 1850.

Grayson County, Texas: Population Schedule for 1880 and 1900.

Jackson County, Oregon: Population Schedules for 1860 and 1870.

Whitesides County, Illinois: Population Schedule for 1860.

Confederate Service Records.

Flemming Collection, Sherman (Texas) Public Library.

Galvin, Lynn. "Olive Ann Oatman—An Indian Captive Returned." Unpublished manuscript, copy in collection of Red River Historical Museum, Sherman, Texas.

Grayson County (Sherman,Texas): Deed and Probate Records.

Pettid, Father Edward J., editor. "Olive Ann Oatman's Lecture Notes." Copy in collection of Red River Historical Museum, Sherman, Texas.

Vertical File on Olive Ann Oatman Fairchild. Red River Historical Museum, Sherman, Texas.

NEWSPAPERS

Dallas Morning News (Dallas, Texas)
Denison Daily Herald (Denison, Texas)
Denison Herald (Denison, Texas)
New York Times (New York)
Sherman Daily Democrat (Sherman, Texas)
Sherman Democrat (Sherman, Texas)
Sherman Register (Sherman, Texas)

CHAPTER FIVE—LUCY KIDD-KEY

PRINTED SOURCES

Domatti, Ruth O. "A History of Kidd-Key College." *Southwestern Historical Quarterly*, Volume 63, October 1959.

Genealogies of Kentucky Families, from the Register of the Kentucky Historical Society: Volumes 1-2. Baltimore, Maryland: Genealogical Publishing Co., Inc., 1981.

Johnson, Frank W. *A History of Texas and Texans: Volume III.* Chicago: The American Historical Society, 1914.

Lane, Mrs. Julian C. *Key and Allied Families.* Macon, Ca: J. W. Burke Company, 1931.

Murray, Nicholas Russell. *Yazoo County, Mississippi: 1845-1900: Marriage Records, Part II.* Hammond, Louisiana: Hunting for Bears, Inc., nd.

North Texas (Female) College and Kidd-Key Conservatory Catalogs.

Smith, Frank E. *The Yazoo River.* New York: Rinehart & Company, Inc., 1954.

Winegarten, Ruthe, editor. *Finder's Guide to the Texas Women: A Celebration of History Exhibit Archives.* Denton, Texas: Texas Woman's University Library, 1984.

Yazoo Historical Association. *Yazoo County Story.* Fort Worth, Texas: University Supply and Equipment Company, 1958.

MANUSCRIPT AND GOVERNMENT SOURCES

Census of the United States:
Yazoo County, Mississippi: Population Schedules for 1840, 1850, 1860, and 1870.
Nelson County, Kentucky: Population Schedule for 1840.
Mercer County, Kentucky: Population Schedule for 1850.

Connelly, Annie Laurie. "The History of Kidd-Key College, Sherman, Grayson County, Texas." Master's thesis, Southern Methodist University, Dallas, Texas, 1942.

Grayson County (Sherman, Texas): Deed Books, Will Books, Marriage Registers, Probate Records.

Interviews: Cecile Sanderson (Denison, Texas), Edwin Worthley (Dallas, Texas).

Kidd-Key Collection in Fondren Library of Southern Methodist University, Dallas, Texas: Clippings; correspondence; photographs; business ledgers; college memorabilia, publications, and catalogs; Methodist Church minutes; and unpublished history by Jennie Hill Barry.

Whitworth College Collection in Lincoln-Lawrence-Franklin Regional Public Library, Brookhaven, Mississippi, including excerpts from *Methodism in the Mississippi Conference* by W. B. Jones; excerpts from "A History of Whitworth College for Women," a doctoral thesis by Kathleen George Rice (The University of Mississippi), 1985; "Whitworth College for Women" (no author or date); Alumnae Rolls, 1877-1890; "The History of Whitworth College, Brookhaven , Mississippi," by Cleo Warren.

Memory Books in Kidd-Key Collection of Red River Historical Museum, Sherman, Texas.

Vertical file: Kidd-Key College. Sherman Public Library, Sherman, Texas.

Yazoo County (Yazoo City, Mississippi): Deed Books, Will Books, Marriage Registers, Probate Records.

NEWSPAPERS

Brookhaven News (Brookhaven, Mississippi)
Dallas Morning News (Dallas, Texas)
Sherman Courier (Sherman, Texas)

Sherman Daily Democrat (Sherman, Texas)
Sherman Daily Register (Sherman, Texas)
Sherman Democrat (Sherman, Texas)
Sunday Gazetter (Denison, Texas)
Yazoo City Herald (Yazoo City, Mississippi)
Yazoo Democrat (Yazoo City, Mississippi)
Yazoo City Weekly Whig (Yazoo City, Mississippi)

CHAPTER SIX—ELA HOCKADAY

PRINTED SOURCES

Acheson, Sam H.; Gambrell, Herbert P.; Toomey, Mary C.; and Acheson, Alex M., Jr., editors. *Texian Who's Who: A Biographical Dictionary of the State of Texas.* (Dallas: The Texian Co., 1937).

Best, Hugh. *Debrett's Texas Peerage.* (New York: Coward McCann, Inc., 1983).

Castleberry, Vivian Anderson. *Daughters of Dallas: A History of Greater Dallas Through The Voices and Deeds of Its Women.* (Dallas, Texas: Odenwald Press, 1994).

Dealey, Ted. *Diaper Days of Dallas.* (Dallas, Texas: Southern Methodist University Press, 1966).

"Dedication of Marker for Hockaday Homestead." *Honey Grove Signal-Citizen/The Ladonia News,* July 2, 1982.

Hodge, Floy Crandall. *A History of Fannin County featuring Pioneer Families.* (Hereford, Texas: Pioneer Publishers).

_____*Fannin County Cemetery Records.* (Privately printed, no date).

Holmes, Maxine and Saxon, Gerald D., editors. *The WPA Dallas Guide and History.* (Dallas Public Library, Texas Center for the Book, and University of North Texas Press, 1992).

Kraeplin, Camille R., editor. *Of Hearts And Minds: The Hockaday Experience, 1913-1988.* (Hockaday Alumnae Association, privately printed, 1988).

The National Cyclopaedia of American Biography. Volume 42. (New York: James T. White & Company, 1958).

Newhouse, Dean and Patricia. *Fannin County, Texas Cemetery Inscriptions.* Volume I. (Honey Grove: Newhouse Publications, 1983).

Rollins, Sarah Finch Maiden. *The Tugwell and Finch Families of Tennessee and Allied Families of Virginia and North Carolina, 1635-1993, including Bobbitt, Hockaday, Lang, Montgomery and Powell.* (Wolfe City, Texas: Henington Publishing Company, 1993).

Saxon, Gerald D., editor. *Reminiscences: A Glimpse of Old East Dallas.* (Dallas, Texas: Dallas Public Library, 1983).

Sherman City Directory, 1899-1904.

MANUSCRIPT AND GOVERNMENT SOURCES

Austin College (Sherman, Texas): Archives.

Census of the United States:
Dallas County, Texas: Population Schedule for 1920.
Fannin County, Texas: Population Schedule for 1870 and 1880.
Grayson County, Texas: Population Schedule for 1900.
Lamar County, Texas: Population Schedule for 1860.
Virginia Population Index for 1830, 1840 and 1850.

Fannin County (Bonham, Texas): Deed, Probate and Marriage Records.

Interview: Personnel Office, Sherman (Texas) Independent School District, May 30, 1995.

Vertical file on Hockaday family in Dallas (Texas) Public Library, including copies of:
Hockaday, Olin S. "The Hockaday Family." (No date)
Sarah B. Trent. "Miss Hockaday, the Founder." (No date)

Denning, Frances Kramer. "A Brief History of Hockaday." (No date, circa 1937)

Hockaday, Ela. "Recollections." (Incomplete, no date)

Hockaday Four-Cast, March 13, 1962.

Dallas Morning News, obituary: March 27, 1956; March 28, 1956.

Dallas Times Herald, obituary: March 26, 1956.

"The Site of the Hockaday Homestead." (No author, no date. Prepared for historical marker application.)

Vertical file on Ela Hockaday at The Hockaday School, including:

Hockaday, O. S. "Descendants of Thomas Hart Benton Hockaday (1835-1918) and Maria Elizabeth Kerr (d. 1881). (1959)

"New Hockaday Trust to Perpetuate School." *Dallas Morning News*, May 6, 1942.

Yancey, Mary Frances. "Past History of Hockaday." (Speech given to new trustees on April 22, 1975.)

NEWSPAPERS

Bonham Favorite (Bonham, Texas)
Dallas Morning News (Dallas, Texas)
New York Times (New York, New York)
Sherman Daily Register (Sherman, Texas)
Sherman Daily Democrat (Sherman, Texas)
Sherman Democrat (Sherman, Texas)

CHAPTER SEVEN—EDNA GLADNEY

PRINTED SOURCES

Fort Worth City Directory, 1901-1960.

Gainesville (Texas) City Directory, 1895-1896.

Harris, Eleanor. "I Gave Away 10,000 Babies." *Woman's Home Companion*, January 1954.

Ours: A Quarterly Publication of the Edna Gladney Home.
Volume 1, No. 3, Special Memorial Issue, October 1961.

Piester, Ruby Lee. *For the Love of a Child: The Gladney Story:
100 Years of Adoption in America.* Austin, Texas: Eakin
Press, 1987.

Sherman City Directory, 1912-1931.

The Texas Digest, Volume XVII, Number 19: May 10, 1941.

MANUSCRIPT AND GOVERNMENT SOURCES

Briney, Priscilla T. "Aunt Edna." Unpublished master's
thesis, Texas Christian University, 1980.

Census of the United States:
Grayson County, Texas: Population Schedule for 1920.
Hunt County, Texas: Population Schedule for 1910.

Center for American History: University of Texas at Austin:
Vertical file on Edna Gladney.

Cooke County, Texas: Marriage, Deed, and Probate Records.

Federal Writers' Project. *Fort Worth and Tarrant County
Research Data*, Series 1 and 2.

Flemming Collection, Sherman (Texas) Public Library:
including newspaper clippings, correspondence,
unpublished article by Guy Yowell.

The Gladney Center: Fort Worth, Texas: Files: Development
and Public Information Offices: including newspaper
clippings, correspondence, scrapbooks, photographs,
brochures.

Grayson County, Texas: Deed and Civil Court Records.

Interview with Mrs. Earl Chester, Fort Worth, Texas: August
24, 1995.

Tarrant County, Texas: Probate Records.

NEWSPAPERS

Austin American-Statesman (Austin, Texas)
Dallas Morning News (Dallas, Texas)
Fort Worth News-Tribune (Fort Worth, Texas)
Fort Worth Press (Fort Worth, Texas)
Fort Worth Star (Fort Worth, Texas)
Fort Worth Star-Telegram (Fort Worth, Texas)
New York Times (New York)
Sherman Daily Democrat (Sherman, Texas)
Sherman Democrat (Sherman, Texas)

CHAPTER EIGHT—ENID MAE JUSTIN

PRINTED SOURCES

Biffle, Kent. "These boots were made for kicking." *Dallas Morning News*, September 21, 1980.

Fenoglio, Helen. "Miss Enid Justin's Story: From Catalog Sacker to Boot Factory." *Wichita Falls Record Times*, December 15, 1968 (?)

Fenoglio, Melvin E., editor. *The Story of Montague County, Texas: Its Past and Present*. Montague County Historical Commission and Curtis Media Corporation, 1989.

Ferguson, Henry N. "Enid Justin: Woman Bootmaker." *Texas Woman*, February 1979.

Fort Worth City Directory.

Henderson, Lt. Col. Jeff S., editor. *100 Years in Montague County, Texas*. Saint Jo, Texas: IPTA Printers, nd.

Jones, Jim W. "Bootmaker 'Miss Enid' Going Strong at 79." *Fort Worth Star-Telegram*, January 2, 1974.

Justin, Enid. As told to Dale Terry. *"Miss Enid:" The Texas Lady Bootmaker*. Austin, Texas: Nortex Press, 1985.

Justin Industries, Inc. *1994 Annual Report*.

"Miss Enid Begins Nocona With A Dream And A Loan." Chicago, Illinois: Derus Media Service, nd.

"Nocona Ads a Real Kick." *Dallas Morning News* (Business), October 26, 1980.

"Nocona Boot Company Founder." *Texas Celebrates the First 150 Years*. Dallas: Southwest Media Corp, 1985.

Nocona Boot Company newsletter. "Miss Enid's Scrapbook."

Nocona's Bicentennial Heritage '76 Committee. *Panorama of Nocona's Trade Area*. Saint Jo, Texas: S.J.T. Printing Co., 1976.

Smith, Donnie. "The bootmaker's daughter did a little fancy footwork." *San Antonio* (Texas) *Express*, February 12, 1975.

Terry, Dale. "Nocona's Lady Bootmaker." *Texas Highways*, January 1975.

Troxel, Navena Hembree. *Montague County, Texas Marriage Books: B & C, 1879-1888*. Privately printed, 1983.

Works, George. "She gets a 'boot' out of work." *Wichita Falls Record Times*, nd.

_____"Joe Justin Named Nocona Boot Officer." *Wichita Falls Record Times*, May 23, 1974.

Yeargin, Bob. "Manufacturing Boots Skill Enid Justin Learned Early." *Las Vegas* (Nevada) *Sun*, January 22, 1973.

MANUSCRIPT AND GOVERNMENT SOURCES

Census of the United States:
Montague County, Texas: 1880 and 1910.

Interviews: Nocona Boot Company, July 19, 1995:
Doris Floyd, Personnel Manager
Pat Keck, Advertising Coordinator
Ann Lawyer, skiver
Darla Linn, supervisor of stitching department

Interview by phone: Betty Stripling, Sherman, Texas: June 20, 1995.

Jenkins, Dr. Floyd. North Texas State University Oral History Collection (Business Archives Project): Number 63: Interview with Enid Justin: November 13, 1981. In collection of Nocona Public Library.

Montague County, Texas: Probate Records.

Texas Woman's University: Women's Collection: file on Enid Justin, including Enid Justin Papers (1939-1965) in Southwest Collection of Texas Tech (Lubbock, Texas).

NEWSPAPERS

Dallas Morning News (Dallas, Texas)
Fort Worth Press (Fort Worth, Texas)

Index

Other Books From Republic of Texas Press

100 Days in Texas: The Alamo Letters
by Wallace O. Chariton
Alamo Movies
by Frank Thompson
At Least 1836 Things You Ought to Know About Texas but Probably Don't
by Doris L. Miller
Black Warrior Chiefs: The History of the Seminole Negro Indian Scouts
by Cloyde Brown
Civil War Recollections of James Lemuel Clark and the Great Hanging at Gainesville, Texas in October 1862
by L.D. Clark
Cow Pasture Pool: Golf on the Muni-tour
by Joe E. Winter
A Cowboy of the Pecos
by Patrick Dearen
Cripple Creek Bonanza
by Chet Cunningham
Daughter of Fortune: The Bettie Brown Story
by Sherrie S. McLeRoy
Defense of a Legend: Crockett and the de la Peña Diary
by Bill Groneman
Don't Throw Feathers at Chickens: A Collection of Texas Political Humor
by Charles Herring, Jr. and Walter Richter
Eight Bright Candles: Courageous Women of Mexico
by Doris E. Perlin
Etta Place: Her Life and Times with Butch Cassidy and the Sundance Kid
by Gail Drago
Exiled: The Tigua Indians of Ysleta del Sur
by Randy Lee Eickhoff
Exploring Dallas with Children: A Guide for Family Activities
by Kay McCasland Threadgill

Exploring the Alamo Legends
by Wallace O. Chariton
Eyewitness to the Alamo
by Bill Groneman
From an Outhouse to the White House
by Wallace O. Chariton
The Funny Side of Texas
by Ellis Posey and John Johnson
Ghosts Along the Texas Coast
by Docia Schultz Williams
The Great Texas Airship Mystery
by Wallace O. Chariton
Henry Ossian Flipper, West Point's First Black Graduate
by Jane Eppinga
Horses and Horse Sense: The Practical Science of Horse Husbandry
by James "Doc" Blakely
How the Cimarron River Got Its Name and Other Stories About Coffee
by Ernestine Sewell Linck
The Last Great Days of Radio
by Lynn Woolley
Letters Home: A Soldier's Legacy
by Roger L. Shaffer
More Wild Camp Tales
by Mike Blakely
Noble Brutes: Camels on the American Frontier
by Eva Jolene Boyd
Outlaws in Petticoats and Other Notorious Texas Women
by Gail Drago and Ann Ruff
Phantoms of the Plains: Tales of West Texas Ghosts
by Docia Schultz Williams
Rainy Days in Texas Funbook
by Wallace O. Chariton
Red River Women
by Sherrie S. McLeRoy
Santa Fe Trail
by James A. Crutchfield
Slitherin' 'Round Texas
by Jim Dunlap

Call Wordware Publishing, Inc. for names of the bookstores in your area: (214) 423-0090

Spirits of San Antonio and South
Texas
by Docia Schultz Williams and
Reneta Byrne
Star Film Ranch: Texas' First
Picture Show
by Frank Thompson
Tales of the Guadalupe Mountains
by W.C. Jameson
Texas Highway Humor
by Wallace O. Chariton
Texas Politics in My Rearview
Mirror
by Waggoner Carr and Byron Varner
Texas Tales Your Teacher Never
Told You
by Charles F. Eckhardt
Texas Wit and Wisdom
by Wallace O. Chariton
That Cat Won't Flush
by Wallace O. Chariton

That Old Overland Stagecoaching
by Eva Jolene Boyd
This Dog'll Hunt
by Wallace O. Chariton
To The Tyrants Never Yield: A
Texas Civil War Sampler
by Kevin R. Young
Tragedy at Taos: The Revolt of
1847
by James A. Crutchfield
A Trail Rider's Guide to Texas
by Mary Elizabeth Sue Goldman
A Treasury of Texas Trivia
by Bill Cannon
Unsolved Texas Mysteries
by Wallace O. Chariton
Western Horse Tales
Edited by Don Worcester
Wild Camp Tales
by Mike Blakely

Seaside Press

The Bible for Busy People
Book 1: The Old Testament
by Mark Berrier Sr.
Critter Chronicles
by Jim Dunlap
Dallas Uncovered
by Larenda Lyles Roberts
Dirty Dining: A Cookbook, and
More, for Lovers
by Ginnie Siena Bivona
Exotic Pets: A Veterinary Guide
for Owners
by Shawn Messonnier, D.V.M.
I Never Wanted to Set the World
on Fire, but Now That I'm 50,
Maybe It's a Good Idea
by Bob Basso, Ph.D.
Jackson Hole Uncovered
by Sierra Sterling Adare
Just Passing Through
by Beth Beggs
Lives and Works of the Apostles
by Russell A. Stultz
Los Angeles Uncovered
by Frank Thompson
Only: The Last Dinosaur
by Jim Dunlap

Pete the Python: The Further
Adventures of Mark and Deke
by Jim Dunlap
San Antonio Uncovered
by Mark Louis Rybczyk
San Francisco Uncovered
by Larenda Lyles Roberts
Seattle Uncovered
by JoAnn Roe
A Sure Reward
by B.J. Smagula
Survival Kit for Today's Family
by Bill R. Swetmon
They Don't Have to Die
by Jim Dunlap
Tucson Uncovered
by John and Donna Kamper
Twin Cities Uncovered
by The Arthurs
Unlocking Mysteries of God's
Word
by Bill Swetmon
Your Kittens' First Year
by Shawn Messonnier, D.V.M.
Your Puppy's First Year
by Shawn Messonnier, D.V.M.

Call Wordware Publishing, Inc. for names of the
bookstores in your area: (214) 423-0090